Inside and Outside Liquid

Inside and Outside Liquidity

Bengt Holmström and Jean Tirole

The MIT Press
Cambridge, Massachusetts
London, England

First MIT Press paperback edition, 2013

© 2011 Massachusetts Institute of Technology

For information about special quantity discounts, please email special_sales@mitpress.mit.edu

This book was set in Palatino by Westchester Book Composition and printed and bound in the United States of America.

Library of Congress Cataloging-in-Publication Data

Holmström, Bengt
Inside and outside liquidity / Bengt Holmström and Jean Tirole.
     p.   cm.
Includes bibliographical references and index.
ISBN 978-0-262-01578-3 (hbk. : alk. paper)—978-0-262-51853-6 (pbk. : alk. paper)
1. Liquidity (Economics) I. Tirole, Jean. II. Title.
HG178.H65   2011
338.4'3—dc22

                    2010036616

10 9 8 7 6 5 4 3

Contents

**Epilogue: Summary and Concluding Thoughts on the Subprime
Crisis   227**

Acknowledgments

The idea of writing this book on inside and outside liquidity started when we were invited to give the Wicksell lectures at the Stockholm School of Economics in 1999. We are grateful for and honored by this invitation. The lectures gave us the impetus for thinking more deeply about the implications of the framework for liquidity that we developed in the mid-1990s.

As usual, our own contribution builds on a large body of research, from the classic works of Wicksell, Keynes, and Hicks on liquidity and macroeconomic policy to the modern corporate finance literature, which forms the foundation for our modeling approach. We are very grateful to the many researchers whose work is cited here, and apologize for inevitable, but inadvertent omissions that have arisen.

We have benefited greatly from the insights and the inputs of many researchers: Tri Vi Dang, Emmanuel Farhi, Gary Gorton, and Jean-Charles Rochet with whom we have collaborated on related topics and who have generously shared their thoughts with us; Pablo Kurlat, who proofread an early version of the book and provided excellent research assistance; Ivan Werning, who corrected an error in our 1998 paper (see chapter 3); Arvind Krishnamurthy for constructive criticism of earlier drafts, and Daron Acemoglu, Tobias Adrian, Bruno Biais, Olivier Blanchard, Jeremy Bulow, Ricardo Caballero, Douglas Diamond, Olivier Jeanne, Anyl Kayshap, Nobu Kiyotaki, Guido Lorenzoni, Thomas Mariotti, Ernesto Pasten, Adriano Rampini, Andrei Schleifer, Jeremy Stein, Robert Townsend, Robert Wilson, and Mark Wolfson for extensive conversations on the subject. Needless to say, we are entirely responsible for any mistakes that remain (comments can be addressed to us at bengt@mit.edu or jean.tirole@tse-fr.eu).

Besides the Lectures at the Stockholm School of Economics, drafts of this book were taught to several generations of students at MIT,

Toulouse School of Economics, Wuhan University, University of Chicago, and the New Economic School, Moscow. We thank all the participants for helpful feedback. Our assistants Emily Gallagher and Pierrette Vaissade did a great job typing the manuscript, always in good cheers; they deserve our sincere gratitude. We are grateful to our MIT Press editor Dana Andrus for her professional editing of the manuscript.

Over the years MIT and TSE have provided us with friendly and very stimulating research environments. One cannot underestimate the benefits of conversations and comments gleaned in corridors, at the coffee machine, and during seminars. As research environments, these institutions played an important role in the conception of this book, and we owe much to our colleagues and students who make these places intellectually exciting.

This book would not exist without generous external support. Jean Tirole is extremely grateful to the partners of TSE and IDEI for their commitment to funding fundamental research; this funding, in particular, includes partners related to finance and macroeconomics: Banque de France, which has taken a particularly keen interest in research on liquidity, and also AXA, BNP Paribas, Caisse des Dépôts et Consignations, Crédit Agricole, Exane, Fédération Française des Banques, Fédération Française des Sociétés d'Assurance, Financière de la Cité, Paul Woolley Research Initiative, and SCOR. Bengt Holmström thanks NBER and the Yrjö Jahnsson Foundation for support, Anyl Kayshap for the invitation to visit the Initiative on Global Markets at the University of Chicago in the Fall 2006, and John Shoven for the invitation to visit Stanford Institute of Economic Policy Research (SIEPR) in the Spring 2010. Some of the work on the book was done during these visits.

Finally, our families and most especially our wives Anneli and Nathalie provided much understanding and love during the long gestation of this book.

Prologue: Motivation and Roadmap

Why do financial institutions, industrial companies and households hold low-yielding money balances, Treasury bills, and other short-term assets? The standard answer to this question, dating back at least to Keynes (1936), Hicks (1967), and Gurley and Shaw (1960), is that these assets are "liquid" as they allow their owners to better weather income shortages.[1]

It is unclear, though, why an economic agent's ability to withstand shocks would not be better served by the broader concept of net wealth, including stocks and long-term bonds. While some forms of equity, such as private equity, may not be readily sold at a "fair price," many long-term securities are traded on active organized exchanges; for example, liquidating one's position in an open-ended S&P 500 index fund can be performed quickly and at low transaction costs. For some reason a big part of the agents' net wealth is not liquid and cannot be used as a substitute for liquid assets. This explains why the yield on liquid assets is lower than could be expected from standard economic models (the "risk-free rate puzzle"). The standard theory of general equilibrium offers no explanation for this phenomenon. In the Arrow–Debreu model, and its variants, economic agents are subject to a single budget constraint, implying that the consumers' feasible consumption sets and the firms' feasible production sets only depend on their wealth.

Similarly financial institutions and industrial companies pay a lot of attention to risk management. They hedge against liquidity risks using short-term securities, credit facilities, currency swaps, and similar

---

1. The book's title *Inside and Outside Liquidity* paraphrases Gurley and Shaw's (1960) "inside and outside money," which distinguishes claims that private parties have on each other versus claims that private parties have on government. Our usage is consistent with this distinction. Wicksell (1898) was one of the first authors to emphasize the dual role of money as a store of value and a medium of exchange.

instruments, adjusting their positions to meet future liquidity needs in the most efficient way. These activities cost billions of dollars. Yet, received theory is not of much help in explaining all the resources and attention spent on them. In an Arrow–Debreu world it does not matter whether economic agents make their consumption and production plans at the initial date or make these decisions later on provided that they can contract on transfers of numéraire from one period to the next (Arrow 1970). In particular, the Modigliani–Miller (1958) irrelevance results imply that the hoarding of liquidity or the hedging of liquidity risk (through choice of leverage, dividend payments, etc.) do not affect a firm's value.

The purpose of this book is to offer an explanation of the demand for and supply of liquid assets. We use insights from modern corporate finance to study how such a theory can explain the pricing of assets, the role of liquidity management, decisions on real investments, and also how this theory relates to some classic themes in macroeconomics and in international finance.

Macroeconomic policy rests on the presumption that the government can do things that the market cannot. Foremost among these is the provision of liquidity. The government provides liquidity in a variety of ways: through industry and banking bailouts, deposit insurance, the discount window, open-market operations, implicit insurance against major accidents or epidemics, unemployment insurance, social security, debt management, and so forth. The result is often a redistribution of income from consumers to producers or from future generations to current ones. The Ricardian equivalence theorem (Barro 1974), the macroeconomic counterpart of the Modigliani–Miller theorem, suggests that these activities are useless, since economic agents can replicate privately optimal outcomes by undoing whatever the government does.

In this book we depart from the Arrow–Debreu paradigm in a small but important way: we assume that some part of a firm's income stream cannot be promised or pledged to investors. Outside investors must share the firm's income with insiders (large shareholder, managers, employees) either because the latter enjoy perks, or can divert resources, or because insiders may exert insufficient effort and so must be given a share of the proceeds to refrain from engaging in moral hazard. Adverse selection also limits the extent to which firms can pledge their future income to investors.

Except for part IV of the book, we assume that arbitrary state-contingent financial claims can be written on the pledgeable part of firm income. But given partial nonpledgeability, the income base on which various kinds of financial claims can be built is smaller than in the Arrow–Debreu world.

We also assume that consumers cannot pledge any of their future income. There are several reasons why this is by and large reality. One reason is that some agents may not participate in markets; they may be too young or not yet born. This type of market incompleteness has been thoroughly investigated in the overlapping-generations literature, starting with Allais (1947), Samuelson (1958), and Diamond (1965). Second, consumers can pledge only a small share of their future labor income for institutional reasons (limited liability, limited slavery, priority of tax claims), verifiability problems (a liability-ridden individual may move abroad), and incentive considerations (future income is endogenous).

The key implication of nonpledgeability is that firms (as well as consumers) can count on liquidating or using as collateral only part of their wealth whenever they need funds. Consequently they must prepare themselves for adverse financial shocks by hoarding liquid assets or by contracting in other ways for the provision of liquidity. Firms are willing to pay a premium for liquidity services. We show that in general, they have to do so because limited pledgeability also constrains the supply of liquid assets. It reduces the amount of wealth in the economy, which in turn limits the ability of investors to promise, in a credible manner, future financing of firms. This observation gives rise to a demand for liquidity (stores of value) that can transfer wealth from today to tomorrow as well as across states of nature tomorrow.

We make a distinction between *inside (aggregate) liquidity* and *outside (aggregate) liquidity*, depending on the source of the pledgeable income.[2] When the pledgeable income is generated by the corporate sector, the

---

2. Our notion of inside and outside liquidity closely parallels the notion of inside and outside money introduced by Gurley and Shaw (1960), as we earlier pointed out, and adopted in modern economics literature. For example, Blanchard and Fischer (1989: ch. 4) state:

Any money that is on net not an asset of the private economy is an outside money. Under the gold standard, gold coins were outside money; in modern fiat money systems currency and bank reserves, high-powered money, and the money base constitute outside money. However, most money in modern economics is inside money, which is simultaneously an asset and a liability of the private sector.

More recently Lagos (2006) defines inside and outside money in a related manner:

Outside money is money that is either of a fiat nature (unbacked) or backed by some asset that is not in zero net supply within the private sector of the economy. Thus, outside money is a net asset for the private sector. ... Inside money is an asset representing, or backed by, any form of private credit that circulates as a medium of exchange. Since it is one private agent's liability and at the same time some other agent's asset, inside money is in zero net supply within the private sector.

claims on it constitute inside liquidity. All claims on goods and services outside the corporate sector constitute outside liquidity.

A basic question we will address concerns the adequacy of inside liquidity. When the corporate sector cannot generate enough inside liquidity, or when it is too expensive to do so, it will make use of outside liquidity. There are three sources of outside liquidity: (1) consumers, who can securitize their assets, notably the houses they own; (2) the government, which can issue claims backed by its exclusive right to tax consumers and producers; and (3) international financial markets, which can offer liquidity in the form of claims on international goods and services.[3] We will pay special attention to how the government supplies liquidity alone and in conjunction with international investors.

The book is organized as follows. Part I builds the foundations for the corporate demand for liquidity. Chapter 1 introduces a simple model of credit rationing with constant returns to scale. Credit rationing of some kind is essential for corporate liquidity demand. Chapter 2 introduces the workhorse model of liquidity demand that we will use throughout the book. In this model, firms with limited pledgeability must plan their liquidity in advance. Firms demand liquidity because they want to insure themselves against credit rationing. Through mechanisms such as credit lines or credit default swaps, investors commit themselves to supplying funds in states of nature in which they would not naturally have done so, namely in states in which liquidity needs exceed the future income that can be pledged to investors. We also examine the provision of liquidity by investors who cannot perfectly monitor the firms' use of funding.

Chapter 2 also compares our model of corporate liquidity demand with the celebrated model of consumer liquidity demand by Bryant (1980) and Diamond and Dybvig (1983). While the two types of models differ in many respects, we show that there is a close formal relationship between them as well. Furthermore the two can readily be merged into a single framework in which corporations and consumers compete for liquidity.

While our use of inside and outside liquidity is consistent with these definitions, our emphasis on liquidity will lead us to a broad view of outside stores of values that do not originate in the corporate sector. Chapters 5 and 6 will show how these can be used to face liquidity shortfalls.

3. In this book we ignore the possibility that asset bubbles, while they last, augment the stock of liquidity in the economy and thereby boost investment. See Farhi and Tirole (2009a) for an analysis of the extent to which bubbles can add to the supply of liquidity.

Part II of the book (chapters 3 and 4) develops our main analysis of liquidity supply and liquidity pricing. Chapter 3 asks whether the private sector provides enough aggregate liquidity on its own. That is, do the firms in the aggregate create enough pledgeable income—inside liquidity—to support the financial claims necessary for implementing a second-best, state-contingent production plan? The answer is yes if the corporate sector is a net borrower and the firms' liquidity shocks are idiosyncratic. In that case the second-best plan can be implemented by each firm holding a share of the market index. However, if the corporate sector is a net lender, there will always be a shortage of aggregate liquidity. The same is true if all firms are hit by the same (macroeconomic) shock and this shock is sufficiently large.

A shortage of liquidity induces the private sector to try and create more stores of value, albeit at a cost. This may involve investing in projects that deliver a safe income or making changes in governance structures that raise the corporations' pledgeable income—such as going public, improving monitoring systems, or employing financial innovations that enable a more efficient use of collateral. Examples of the latter include bilateral and tri-party repos (legal innovations that free posting of collateral from the vagaries of bankruptcy processes), and securitization, which transforms illiquid, low-grade loans into publicly traded assets of higher quality. Such efforts fit well with de Soto's (2003) view that a major role of a financial system is to transform "dead capital" into "live capital." He thought of the opportunities to create collateral in developing economies. What seems to have take place at the beginning of the new century is that excesss savings from China, and other emerging economies with underdeveloped financial markets, flowed to developed countries, and especially the United States which could meet the increased demand for stores of value at a lower cost.

Chapter 3 also offers a preliminary analysis of the pricing of outside liquidity and assets, which in broad terms fits the empirical evidence on liquidity premia of Treasury bonds in Krishnamurthy and Vissing-Jorgenson (2010). Chapter 4 goes on to develop a general equilibrium model in which only pledgeable income can be used as the basis for contingent claims. While the basic logic of our Liquidity Asset Pricing Model (LAPM) is identical to that of the Arrow–Debreu model, LAPM prices do not merely reflect the yield of the assets, but also the value that they bring as collateral, which helps firms withstand liquidity shocks. The chapter also illustrates how one can use state prices to derive an optimal policy for risk management at the firm level.

If the corporate sector cannot produce enough inside liquidity it may obtain insurance from providers of outside liquidity. More generally, firms will turn to outside liquidity whenever it is less expensive than inside liquidity. In part III (chapters 5 and 6) we study the supply of outside liquidity by the government as well as international investors. Our main interest is in understanding how the government should manage public liquidity.

In chapter 5 the government acts without the help of international investors. Given that consumers cannot directly pledge their future income to firms, at least in states of nature where the latter are short of liquidity, we argue that the state, through its regalian taxation power, can increase the pledgeability of consumers' future income and thereby create liquidity for the corporate sector. Consumers and firms can be made better off by having the government act as an insurance broker, transferring funds from consumers to firms when the latter are hit by aggregate liquidity shocks. We study government policy assuming that an explicit insurance contract can be drawn up ex ante, but we argue that a number of ex post policy interventions emulate the patterns of optimal government insurance. In fact the ability of the government to provide liquidity ex post gives it a potential advantage over privately supplied liquidity. Privately supplied liquidity often requires ex ante investments in short-term assets, incurring an opportunity cost whether or not liquidity is needed. In contrast, an ex post government policy that does not waste liquidity can be much cheaper, especially when covering liquidity shortages that occur rarely.

Chapter 6 pursues the analysis of public provision of liquidity by asking whether the presence of efficient international financial markets could eliminate all potential liquidity shortages. The answer is no, in general. A country's access to international financial markets is limited by its ability to generate pledgeable income that is tradable. We study the relationship between international and domestic liquidity in an open economy with both tradable and nontradable goods and conclude that when there is a shortage of international liquidity, the insights about the value of domestic liquidity continue to hold.

Part IV (chapters 7 and 8) departs from the assumption of perfect coordination of liquidity within the corporate sector and look at situations where each firm individually arranges its own supply of liquidity without any ex ante coordination with the other firms. The only type of coordination occurs ex post in spot markets that can reallocate liquidity. One could ask how close this kind of self-provided liquidity arrangement comes to the second best. We show that it will, in general, not replicate the second-best optimum because firms may hoard either too much or too little liquidity. Yet the government may be unable to improve on the situation, in contrast to the large literature on incomplete insurance markets.

The epilogue summarizes the main lessons to be drawn from our particular approach toward the supply of inside and outside liquidity and relates it to the subprime crisis.

On terminology: Throughout the book we take the terms *pledgeable income, liquidity,* and *collateral* to mean the same thing and use them interchangably.[4] The financial crisis that began in 2007 we call *the subprime crisis* for brevity.

---

4. Clearly, in many settings collateral can be different from pledgeable income. The value of the assets backing up debt is often higher than the value of debt (the debt is over-collateralized). This may be because the underlying assets are risky and do not protect the investor's claim in all states of nature. Or it may be because the value of collateral is worth less to the investor than it is to the borrowing firm. Note that even if the collateral is worth very little to the investor, it can provide proper incentives for repayment of debt as long as the borrower prefers to repay the debt than lose his collateral and has the means to do so.

In our complete market model the amount of collateral is exactly equal to the amount promised in any given state. Considerations of default are already built into the notion of pledgeable income. Promising more than the pledgeable income would not be credible and promising less would waste collateral.

I   Basics of Leverage and Liquidity

In standard microeconomic theory a firm that confronts financial needs can meet these needs as they arise by taking out loans or by issuing new securities whose repayments and returns are secured by the cash flows that the firm generates. As long as the net present value of a reinvestment is positive, investors will agree to supply the needed funds.[1] Reality is very different. Firms keep a close watch on their current and forecasted cash positions to ensure that their essential liquidity needs can be met at all times. They do not wait until the cash register is empty. To guard against liquidity shortages, firms arrange financing in advance using both the asset and the liability sides of their balance sheets. On the asset side, they may hoard liquidity by buying Treasury bills and other safe assets that can be easily sold when necessary.[2] On the liability side, they may take out credit lines or issue securities that give them flexibility in their management of cash, such as long-term debt, preferred equity, and straight equity.[3] The recent subprime crisis is a cogent demonstration of how costly—and in some cases impossible—it can be to face a maturity mismatch and to seek financing in times of distress. Financial institutions have been struggling to replace with alternative sources of funding the short-term, market-based financing that they had grown used to in boom times. At the same time they have been forced to delever significantly by selling assets at distressed prices. The troubles in the financial sector in turn have shut off normal credit channels for the nonfinancial sector, causing bankruptcies and distress throughout the economy. A crisis of this magnitude is obviously rare, but it certainly is a stark reminder of how important it is to think about one's liquidity needs in advance rather than wait until the need materializes.

By now there are several related theories in modern corporate finance that can explain why firms demand liquidity. Each theory provides a rationale for why a firm wants to buy insurance against higher credit costs or outright credit rationing stemming from information problems. In von Thadden (1995) a firm that waits may be unable to get access

---

1. In the case of a debt overhang, additional financing will require previous contracts to be renegotiated.

2. Some nonfinancial firms hold surprising amounts of liquid assets at any given time. Big technology firms like Microsoft have at times held tens of billions of dollars in liquid instruments, mostly, if not exclusively, in the form of safe, low-yielding debt. Large accumulations of cash like this provide a readiness to make major acquisitions, and also a hedge against liquidity shocks.

3. Brunnermeier and Pedersen (2009) talk about *funding liquidity* when the liability side is used and *market liquidity* when the asset side is used.

to funding because of adverse selection problems. Adverse selection can make it very costly for a firm to obtain funding and in the worst case, asset and credit markets may dry up entirely.[4] The cost of "signal-jamming" is an alternative reason for advanced funding (e.g., Bolton and Scharfstein 1990; Fudenberg and Tirole 1985). If financiers base tomorrow's refinancing decision on a firm's current performance, competitors have an incentive to prey on each other by choosing hidden actions, such as secret price cuts, that hurt rivals and make them look financially weak. In equilibrium, the market can see through this, but nevertheless the wasteful signaling behavior is rational. To prevent such predation, a firm has an incentive to secure its funds in advance (in a publicly observable fashion).

Throughout this book we employ a very simple information-based model as the driver of liquidity demand. The key assumption is that firms are unable to pledge all of the returns from their investments to the investors. Insiders—from control shareholders to managers to ordinary employees—enjoy private benefits of various kinds that create a wedge between total returns and pledgeable returns. The insiders may consume employment rents, enjoy perks, engage in empire building, or receive inducements to perform that give them an extra share of the firm's payoff. To the extent that these benefits cannot be transferred or paid for up front, a part of the total surplus will not be pledgeable to outside investors.

This partial nonpledgeability of investment returns can make it more costly or impossible to finance a project. And even when the project can get off the ground, private benefits can make future reinvestments difficult. In general, we show that firms will face credit rationing not just at the start but also in the future. There is, however, a key difference between credit rationing at the initial financing stage and the refinancing stages: in the latter case, credit rationing can be anticipated and therefore measures can be taken to insure against it.

---

4. The idea that adverse selection may lead to market freezes dates back to Akerlof (1970). Some recent papers have used Akerlof's model to show how the inability to sell legacy assets may hamper reinvestment policies: see, for example, House and Masatlioglu (2010) and Kurlat (2010). Philippon and Skreta (2010) and Tirole (2010) study how the state can jump-start asset markets when financial institutions can opt to be refinanced in a (cleaned-up) financial market. Daley and Green (2010) show how the thawing of an illiquid market is affected by the accrual of news about the quality of individual assets and by waiting strategies of sellers who try to signal a high quality of their assets by conveying the message that they are not particularly eager to part with them.

We begin by showing (in chapter 1) how a simple moral-hazard model with limited liability can give rise to a wedge between total and pledge-able income. Chapter 2 introduces a "liquidity shock" that may hit the firm after it has sunk its initial investment. This gives rise to a demand for liquidity. We show that if the potential liquidity shock is severe enough, the firm needs to arrange financing in advance to avoid facing costly credit rationing. Firms face both a solvency concern (the need to be adequately capitalized in order to attract financing in the first place) and a liquidity concern (the risk of facing solvency concerns in the future). The optimal design exhibits a trade-off between liquid and illiquid investments: the higher the insurance purchased by the firm in the form of a liquidity backup, the lower the investment in illiquid assets. Put differently, the firm can opt for a large scale with a maturity mismatch (much long-term illiquid assets and little short-term liquidity), or for a smaller, but more secure balance sheet.

Appendix 2A shows how private information about the magnitude of the liquidity shock limits contracting possibilities and affects the optimal solution and the demand for liquidity. Appendix 2B addresses an obvious question: how does our model of liquidity demand by firms compare with the extensively studied case of consumer liquidity demand?

1 Leverage

We use a very simple model of credit rationing as the basic building block for our liquidity analysis. An entrepreneurial firm has an investment opportunity with a known outcome, but only part of the return is pledgeable to investors. When the pledgeable income is insufficient to cover the full investment cost, the firm has to cover the gap with funds it has accumulated from the past. As a result the firm's investment is constrained by the firm's net worth (unlike in classic theory). We start with a version of the model where the investment scale is fixed. We then introduce a constant-returns-to-scale version, which allows us to study (in chapter 3) the critical trade-off between investment in scale versus investment in liquidity that credit rationed firms inevitably face.

There are many ways to rationalize the assumption that not all of a firm's income is pledgeable. We present a simple moral hazard model with limited liability as an illustration and a reference point for later discussion.

1.1 A Simple Model of Credit Rationing with Fixed Investment Scale

Consider a risk-neutral entrepreneur with an investment opportunity that is worth Z_1 but only $Z_0 < Z_1$ to outside investors. We assume that the initial investment I satisfies $Z_1 > I > Z_0$ (see figure 1.1). The investment has a *positive net present value*, $Z_1 > I$, but it is *not self-financing* because the most that investors can be promised is less than the investment, $Z_0 < I$. The shortfall $I - Z_0 > 0$ must be paid by the entrepreneur (or covered by claims on the market value of the firm's existing assets).

There are a variety of reasons why the full returns of a project cannot be paid out to the investors, that is, why there is a *positive wedge*

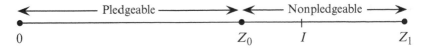

Figure 1.1
Limited pledgeability

(entrepreneurial rent) $Z_1 - Z_0 > 0$. We can put the explanations into two general categories: one based on *exogenous* constraints on payouts and another based on *endogenous* constraints. The prime example of exogenous constraints is a private benefit that only the entrepreneur can enjoy, such as the pleasure of working on a favorite project or the increased social status that comes with its success. A related intangible benefit arises from differences in beliefs. Entrepreneurs often have an inflated view of the chance that their project will succeed.[1] To the extent that the differences in beliefs are not based on better information, the extra utility the entrepreneur derives from overoptimism can, in a one-shot setting, be modeled as a private benefit that investors do not value. There are also tangible benefits that may be impossible to transfer fully, such as the increased value of human capital that comes with investment experience, or the future value that an entrepreneur may enjoy from the option to move after he has been revealed to be a good performer.[2]

In the second category, entrepreneurial rents are endogenous in the sense that while it is feasible to pay out all of the project's returns to the investors, attempts to reduce the entrepreneur's share below $Z_1 - Z_0 > 0$ will inevitably hurt the investors. Therefore it is optimal to let the entrepreneur enjoy a minimum rent. The simplest example is one where the entrepreneur can steal some of the output for private consumption or, equivalently, where the entrepreneur has to be given a share of the output in order to discourage him from diverting output to private consumption (Lacker and Weinberg 1989). Below we consider

---

1. Of course, the fact that entrepreneurs often fail, or that they express a high confidence in a project when asked, is as such no evidence of overconfidence and can be explained by either agency costs or confidence-maintenance strategies. However, Landier and Thesmar (2009) provide evidence of entrepreneurial overconfidence that is consistent with Van den Steen (2004). Simsek (2010) analyzes financing of projects sponsored by optimistic entrepreneurs. He shows that heterogeneity in beliefs has an asymmetric impact on financing, as financial market discipline operates only when entrepreneurial optimism concerns the likelihood of bad events. By contrast, entrepreneurs who are optimistic about good events can raise substantial amounts.

2. See, for example, Terviö (2009).

a standard moral hazard model with limited liability that leads to the same conclusion.

Because we assumed that the project is not self-financing, $I - Z_0 > 0$, investment will require a positive contribution from the entrepreneur. Let A be the maximum amount of capital that the entrepreneur can commit to the project either personally or through the firm. The project can go forward if and only if the pledgeable income exceeds the project's net financing need $I - A$, that is, when

$$A \geq \bar{A} \equiv I - Z_0 > 0. \tag{1.1}$$

Condition (1.1) puts a lower bound $\bar{A}$ on the amount of assets that the firm or the entrepreneur needs to have in order to be able to attract external funds. A firm with less capital than $\bar{A}$ will be *credit rationed*. It is, of course, possible that $A > I$, in which case no external funds are needed. This is an uninteresting case in the current model, so we will rule it out for the time being. But when we study liquidity shortages in chapter 3, $A > I$ is a legitimate and interesting case.

It bears repeating that a positive entrepreneurial rent $Z_1 - Z_0 > 0$ is necessary for credit rationing. If $Z_1 = Z_0$, then all projects with positive net present value $(Z_1 > I)$ are also self-financing $(Z_0 > I)$ and hence can move forward. Another necessary condition for credit rationing is that the firm is *capital poor* in the sense that

$$A < Z_1 - Z_0. \tag{1.2}$$

When (1.2) is violated, the firm has enough capital up front to pay for the ex post rents it earns, and therefore all projects with positive net present value can go forward. One can see this formally by rewriting (1.1) in the form

$$Z_1 - I \geq Z_1 - Z_0 - A. \tag{1.3}$$

The left-hand side is the net present value of the project. The right-hand side is the net rent enjoyed by the entrepreneur after investing all his net worth in the project. If the right-hand side is negative, all projects with a positive net present value can proceed. It is only when the firm is capital poor and (1.2) holds that valuable projects may be rejected. Stated more strongly, condition (1.2) has the important implication that for a capital poor firm there will always be projects with a positive net present value that have to be rejected because the firm does not have enough capital.

Let us finally note that the internal cost of capital is above the market rate (0) below the point where the firm is credit rationed as can be seen by considering the entrepreneur's utility payoff U.

$$U = A + Z_1 - I, \quad \text{if} \quad A \geq \bar{A},$$
$$U = A, \qquad \text{if} \quad A < \bar{A}. \tag{1.4}$$

Because utility jumps up at $A = \bar{A}$, the value of funds inside the firm is strictly higher than outside the firm below $\bar{A}$.[3] When $A < \bar{A}$, total output can be increased by transferring funds from investors to capital poor entrepreneurs, but such transfers will not be Pareto improving. In models with non-transferable utility, Pareto optimality does not imply total surplus maximization.

1.2 A Simple Moral Hazard Model of the Wedge between Value and Pledgeable Income

1.2.1 The Wedge as an Incentive Payment

Our liquidity analysis proceeds largely without reference to the particular reasons behind the nonpledgeable income wedge $Z_1 - Z_0$. But to gain a better grasp of the economic significance of this analysis, it is worth going beyond the reduced-form model. In this section we analyze a specific model in which the wedge appears endogenously.[4] The analysis will highlight important determinants of the firm's debt capacity, illustrate the impact that credit rationing may have on the firm's choice of investments, and indicate the benefits and costs of using different kinds of collateral.

We employ a standard model of investment with moral hazard.[5] There is a single entrepreneur (firm) and a competitive set of outside investors. All parties are risk neutral. There is a single good used for consumption as well as investment. There are two periods. In the initial period, indexed $t = 0$, there is an opportunity to invest. The investment costs I. The gross payoff of the investment one period later ($t = 1$) is either R (a success) or 0 (a failure). The probability of success depends on an

---

3. Formally, the marginal internal cost of capital is equal to 0 up to $\bar{A}$ and jumps to infinity at $\bar{A}$. With a continuous investment choice this cost varies more smoothly and exceeds the market rate; see section 1.3.

4. Note that even if a number of explanations can be given for a positive wedge, we will take the wedge as a primitive in our analysis. This is why we provide an explicit model that justifies treating the wedge as exogenous in the analyses we will be considering.

5. The model is taken from Holmström and Tirole (1998), but it has many antecedents.

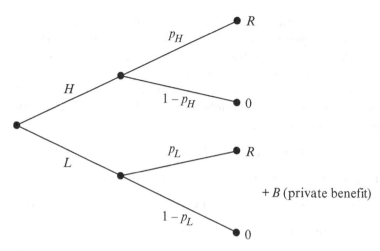

Figure 1.2
Description of moral hazard

unobserved action taken by the entrepreneur. The action represents the entrepreneur's choice of where to invest the funds, I. The intended purpose is to invest in an efficient technology H, which gives a high probability of success p_H. The entrepreneur also has the option to invest in an inefficient technology L, which gives a lower probability of success $p_L < p_H$, but provides the entrepreneur with a private benefit B. (For instance, the inefficient technology may only cost $I - B$, leaving B for the entrepreneur's private consumption.) The choice and payoff structure is described in figure 1.2.

We assume that there is no discounting between the periods and that the expected return of the investment is negative if the low action is taken and positive if the high action is taken:

$$p_H R - I > 0 > p_L R - I + B \tag{1.5}$$

Thus it is better not to invest at all than to invest and have the firm choose the inefficient technology L.

The entrepreneur has assets worth A. These assets are liquid in the sense that they have the same value in the hands of the entrepreneur as in the hands of investors. The firm is protected by limited liability. We assume again that $A < I$ so that the firm needs to raise $I - A > 0$ from outside investors in order for the project to go forward. Investors can access an unlimited pool of funds, and they demand an interest rate that we normalize to 0.

Investors can be paid contingent on the outcome of the project. Let X_s (X_f) be the entrepreneur's date-1 wealth in case the project succeeds (fails). Limited liability requires that $X_i \geq 0$, $i = s, f$. Investors receive $Y_s = R - X_s$ if the project succeeds and $Y_f = -X_f$ if it fails.

We are interested in the conditions under which the investment can go ahead. There are two constraints that must be satisfied. First, the investors need to break even,

$$p_H(R - X_s) + (1 - p_H)(-X_f) \geq I - A. \tag{1.6}$$

Second, the entrepreneur must be induced to be diligent,

$$p_H X_s + (1 - p_H) X_f \geq p_L X_s + (1 - p_L) X_f + B. \tag{1.7}$$

Simplified, this incentive compatibility constraint reads as

$$X_s - X_f \geq \frac{B}{\Delta p}, \tag{1.8}$$

where

$$\Delta p \equiv p_H - p_L > 0. \tag{1.9}$$

Incentive compatibility (1.8) paired with limited liability implies that the entrepreneur earns a positive rent. This rent is minimized by setting $X_f = 0$ and $X_s = B/\Delta p$. The rent cuts into the amount that can be paid out to investors. The firm's *pledgeable income* is defined as the maximum expected amount that investors can be promised when the entrepreneur is paid the minimum rent. The pledgeable income is

$$Z_0 = p_H \left(R - \frac{B}{\Delta p} \right). \tag{1.10}$$

To complete the link to the reduced form discussed earlier, denote the output $Z_1 = p_H R$. The positive wedge is then equal to the entrepreneur's minimum rent $Z_1 - Z_0 = p_H(B/\Delta p)$.

1.2.2 Factors Influencing Pledgeable Income

Bias toward Less Risky Projects   The net worth of a firm may altogether prohibit it from investing, as discussed above. More generally, a firm's net worth will merely limit which projects it can invest in. Assume that there is a set of projects that the firm and the investors can jointly choose from. The firm can more easily satisfy (1.1) by choosing projects with a smaller investment scale I or a higher pledgeable income.

For example, in the incentive payment illustration, each project is characterized by a tuple (I, R, p_H, p_L, B). Pledgeable income increases in p_H and R and decreases in p_L and B, reflecting the fact that the entrepreneur's incentive problem is less severe when the efficient choice H becomes more attractive relative to the inefficient choice L. More interesting, consider variations in p_H and R that leave the expected payoff of the desired project Z_1 and the other parameters unaltered. Specifically, assume that p_H goes down while R goes up so that the project becomes more risky. Other things equal, the firm's pledgeable income decreases with such risk. A decrease in p_H increases the rent $p_H B / \Delta p$ that goes to the entrepreneur, since the entrepreneur's reward in the successful state (the only incentive instrument available) is less potent the lower is p_H. With a higher entrepreneurial rent, less can be promised to investors (Z_0 is lower), which raises the cutoff value $\bar{A}$. At the margin, capital-constrained firms will therefore accept safer projects at the expense of lower expected returns.

Diversification   A variant on the theme above occurs when diversification helps reduce the need for own funds. Suppose that a single project can be replaced by two identical, half-sized projects of the sort we have discussed. Assume that the projects are stochastically independent and that the entrepreneur chooses separately, but simultaneously, whether to be diligent in executing each project. One can show that in this case the optimal incentive scheme pays the entrepreneur a positive amount only when both projects succeed. The entrepreneur in effect pledges the rewards that accrue from a successful project as collateral for the other project. This maximizes the pledgeable income.

For diversification to be of value, it is important that the projects be independent. If the projects are perfectly correlated (or the entrepreneur opportunistically choses them to be perfectly correlated), diversification does not raise the pledgeable income.[6]

Intermediation   Another way of increasing the pledgeable income is to reduce the entrepreneur's opportunity cost of being diligent. Some projects are more conducive to misbehavior than others, for instance, projects that are exceptional, that do not have tangible investments, or that involve poor accounting. A capital poor firm can sometimes increase

---

6. For more on diversification in this type of model, see Conning (2004), Hellwig (2000), Laux (2001), and Tirole (2006, ch. 4).

its pledgeable income by turning to an intermediary that has monitoring expertise. A simple way to model monitoring is to assume that the intermediary can reduce B to a lower level b (and perhaps simultaneously reduce p_L) because it can place constraints on what the firm can do. Loan covenants serve this purpose: for instance, lending contracts frequently forbid the firm from paying dividends if certain financial conditions are violated. Covenants may also give the bank veto rights on the sale of strategic assets and spell out circumstances under which the bank can intervene even more aggressively by getting the right to nominate all or part of the board. Another potential interpretation of the monitoring activity is that the bank acquires information that is relevant for decision-making and uses it to convince the board not to rubberstamp (what turns out to be) the management's pet project. In the model, and apparently in reality, giving the firm less attractive outside options reduces entrepreneurial rents, increases pledgeable income and thus lowers $\bar{A}$. The carrot can be smaller if the stick is bigger.

Of course, intermediation is not free. To determine whether intermediaries can really increase pledgeable income, monitoring costs must also be taken into account. One can distinguish at least three kinds of monitoring costs from intermediation:

1. Direct costs are incurred by the intermediary as well as the firm due to the additional work involved in evaluating investments, processing loans, and monitoring compliance with covenants.

2. Constraints imposed on a firm as part of a loan covenant do not merely cut out illegitimate opportunities, they also cut out legitimate ones. A firm that cannot sell or acquire significant assets without the approval of a bank may have to forego valuable deals. Excluding profit opportunities of this kind lowers Z_1 and reduces the project's expected return.

3. Monitoring expertise is scarce and commands rents that depend on market conditions. In Holmström and Tirole (1997), we study a model where the monitor can itself act opportunistically and therefore has to be given a share in the firm's payoff. This increases $\bar{A}$ by an amount that gets determined by the demand for intermediation among credit-constrained firms. In equilibrium firms sort themselves into three groups as a function of their net worth: firms that have too little own capital to be able to invest, firms that have enough own capital to go directly to the market and so do not need intermediation, and firms that have

intermediate amounts of capital and invest with the help of intermediaries. In the last instance, funding comes both from the informed
investors (intermediaries) and from the uninformed investors (the general market) that invest only because the intermediary's participation
has reduced the risk of opportunism.

1.3 Variable Investment Scale

For the upcoming liquidity analysis we need a model where investment
is variable so that we can study the important trade-off between the
scale of the initial investment and the decision to save some funds to
meet future liquidity shocks. A simple, tractable model is obtained by
letting the investment vary in a constant-returns-to-scale fashion.

Let I be the scale of the investment (measured by cost), let ρ_1 be the
expected total return, and ρ_0 the pledgeable income, both measured *per
unit invested*. Thus I results in a total payoff $\rho_1 I$ of which $\rho_0 I$ can be
pledged to outside investors. The residual $(\rho_1 - \rho_0)I$ is the minimum
rent going to the entrepreneur.[7]

The moral-hazard model of section 1.2 fits this framework if we
assume that a successful project returns RI and the private benefit to
the entrepreneur from cheating is BI. In that case,

$$\rho_1 = p_H R,$$

$$\rho_0 = p_H \left(R - \frac{B}{\Delta p} \right). \tag{1.11}$$

As before, we assume that projects are socially valuable but not self-
financing:

$$0 < \rho_0 < 1 < \rho_1. \tag{1.12}$$

Consequently the entrepreneur needs own funds $A > 0$ to invest. For
each unit of investment the firm can raise ρ_0 from outside investors,
leaving the *minimum equity ratio* $1 - \rho_0 > 0$ to be covered by own funds.
The repayment constraint is

$$A \geq (1 - \rho_0)I,$$

---

7. The parameters ρ_1 and ρ_0 correspond to the parameters Z_1 and Z_0 of the fixed investment model in section 1.1 at $I = 1$.

implying a maximum investment scale

$$I = kA = \frac{A}{1 - \rho_0}.$$ (1.13)

The *equity multiplier* $k \equiv 1/(1 - \rho_0) > 1$, the inverse of the (minimum) equity ratio, defines the firm's maximum leverage per unit of own capital. A firm with 10 units of own capital and a required minimum equity ratio of 20 percent can invest a maximum of 50 units.

If the firm chooses the maximum investment scale, the entrepreneur's gross payoff is

$$U^g = \frac{(\rho_1 - \rho_0)A}{1 - \rho_0} = \mu A,$$

where

$$\mu \equiv \frac{\rho_1 - \rho_0}{1 - \rho_0}.$$ (1.14)

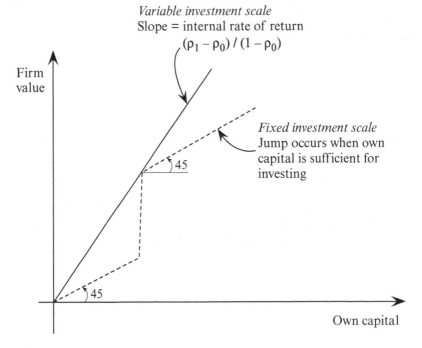

Figure 1.3
Internal rate of return

The entrepreneur's net utility is

$$U = (\mu - 1)A = \frac{\rho_1 - 1}{1 - \rho_0}A.$$

For each unit invested, the entrepreneur enjoys a rent $\rho_1 - \rho_0$. Thanks to the equity multiplier $k > 1$, the rent gets magnified, resulting in a gross rate of return on own capital $\mu > 1$; see figure 1.3. The rate is constant because of the constant-returns-to-scale technology. More important, the rate is greater than 1 because of (1.12), implying that the internal rate of return exceeds the market rate of interest. By transferring a unit of the good from investors to the entrepreneur, total social surplus ($\rho_1 I - I$) could be increased by more than one unit. But such transfers are not Pareto improving, since the increase in total surplus cannot be arbitrarily split between the investors and entrepreneurs.

To see this, note that the entrepreneur maximizes his utility by choosing the maximum investment scale (1.14), since the rate of return on entrepreneurial capital exceeds the market rate. He puts all his wealth in the illiquid portion of the return (the nonpledgeable return ($\rho_1 - \rho_0)I$), leaving outsiders holding the firm's liquid assets. While total output could be raised by transferring wealth from passive investors to active entrepreneurs, investors cannot be compensated as they already hold all the firm's liquid claims. There is nothing that the government can do to improve on private contracting.

1.4 Comparative Statics and Investment Implications

Factors that increase ρ_0 or ρ_1 (or both) will increase the entrepreneur's utility and an increase in ρ_0 will also increase the investment scale I. Investors are simply paid their market rate of return, so they remain unaffected by these changes.

Recall that in the moral-hazard model, ρ_0 increases with R and p_H and decreases with B and p_L, while ρ_1 increases with R and p_H. If the firm could choose among investments that differed in their attributes ρ_0 and ρ_1, the firm would not simply choose the investment that maximizes the social net present value per unit, that is, the investment with the highest ρ_1. The pledgeable income is also critical as it determines the extent to which the firm can lever its capital. From (1.14) we see that the firm's willingness to substitute ρ_0 for ρ_1 is given by

$$\frac{d\rho_1}{d\rho_0} = 1 - \mu < 0. \tag{1.15}$$

The firm will choose projects with lower ρ_1 up to the point where the reduction in ρ_1 per unit of increase in ρ_0 equals the difference between the internal rate of return and the market rate of return. Each unit of pledgeable income ρ_0 is worth $\mu - 1$ units of ρ_1 because of scale expansion. This illustrates one of the central themes of credit constrained lending: the willingness to sacrifice net present value for an increase in pledgeable income.

1.5 Concluding Remark

This chapter introduced a simple agency model to create a link between a firm's net worth and its scale of investment. Even at this basic level it shows how moral hazard problems influence the firm's leverage and economic activity.[8] In all models of credit rationing, the leverage of net worth implies that the return on inside funds is higher than the market return on capital. Therefore the economy's total output can be increased by redistributing capital from investors to entrepreneurs. In reality the effectiveness of such redistributions is limited by the difficulty of identifying which entrepreneurs are able to use the capital constructively. The limited scope of venture capital funding makes this evident. In our model (and many others) there are no such informational limitations. However, as we argued, even if one were able to identify deserving entrepreneurs and redistribute to them funds from passive investors, this cannot be done in a manner that makes both entrepreneurs and investors better off. The next chapter shows that the situation changes when one adds to the model a period in which firms can anticipate future liquidity needs and make arrangements to fund them. What is redistribution in the one-period model becomes insurance in this two-period model. This simple observation about insurance lies at the heart of the analysis of liquidity provision both privately and publicly.

---

8. Bernanke and Gertler (1989) were the first to demonstrate the importance of net worth for investment and economic activity. They used a different model of moral hazard (the costly state verification model due to Townsend 1979).

2   A Simple Model of Liquidity Demand

Firms demand liquidity in anticipation of future financing needs either because it is cheaper to get financing now or because there is a risk that financing will not be available if the firm waits until the need for funding arises. In this chapter we analyze the demand for liquidity in a simple extension of the two-period model from section 1.3. The basic idea is easy to understand. Suppose that there is an intermediate period when additional funds have to be invested in order to continue the project and realize any payoffs. We refer to this reinvestment need as a *liquidity shock* and denote it ρ (per unit of investment). If the liquidity shock ρ turns out to be larger than the pledgeable amount ρ_0, the firm cannot get outside funding to continue the project unless it has arranged for such funding in advance. This creates a demand for liquidity, as firms look to insure against shocks that have a positive total return ($\rho_1 - \rho > 0$), but a negative net present value for investors ($\rho_0 - \rho < 0$). Note that the wedge $\rho_1 - \rho_0 > 0$ is crucial for the argument. If $\rho_1 = \rho_0$, the liquidity shock ρ cannot fall strictly between the total and the pledgeable return.

The ex ante demand for liquidity will depend on the size of the liquidity shock. Shocks that are high enough will not be insured (financed in advance). The second-best policy trades off the scale of the initial investment against the ability to withstand higher liquidity shocks. In general, there will be credit rationing both at the initial period and in the intermediate period, since entrepreneurial capital is scarce and commands a premium relative to the market.

By assumption, no external claims can be issued on the private (illiquid) return $\rho_1 - \rho_0$, while arbitrary external claims can be issued on the pledgeable (liquid) return ρ_0. In particular, these claims can be made contingent on the liquidity shock ρ. In effect we are assuming complete contracting on the liquid portion of the firm's return. This is perhaps unrealistic, but it has the attraction that it is a minimal departure from the standard Arrow–Debreu world. After studying optimal contingent contracts, we discuss how they can be implemented using common means such as credit lines, equity issues (involving dilution), and holding liquid (marketable) assets in anticipation of future liquidity needs. Relaxing the assumption that the liquidity shock is observed by investors, we also show that the implementation of the second-best policy hinges crucially on the ability of investors to keep the firm from spending funds on unauthorized projects.

2.1 The General Setup

There are three dates, $t = 0, 1, 2$, and a single good. At date 0, the firm chooses the scale of the project I. At date 1, the *liquidity shock* $\rho \geq 0$ takes place. The value ρ determines how much more needs to be invested per unit to continue. Continuing at a smaller scale than I is feasible. Let $i(\rho) \leq I$ denote the continuation scale when the liquidity shock is ρ. Continuing at this scale requires a date-1 investment $\rho i(\rho)$ and yields a date-2 liquid (pledgeable) return $\rho_0 i(\rho)$ and an illiquid (private) return $(\rho_1 - \rho_0) i(\rho)$ to the entrepreneur. There are no returns from the portion of the project that is not carried forward. If $i(\rho) = 0$, then the firm is closed down and the payout, both pledgeable and private is zero; see figure 2.1.

To be concrete, one can think of I as the cost of purchasing a machine. The variable cost of production—which includes payments for intermediate inputs, labor, and so on—is ρ. At date 1, after observing ρ, the firm can decide at what scale to operate the machine. Another example would be the initial purchase of land and the subsequent decision to develop all or some fraction of the land. More generally, I represents a sunk, fixed cost that caps the scale at which production can be carried out at date 1. We thus assume that it is infinitely costly to increase the scale I at date 1 (it takes time to build).

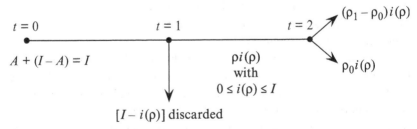

Figure 2.1
Timing

The liquidity shock is modeled this way mainly for convenience. The basic ideas we want to get across at this point are not dependent on the particular way we model the liquidity shock. In section 2.5 we show how the analysis extends to more general cases (uncertain returns, a positive value of liquidation, an intermediate income, etc.) that are of interest, for instance, when we discuss implementation issues and risk management policies.

2.2 Two Liquidity Shocks

We start with the case where the liquidity shock ρ can take only two values, high (ρ_H) or low (ρ_L), which are constrained to satisfy

$$0 \leq \rho_L < \rho_0 < \rho_H < \rho_1. \tag{2.1}$$

The reason for limiting the shocks in this manner is that shocks below ρ_0 do not require pre-arranged financing, whereas shocks above ρ_0 do. The high and low shocks in (2.1) cover these two leading cases. Let f_L and f_H denote the probabilities of a low, respectively high, liquidity shock. We assume that

$$\rho_0 < \min \left\{ 1 + f_L \rho_L + f_H \rho_H, \frac{1 + \rho_L f_L}{f_L} \right\} < \rho_1. \tag{2.2}$$

The middle term in (2.2) is the minimum expected cost of carrying one unit of the project to completion (see below). If the project is continued in both states, the expected cost is the first term in the brackets. If the project is continued only in the low state, the second term measures the expected cost per unit completed. The inequality on the right implies that the project is socially desirable, while the inequality on the left assures that the project is not self-financing (the pledgeable income does not cover the total cost of investment for any policy). A self-financing project could be carried out at any scale, which would lead to unbounded payoffs.

We are looking for a second-best contract. A contract specifies the level of investment I and the continuation scales $i_L \equiv i(\rho_L)$ and $i_H \equiv i(\rho_H)$ (both $\leq I$) corresponding to the low and high liquidity shocks, respectively. A contract also specifies final payments to investors and the entrepreneur, but just as in the simpler two-period model, it is easy to see that it is optimal to assign all the liquid returns $\rho_0 i(\rho)$ to the investors, leaving the entrepreneur holding only the illiquid part $(\rho_1 - \rho_0)i(\rho)$. The entrepreneur only holds illiquid claims because the return on internal liquid funds exceeds the market rate (which we take to be 0).

The second-best solution solves

$$\max_{\{I, i_L, i_H\}} \left\{ f_L(\rho_1 - \rho_L)i_L + f_H(\rho_1 - \rho_H)i_H - I \right\}, \tag{2.3}$$

subject to

$$f_L(\rho_0 - \rho_L)i_L + f_H(\rho_0 - \rho_H)i_H \geq I - A, \tag{2.4}$$

$$0 \leq i_L, i_H \leq I. \tag{2.5}$$

The objective function is the expected social return on the investment. Evidently the budget constraint (2.4) will bind at the optimum. By substituting the budget constraint into the objective function, eliminating I, we get an equivalent program in which the entrepreneur's expected rent, rather than the expected social return, is maximized. Since investors all earn the market rate of interest (0), the full social surplus goes to the entrepreneur. We will often take the entrepreneur's rent, which equals his expected *net utility*, as the objective.

The budget constraint makes clear that investors provide insurance against liquidity shocks. When the low shock occurs, the firm pays the investors $\rho_0 - \rho_L > 0$ per unit of continued investment. When the high shock occurs, investors pay the firm $\rho_H - \rho_0 > 0$.

Since $\rho_1 - \rho_L$ and $\rho_0 - \rho_L$ are both positive, it is in the interest of the investors as well as the entrepreneur to continue at full scale when a low shock occurs; hence $i_L = I$.[1] The program then boils down to choosing just two values: the initial scale I and the continuation scale i_H in the high shock state. There is a trade-off between these two investments. The bigger one chooses I, the lower must i_H be, since both imply net outlays for the investors (in contrast to i_L, which relaxes the budget constraint). Let $x = i_H/I$ denote the fraction of the project that is being continued when the high shock occurs at date 1, and let

$$\bar{\rho}(x) \equiv f_L \rho_L + f_H \rho_H x \tag{2.6}$$

denote the expected unit cost of continuing. The maximal scale of the initial investment $I(x)$ as a function of the fraction x of the project that is

---

1. Because the project always continues at full scale when the low shock occurs, we could have counted the low shock as part of the initial investment and adjusted both the low and the high shock correspondingly; that is, we could have chosen $\rho_L = 0$ without loss of generality. When there is a positive liquidity premium, as will be the case later on, the same nominal expenditure may have a different value in different periods; hence we refrain from this simplification.

continued in the high-shock state is given by the budget constraint (2.4):

$$I(x) = \frac{A}{1 + \bar{\rho}(x) - \rho_0(f_L + xf_H)}. \tag{2.7}$$

The entrepreneur's expected net utility (equal to the social surplus) is

$$\begin{aligned} U(x) &= [\rho_1(f_L + f_H x) - (1 + \bar{\rho}(x))]I(x) \\ &= (\mu(x) - 1)A, \end{aligned} \tag{2.8}$$

where $\mu(x)$ is the gross value of an additional unit of entrepreneurial capital and takes the form

$$\mu(x) = \frac{(\rho_1 - \rho_0)(f_L + f_H x)}{(1 + \bar{\rho}(x)) - \rho_0(f_L + f_H x)}. \tag{2.9}$$

Because the Lagrangian of the program (2.3) through (2.5) is linear, we only need to evaluate the utility levels corresponding to $x = 0$ (continuing only when the shock is low) and $x = 1$ (always continuing). In either case continuation is at full scale I; partial continuation is not relevant. A direct evaluation of $U(1) - U(0)$, the difference in utility between the two cases, shows that it is optimal to cover both liquidity shocks (choose $x = 1$) if and only if

$$\frac{(\rho_1 - \rho_0)f_L}{(1 + \rho_L f_L) - \rho_0 f_L} = \mu(0) \leq \mu(1) = \frac{(\rho_1 - \rho_0)}{(1 + \bar{\rho}(1)) - \rho_0}. \tag{2.10}$$

When $\rho_H = \rho_0$, inequality (2.10) holds and the project will be continued in both states. As ρ_H is increased from ρ_0 to ρ_1, the difference $\mu(0) - \mu(1)$ moves monotonically from being strictly negative to strictly positive. Therefore in between the two extreme ρ_H-values there is a cutoff value c, satisfying $\rho_0 < c < \rho_1$, such that the project will continue if and only if

$$\rho_H \leq c. \tag{2.11}$$

Simple manipulations of the cutoff condition $\mu(0) \leq \mu(1)$ allow us to write

$$c = \min\left\{1 + f_L \rho_L + f_H \rho_H, \frac{1 + f_L \rho_L}{f_L}\right\}. \tag{2.12}$$

We can interpret c as the *unit cost of effective investment*, namely what it costs on average to bring one unit of investment to completion. Condition (2.11) therefore has the intuitive interpretation that it is optimal to continue in the high-shock state if and only if the unit cost of effective investment (the expected cost of increasing scale) is less than the cost of the shock (the cost of liquidity). We will see that an analogous condition holds in the continuum case.

We can also restate the inequality (2.10) as the following necessary and sufficient condition for continuing in both the low and the high states.[2]

$$f_L(\rho_H - \rho_L) \leq 1. \tag{2.13}$$

The effects of ρ_H and ρ_L in (2.13) are intuitive. They reflect the fact that both an increase in ρ_H and a decrease in ρ_L will work in favor of larger ex ante scale at the expense of less ex post liquidity; a lower ρ_L increases the return to initial scale, while a higher ρ_H makes it more costly to continue ex post. The role played by f_L in (2.13) is less obvious, since both the benefits and costs of continuing in the high state go up as f_L decreases. The issue then is how the firm should divide an extra unit between the initial investment I and liquidity provision at date 1. As f_L goes to zero, the net return from investing only in the low-shock state goes to zero, while the net return from continuing in both states is bounded below by a strictly positive number. Hence, if f_L is small enough, it is better to continue also in the high state.

Remark (Repeated Liquidity Shocks)   A limitation of our analysis is that it does not do justice to the rich dynamics of liquidity management. After the initial contracting stage, date 0, there is only one period, date 1, at which the firm will possibly need new cash. There is accordingly no point hoarding liquidity at date 1. Relatedly, all liquidity hoarded at date 0 is usable,[3] with the caveat, studied in appendix 2A, that available liquidity may be abused in the presence of alternative uses of this liquidity. Recent work has studied optimal liquidity management in related, but infinite-horizon models of repeated moral hazard. Biais et al. (2007, 2010) and DeMarzo and Fishman (2007a, b) shed light on how, over time, investment and available liquidity adjust to profit realizations in an optimal contract. For example, Biais et al. show that liquidity is not meant to be fully depleted even though it is in fact reduced after an adverse shock. Discipline is ensured by downsizing when things go

---

2. That neither ρ_0 or ρ_1 show up in (2.13) is a consequence of the constant returns to scale technology; however, they enter implicitly through the parameter restrictions (2.1) and (2.2).

3. See Goodhart (2008) for a discussion of usable liquidity.

wrong, not by a complete exposure to liquidity risk. This policy is in the spirit of proportionality for compulsory reserves as well as for capital requirements in banking regulation.

2.3   Implementation of the Second-Best Contract

The implementation of the second-best contract presents two kinds of problems. The first problem is that the entrepreneur may use the funds in a different way than the contract specifies (either at date 0 or at date 1). The second problem is that investors may not be able to deliver on the promise to provide funds at date 1. Such promises must be backed up by claims on real assets that the investor owns at date 1 and can use as collateral. We will discuss collateral problems at length in the coming chapters. The purpose of this section is to illustrate some of the problems that may arise on the firm's side.

One potential problem is that when the second-best optimum specifies that the firm should not continue when facing the high shock, the entrepreneur may still want to invest less than the agreed-upon amount I at date 0 in order to keep extra funds in store to meet the high liquidity shock. Alternatively, when the second-best optimum recommends that the firm withstand even the high liquidity shock, the entrepreneur may not want to save funds for reinvestment in the high state and instead spend the funds on a higher initial investment I. This may be a tempting possibility, since the entrepreneur knows that investors will always finance a low shock even if the scale is higher than initially intended. The entrepreneur can rely on a soft-budget constraint for the low shock because investors face a fait accompli. The downside to the entrepreneur of such a policy is that there will not be enough funds to fully finance the high shock, as no investor will be ready to make up the shortfall at date 1.

In order to implement the second-best policy, there must be a way to enforce the right levels and kinds of investment at date 0 as well as date 1. Intermediaries, venture capitalists, large block holders, and others, monitor in varying degrees and in different ways a firm's use of funds. A rich literature in corporate finance has investigated these issues in depth. We will not study intermediation explicitly, even though it constitutes an integral part of the financing of firms.[4] We will assume

---

4. See Holmström and Tirole (1997) for an analysis of intermediation using the same basic model as here and Tirole (2006) for a more extensive treatment.

instead that investors can directly monitor the firm's liquidity position but not the firm's liquidity shock and consider two illustrative cases: in the first, the firm has no alternative uses of funds and will therefore behave; in the second, the entrepreneur can divert funds for some personal benefit.

2.3.1 Costless Implementation: Firm Has No Alternative Use of Funds

Assume that condition (2.10) holds so that reinvestment is desirable in both the low-and the high-shock states. Consider, first, a hypothetical scenario where the entrepreneur has no alternative use of date-1 funds; date-1 liquidity is of value only because it allows the firm to meet liquidity shocks. Under this scenario there are many alternative ways to implement the second-best solution.

One option is to give the firm a line of credit up to $\rho_H I$, which it can freely use at date 1. This allows the firm to meet both kinds of shocks. If the low shock occurs, the firm will leave $(\rho_H - \rho_L)I$ unspent, since we assumed that there is no alternative use for the excess funds. If the high shock occurs, the firm will draw down the full line of credit, which has a negative net present value, because the firm's pledgeable date-2 income $\rho_0 I$ is less than the credit $\rho_H I$ used. A minor variant would be to reduce the credit line to $(\rho_H - \rho_0)I$ but give the entrepreneur the right to dilute the initial investors' up to their maximum stake $\rho_0 I$. Either way, the entrepreneur has to pay for the expected use of liquidity up front.

One may wonder to what extent banks actually honor credit lines in states of nature where they would prefer not to lend. Empirically it is not so easy to distinguish involuntary lending from voluntary lending or lending that is done to preserve a reputation in the credit market as has been suggested by Boot, Thakor, and Udell (1987).[5] However, studies of bank lending during the subprime crisis, as well as the 1998 crisis associated with the collapse of Long Term Capital Management (LTCM), indicate that drawdowns on existing credit lines can be substantial. Ivanisha and Scharfstein (2009), who compare patterns of bank lending in the period August to November 2008 note that while new commercial and industrial loans fall dramatically (37 percent) in this period compared with the same period in 2007, firms that secured credit

---

5. Implicit bank liabilities are common and create serious issues for prudential regulators as they are not really covered by any capital charge. For example, in the summer of 2007 Bear Stearns bailed out two funds it had sponsored even though it had no legal obligation to do so.

lines made extensive use of them, since the level of loans on bank balance sheets increased somewhat during that time. They identify $16 billion worth of drawdowns from press releases alone, but considering the large stock of credit lines (about $3,500 billion), the total drawdowns must be much larger. The paper further documents that banks that were liquidity constrained had to reduce their other lending in order to handle drawdowns—an opportunity cost argument that points to the involuntary nature of honoring credit lines. Anecdotal evidence indicates that a large number of firms also drew down credit lines in anticipation of future liquidity problems caused by the crisis, suggesting that firms were concerned about either the credit worthiness of banks or changes in the terms of credit. Strahan, Gater, and Schuermann's (2006) study of the LTCM crisis likewise concludes that banks and other credit institutions had to accept costly drawdowns, though the overall effect on the banking system was moderated by the fact that the funds came back in the form of deposits. On balance, the evidence indicates that credit lines do serve an insurance role of the sort envisioned in our model.[6]

Another common arrangement to guarantee that the firm will have enough resources in adverse circumstances is for the firm to buy insurance. Credit default swaps (CDSs), which amounted to $62 trillions at the onset of the recent crisis, allow firms to buy protection against the default of other firms.[7] For example, if an amount exceeding $(\rho_H - \rho_0)I$ constitutes a shortfall of income due to the default of trading partners, the shortfall can be offset through the use of CDSs.

Finally, firms routinely hoard liquid funds, sometimes very large ones, both to cushion smaller liquidity shocks as well as in anticipation of future spending needs such as acquisitions and other kinds of investments.[8] This can be represented in our model by investors paying the

---

6. Credit lines are often contingent on satisfying loan covenants, which could be interpreted as an effort to deal with states where firms, even in the second-best, should not be extended credit. In the recent crisis and especially in the final years before the collapse, many banks appear to have abandoned the usual precautions and extended "covenant-light" credit lines, tempted by the generous up-front fees for contingent credit.

7. The $62 trillions figure is the gross value of CDSs and greatly overstates the actual insurance coverage for this reason. Also many participated in these markets for reasons other than insuring themselves. The CDS market was in part a place where bets could be placed on the future of the economy.

8. For instance, Microsoft had at one point over $40 billion in liquid assets. Very little is typically invested in the stock of other companies, unless there is some strategic purpose to do so or the firm is in the investment business as such. Our focus is on liquidity shocks, but as the analysis in section 2.5 shows, we could include other motives.

firm $I + (\rho_H - \rho_0)I - A$ at date 0 and making sure that the firm hoards liquid assets, for instance, Treasury bonds, at date 0 in the amount $(\rho_H - \rho_0)I$. At date 1 the firm can raise up to $\rho_H I$ in fresh funds by selling the bonds and by diluting the stake of the initial investors through additional equity. If the liquidity shock is low, the firm simply leaves the excess liquidity unused—does not issue new equity and/or does not use all of the bonds. Note that this way of implementing the second-best outcome, while equivalent to a credit line, does not require the firm to raise fresh funds at date 1 for a project that has a negative net present value. The funds covering negative net present value actions at date 1 have been paid already at date 0. Naturally one can mix hoarding with credit lines in a lot of ways as long as the firm can access the right amount of liquidity at date 1.

2.3.2   Costly Implementation: Firm Can Divert Funds at Date 1

The assumption that the firm has no alternative use for excess liquidity is extreme. Firms always have alternative investments to consider, especially if the funds come at no extra charge as above. In appendix 2A we illustrate with a simple example how the optimal contract responds to the presence of an alternative investment option.

Consider again the two-shock model in which (2.10) holds, so that the second-best contract prescribes continuation for both the low (ρ_L) and the high (ρ_H) liquidity shock. Suppose that the firm can divert funds at date 1 to a project that only generates private benefits. Each unit diverted into the alternative project generates a benefit to the entrepreneur that is equal to ξ units of consumption. We assume that the value of a diverted unit satisfies

$$\xi \leq 1, \tag{2.14}$$

so that it is more efficient for the entrepreneur to receive one unit from the pledgeable income at date 2 than to divert one unit at date 1.

Investors can observe how much funds the firm uses in total at date 1 as well as the scale at which the project is continued, but they cannot see how much is used for reinvestments and how much for diversion, nor can they observe the realization of the date-1 liquidity shock. The presence of the alternative project makes the design of liquidity provision more challenging. In general, the second-best solution from section 2.2 can no longer be implemented, since the optimal contract must ensure that the entrepreneur does not want to divert funds for private benefit.

Appendix 2A determines the optimal second-best contract with potential diversion, using a standard mechanism design approach. To summarize our findings briefly, we find that diversion can be avoided most efficiently in one of two ways. Either the entrepreneur is asked to hold more than the minimum stake at the beginning, which he forgoes if he claims that the high shock has occurred, or investors scale down the investment in response to a reported high shock. Which of the two options are used depends on parameter values. Both schemes add to the cost of financing and therefore reduce the social surplus. The idea of discouraging false reporting (claiming high costs) by lowering the continuation scale of investment corresponds to standard distortions in adverse selection models. The other solution, which forces the entrepreneur to hold some of the pledgeable income in addition to the nonpledgeable one, is more interesting. The entrepreneur's incentives are made to align with the investors by having his extra shares diluted along with the initial investors' shares when a high-liquidity shock occurs. Both solutions resonate with practice.

Finally, we note that when $\xi = 1$, namely when there is no deadweight loss for the entrepreneur to consume unneeded funds, the option to divert destroys all outside insurance opportunities. In that case the firm is left to take care of itself using market instruments that are not contingent on idiosyncratic shocks.[9]

2.4   Continuum of Liquidity Shocks

For some applications (e.g., risk management; see section 4.3) it is analytically more convenient to deal with a continuum of liquidity shocks. We provide only a brief treatment here. For a more detailed analysis see Holmström and Tirole (1998) and Tirole (2006).

Let $F(\rho)$ be the distribution function and $f(\rho)$ the density function of the liquidity shock ρ. A contract specifies the initial investment level I and the continuation levels $i(\rho) \leq I$ for each contingency ρ. The contract also specifies payments to each party. As in the two-shock case, it is optimal to let the investors retain all of the pledgeable income $\rho_0 i(\rho)$ and have the entrepreneur hold only the illiquid part $(\rho_1 - \rho_0)i(\rho)$. This maximizes the return on the entrepreneur's initial assets A.

---

9. There are other technologies that result more readily in self-insurance. For instance, in Caballero and Krishnamurthy's (2003b) closely related model of liquidity demand, reinvestments only create nonpledgable income. Since the reinvestment cannot be observed and controlled by the investors, self-insurance is the only option in their model.

The second-best solution can therefore be found by solving the following program:

$$\max_{\{I,i(\rho)\}} \int (\rho_1 - \rho_0)i(\rho)f(\rho)d\rho, \tag{2.15}$$

subject to

$$\int (\rho_0 - \rho)i(\rho)f(\rho)d\rho \geq I - A, \tag{2.16}$$

$$0 \leq i(\rho) \leq I, \quad \text{for every } \rho.$$

Note that we have taken the entrepreneur's rent as the objective function because the budget constraint binds. The left-hand side of the budget constraint is the expected pledgeable income given the reinvestment policy. This has to cover the investors' date-0 contribution $I - A$.

It is intuitive, and also easy to show, that the solution to the second-best program takes the form of a cutoff value $\hat{\rho}$ such that the project continues at full scale ($i(\rho) = I$) if $\rho \leq \hat{\rho}$ and it is discontinued ($i(\rho) = 0$) if $\rho > \hat{\rho}$. We show that the optimal cutoff level, denoted ρ^*, falls strictly between the pledgeable and the total income:

$$\rho_0 < \rho^* < \rho_1. \tag{2.17}$$

To this end, consider the maximal investment level consistent with an arbitrary cutoff level $\hat{\rho}$. This level, obtained from the budget constraint (2.16), can be written

$$I = k(\hat{\rho})A, \tag{2.18}$$

where the *investment multiplier* $k(\hat{\rho})$ is

$$k(\hat{\rho}) = \frac{1}{1 + \int_0^{\hat{\rho}} \rho f(\rho)d\rho - F(\hat{\rho})\rho_0}. \tag{2.19}$$

The denominator of the investment multiplier gives the amount of entrepreneurial funding that is required per unit of investment. Substituting the maximal investment level into the objective function (2.15), the entrepreneur's net expected utility can, after some algebraic manipulations, be written

$$U(\hat{\rho}) \equiv (\mu(\hat{\rho}) - 1)A = m(\hat{\rho})k(\hat{\rho})A = \frac{\rho_1 - c(\hat{\rho})}{c(\hat{\rho}) - \rho_0}A, \tag{2.20}$$

where the *total expected return per unit of investment* $m(\hat{\rho})$ is

$$m(\hat{\rho}) = F(\hat{\rho})\rho_1 - 1 - \int_0^{\hat{\rho}} \rho f(\rho)d\rho, \tag{2.21}$$

and the *expected unit cost of effective investment* $c(\hat{\rho})$ is

$$c(\hat{\rho}) \equiv \frac{1 + \int_0^{\hat{\rho}} \rho f(\rho)d\rho}{F(\hat{\rho})}. \tag{2.22}$$

The interpretation of $c(\hat{\rho})$ parallels that of c in the two-shock case. It is the expected cost of completing one unit of investment; see (2.12). It is intuitive that the entrepreneur's expected utility is the product of the total expected return per unit invested $m(\hat{\rho})$ times the maximal investment scale $I(\hat{\rho}) = k(\hat{\rho})A$ for the cutoff $\hat{\rho}$. To see why the optimal cutoff ρ^* falls strictly between ρ_0 and ρ_1 as posited in (2.17), note first that the investment scale $k(\hat{\rho})$ is largest at $\hat{\rho} = \rho_0$, since the investor's date-1 expected net income is maximized by continuing at full scale whenever the financial return is nonnegative ($\rho_0 - \rho \geq 0$). On the other hand, the total expected return per unit of investment $m(\hat{\rho})$ is maximized by continuing at full scale whenever the total return from continuing is positive ($\rho_1 - \rho \geq 0$), that is, by setting $\hat{\rho} = \rho_1$. The second-best cutoff ρ^* is set strictly above ρ_0 because $m(\hat{\rho})$ is strictly increasing at ρ_0; it is set strictly below ρ_1 because $k(\hat{\rho})$ is strictly decreasing at ρ_1.

The model with a continuum of shocks highlights the fundamental trade-off facing the firm: that between investing in initial scale versus saving funds to meet liquidity shocks. The argument above shows that the *the second-best solution is a compromise featuring credit-rationing both at the initial investment date 0 and at the reinvestment date 1*.[10]

From the entrepreneur's expected utility (2.20) follows immediately that the optimal cutoff value $\hat{\rho} = \rho^*$ is determined by minimizing the expected unit cost of effective investment $c(\hat{\rho})$. The first-order condition for minimizing $c(\hat{\rho})$ can after some manipulation be expressed as

$$\int_0^{\rho^*} F(\rho)d\rho = 1. \tag{2.23}$$

---

10. With our constant-returns-to-scale technology, the cutoff ρ^* does not depend on the entrepreneur's endowment. Rampini and Viswanathan (2010), in a richer model, show that if the initial investment exhibits decreasing returns to scale, then the trade-off will depend on the entrepreneur's endowment. Most important, entrepreneurs with little wealth will buy no insurance at all, since the return from the initial investment trumps the value of liquidity.

Using (2.21), we can also write the condition for the optimal cutoff ρ^* as

$$c(\rho^*) = \rho^*, \tag{2.24}$$

which is the natural counter-part to the cutoff condition for the two-shock case; see (2.11).

Equation (2.23)—or, equivalently, (2.24)—determines implicitly the second-best cutoff value ρ^*. Note that the optimal cut off ρ^* does not depend on the parameters ρ_0 or ρ_1 (as long as it is desirable to invest in the project at all). Equation (2.23) implies that a mean-preserving spread of the distribution F lowers ρ^*.[11] Substituting (2.24) into (2.22), it follows that a mean-preserving spread also reduces $c(\rho^*)$, implying that more uncertainty raises the value of the project. The simple intuition behind these conclusions is that higher uncertainty increases the option value of terminating the project when the liquidity shock exceeds ρ^*. Indeed it is essential that ρ be stochastic. If the liquidity shock were a constant, the firm could raise external funds only if this constant were less than ρ_0. To finance shocks above ρ_0, there must also be shocks below ρ_0.

Finally, it is worth noting that the implementation options described in section 2.4 would not work with a continuum of liquidity shocks. In the continuum model both a credit line and the purchase of bonds would permit the entrepreneur to continue at a scaled-down level even when the shock exceeds ρ^*, the second-best cutoff. Unless prevented, the entrepreneur would take advantage of such an opportunity.

2.5   General Shocks

It is easy to generalize the model to include income at date 1 as well as a payoff from liquidation. We can also let all the variables, including the date-2 payoffs, be uncertain until date 1. The purpose of looking into such an extension is twofold. It gives a richer interpretation of the liquidity shock by pointing to a variety of sources that give rise to a

---

11. Consider two cumulative distribution functions $F(\rho)$ and $G(\rho)$ on $[0,\ \bar{\rho}]$. Distribution G is a mean-preserving spread of distribution F if for all $\hat{\rho}$,

$$\int_0^{\hat{\rho}} G(\rho)d\rho \geq \int_0^{\hat{\rho}} F(\rho)d\rho$$

and

$$\int_0^{\bar{\rho}} G(\rho)d\rho = \int_0^{\bar{\rho}} F(\rho)d\rho$$

(they have the same mean).

demand for liquidity. The general model will also be the basis for discussing risk management in section 4.3. Our original focus on shocks to the cost of reinvestment ρ was mainly for convenience.

Let ω describe the state of nature at date 1 and $F(\omega)$ be the probability distribution as seen by the parties at date 0. Contracts at date 0 can be made contingent on ω as before. Let $\rho(\omega)$, $\rho_0(\omega)$, $\rho_1(\omega)$ be the various per-unit costs and payoffs in state ω, and $i(\omega)$ be the corresponding reinvestment level at date 1. Liquidation is also possible at date 1: the value of liquidation is $(I - i(\omega))w(\omega)$, where $I - i(\omega)$ is the amount liquidated and $w(\omega)$ represents the per-unit value of liquidation. We also allow for uncertain income at date 1. It takes the form $r(\omega)I + y(\omega)$, where $r(\omega)$ is the per-unit income from the initial investment and $y(\omega)$ is income from old assets in place.

The problem is the same as before: to decide the level of the date-0 investment I and the date-1 continuation scale $i(\omega)$. This problem is solved by the following program, which is a straightforward extension of (2.15) and (2.16):

$$\max_{\{I, i(\cdot)\}} \int b(\omega)i(\omega)dF(\omega), \tag{2.25}$$

subject to

$$\int \{(\rho_0(\omega) - \rho(\omega))i(\omega) + w(\omega)(I - i(\omega))\}dF(\omega)$$
$$+ \int [r(\omega)I + y(\omega)]dF(\omega) \geq I - A,$$

$$0 \leq i(\omega) \leq I, \quad \text{for every } \omega. \tag{2.26}$$

We have chosen to replace $\rho_1(\omega)$ with the entrepreneur's private benefit $b(\omega) = \rho_1(\omega) - \rho_0(\omega)$ (per unit of continuation investment) to separate the effect that $\rho_0(\omega)$ has on the objective function from the effect it has on the budget constraint. The budget constraint includes the value of liquidation as well as the date-1 incomes from investment and from legacy assets. As before, assume that $I > 0$ and that the budget constraint binds, so that the maximization of social surplus is equivalent to the maximization of the entrepreneur's expected rent.

Let $1 + \lambda \geq 1$ be the shadow price of the budget constraint. Then the optimal choice of $i(\omega)$ is determined by the sign of

$$\Psi(\omega) = b(\omega) - (1 + \lambda)[\rho(\omega) + w(\omega) - \rho_0(\omega)] \tag{2.27}$$

as follows:

$i(\omega) = 0$ if $\Psi(\omega) < 0$,

$i(\omega) = I$ if $\Psi(\omega) > 0$,

$i(\omega) \in [0, I]$ if $\Psi(\omega) = 0$.

We see that variations in date-1 income $r(\omega)I + y(\omega)$ do not affect the decision rule directly. However, the expected value of $r(\omega)$ does influence the return on the initial investment I and that way the cost of capital $1 + \lambda$. The expected value of $y(\omega)$ merely changes the value of entrepreneurial capital and therefore the scale of investment, but it does not influence the balance between date-0 and date-1 investments. We return to these observations when we discuss risk management in chapter 4.

The decision to continue in any given state ω depends on three terms: (1) the entrepreneur's private value of continuing, $b(\omega) = \rho_1(\omega) - \rho_0(\omega)$; (2) the net financial cost $\rho(\omega) + w(\omega) - \rho_0(\omega)$ of continuing, including the cost of forgoing the opportunity to liquidate the project; and (3) the entrepreneur's cost of capital $1 + \lambda$. Thus $\Psi(\omega)$ is the marginal social as well as entrepreneurial value of continuing in state ω. The higher the private benefit or the pledgeable income in a state, the more likely it is that the project is continued in that state. The reverse is true, the higher is the total cost of continuing, where total cost is the sum of the direct reinvestment cost $\rho(\omega)$ and the liquidation benefit $w(\omega)$.

For empirical work, it is important to note that these "comparative statics" results pertain to variations across realized states of nature. Changes in the (random) parameters of the model would in general affect λ and that way investments as well as the cutoff. This should be contrasted with comparative statics performed on the parameters of the basic model. In that model, changes in the parameters ρ_0 and ρ_1 had no effect on continuation decisions (the cutoff rule implicit in (2.23) does not include these parameters) as long as the parameter values are such that I is strictly positive but finite. Nevertheless, most of the qualitative features of the basic model are retained. In particular, instead of taking ρ to be random, we can let the liquidation value w or the pledgeable income ρ_0 be random (keeping $b(\omega)$ fixed) without changing our main conclusions (e.g., the optimality of a cutoff rule and the incomplete insurance result). In this sense, the liquidity shock can be given a broader interpretation (also for many of the qualitative results that follow up to part IV).

2.6 Summary and Concluding Comments

In this chapter we have introduced our basic model of liquidity demand. Firms demand liquidity, because they want to insure themselves against credit rationing. Credit rationing is caused by the wedge between the pledgeable income to investors and the total income to the firm. When the cost of continuing a project falls between the pledgeable income and the total income, the project can continue only if its funding has been arranged in advance. This is the sense in which firms demand liquidity. In traditional financial models, firms never demand liquidity.[12]

As in many corporate finance models, investments have, at least at the margin, a negative net present value based on pledgeable income, so the entrepreneur has to put in some of his own capital to get the project off the ground. Because entrepreneurial capital has a higher rate of return than investor capital, it is optimal for the entrepreneur to commit all of the firm's pledgeable income to the investors and only hold the illiquid claims for himself. The amount of entrepreneurial capital determines the scale of operations.

Adding a liquidity demand to this standard solvency-requirement story, we have shown how the firm must also plan for its liquidity. The model is one of asset–liability management. Not hoarding liquidity is akin to accepting a maturity mismatch. Liquidity hoarding is akin to purchasing insurance. In general (and always with a variable investment scale and a continuum of liquidity shocks), the firm is credit rationed both ex ante (initial investment) and ex post (continuation investment). All strictly positive net present value investments and reinvestments will not be undertaken.

It may at first be surprising that investors knowingly fund projects with a negative continuation value, yet this is an essential ingredient of the theory of liquidity shortages. If all liquidity shocks were associated with a positive continuation value for the investors, there would be no need to seek funding in advance.[13] The demand for insurance is always

---

12. This statement is just a variant on the indeterminacy of the firm's capital structure in traditional finance.

13. With a strictly concave production function, it is possible to have a demand for liquidity even if continuation yields a positive net present value. The ex ante commitment required from investors occurs at the margin: they may prefer a smaller scale than is optimal. More formally, if the pledgeable income $\rho_0(I)$ is concave, one can have $\rho_0(I) \geq \rho I$ while $\rho_0'(I) < \rho$. There is no need to hoard stores of value or to obtain a credit line, but the entrepreneur must still plan liquidity by securing in advance the right to dilute the stake of investors.

associated with one side winning and the other side losing ex post. In that sense, our model is conceptually no different than Diamond and Dybvig's (1983) seminal model of consumer liquidity demand. Indeed the two models are formally similar, though liquidity shocks to the productive sector have quite different implications for the economy as we will see later.

The extent to which investors can commit additional funds to projects that have a negative continuation value depends on their ability to monitor the contingencies. If investors cannot observe the firm's liquidity shock, a contingent contract has to rely on information reported by the firm. This is not a problem if the firm has no alternative use for funds. However, if the firm can divert excess funds for private benefit, the contract needs to be adjusted as shown in appendix 2A. Diversion can be avoided in one of two ways. Either the entrepreneur is asked to hold more than the minimum stake at the beginning, which he forgoes if he claims that a high shock has occurred, or investors scale down the investment in response to a reported high shock. In either case the solution is less efficient than when the shock is contractible.

In appendix 2B we develop in more detail the formal relationship between consumer liquidity demand and producer liquidity demand by reinterpreting our firms as Diamond–Dybvig consumers. Here is a brief summary of the key points. The basic model of consumer liquidity demand has a three-period structure like the model with producer liquidity demand. Consumers hoard liquidity to smooth consumption and meet unexpected liquidity needs. Modeling this has traditionally assumed that consumers save at date 0 because they face uncertainty about the timing of their consumption needs, that is, they are unsure about their marginal rate of substitution between consumption at date 1 and date 2. If one is to compare the models of producer and consumer liquidity demand, this suggests considering firms that have net savings at date 0 ($I < A$) and, as discussed in this chapter, a random liquidity need that accrues either at date 1 or at date 2 (and income accruing at date 3).

With firms as net lenders, we are able to show the precise sense in which the two models are isomorphic. The central optimal insurance result in the Diamond–Dybvig analysis, whereby patient consumers end up subsidizing impatient ones (provided relative risk aversion is greater than 1), has an exact counterpart in the producer liquidity context as long as one interprets the entrepreneur's "consumption" as the "average liquidity withdrawals." We also discuss Jacklin's (1987) critique of a breakdown in insurance (cross-subsidization) between patient and impatient consumers when consumers have access to financial markets. Jacklin's critique in our context comes down to whether firms have alternative uses for excess funds withdrawn at date 1.

Finally, it is worth noting that our model can be used to support some degree of cross-subsidization within a firm. Conglomerates are often criticized for subsidizing divisional investments, though the empirical evidence by now is rather mixed (for a survey of the evidence, see Stein 2003). In light of the model presented here, subsidies can be viewed as optimal insurance policies for the human capital invested in the firm or alternatively as efficient ways to motivate the management and employees of divisions. Conglomerates have specific information about divisional circumstances as well as the right to reallocate capital based on this information. Reputation and culture can provide the necessary commitment power to implement such policies (see Shleifer and Summers 1988 for a related argument).

Appendix 2A: Mechanism Design under Fund Diversion

In this appendix we provide a full treatment of the second-best optimum and its implementation when the entrepreneur can divert funds at date 1 as reviewed in section 2.3. By the revelation principle, the optimal mechanism or contract will have to induce the firm to truthfully reveal its type (the date-1 liquidity shock ρ). A generic contract specifies the initial investment level I—and for each state $j = L, H$—the level of reinvestment i_j, and payments t_{1j} and t_{2j} made to the firm at dates 1 and date 2, respectively. The date-1 payment t_{1j} will at the optimum be used to cover the firm's liquidity shock as it is not optimal to induce the entrepreneur to divert funds at date 1. We assume that the payment t_{2j} does not vest until date 2 and cannot be used to secure additional funding for the firm at date 1 (this feature is common in executive incentive schemes, e.g., restricted stock). The vesting constraint is important, since it provides an additional instrument for screening. If the firm could use t_{2j} as collateral for borrowing at date 1, there would be no distinction between t_{1j} and t_{2j}.

It is clear that we can restrict attention to cases where the entrepreneur at date 1 is given no more than he claims to need; that is, $t_{1j} = \rho_j i_j$. Indeed, keeping liquidity t_{1L} at its minimum level makes it infeasible for an H-firm to claim that it is an L-firm; since $t_{1L} = \rho_L i_L < \rho_H i_L$, there will not be enough date-1 funds for the H-firm to invest i_L. Any additional compensation for the entrepreneur is most efficiently paid by increasing t_{2j}.

The diversion option creates the following incentive problem: an L-firm can claim a high liquidity shock ρ_H and then divert the excess funds $(\rho_H - \rho_L)i_H$ for private consumption; the entrepreneur cannot turn more of the date-1 funds into private consumption because the scale of the continuation investment is verifiable. Note that diversion is an issue only if without diversion it is optimal to continue in both states, namely (2.10) holds, which we will assume in this appendix. Otherwise, $i_H = 0$ without diversion, and diversion would not feasible in the first place.

With these preliminary observations, the second-best program can be written

$$\max_{\{I, i_j, t_{1j}, t_{2j}\}} \left\{ \sum_j f_j \left(t_{2j} + (\rho_1 - \rho_0)\, i_j \right) \right\},$$

subject to

$$\sum_j f_j(\rho_0 i_j - t_{1j} - t_{2j}) \geq I - A, \tag{2.28}$$

$$t_{2L} + (\rho_1 - \rho_0)\, i_L \geq t_{2H} + (\rho_1 - \rho_0)\, i_H + \xi(\rho_H - \rho_L)i_H, \tag{2.29}$$

$$t_{1j} = \rho_j i_j,\ j = L,\ H, \tag{2.30}$$

$$0 \leq i_j \leq I,\ j = L,\ H, \tag{2.31}$$

$$t_{2j} \geq 0,\ j = L,\ H. \tag{2.32}$$

Constraint (2.28) is the budget constraint, and constraint (2.29) the (remaining) incentive constraint. We argued that the liquidity constraint (2.30) is binding. This fact has been used to eliminate the t_{1j} terms from the objective function and the incentive constraint. The last term on the right-hand side of the incentive constraint is the L-type's private benefit when claiming to be an H-type and diverting the excess funds for private consumption.

The budget constraint (2.28) will obviously bind. If the incentive constraint (2.29) did not bind, the solution would be the same as without diversion. Since we assumed that (2.10) holds, that solution sets $i_L = i_H = I$; then $t_{2L} = 0$ because the entrepreneur's utility (and the initial investment scale) is maximized by distributing all the pledgeable income to investors. But these values violate the incentive constraint, so (2.29) must hold as an equality.

Suppose $t_{2H} > 0$. By reducing t_{2H} to 0 and increasing t_{2L} by the amount $f_H t_{2H}/f_L$, we can relax the incentive constraint (2.29) while keeping the objective function and the budget constraint intact. This cannot be optimal, hence $t_{2H} = 0$. Put differently, setting $t_{2H} = 0$ maximizes the leverage of A.

It is easy to see that $i_L \geq i_H$. This is true already without the diversion option, and the incentive constraint (2.29) pushes in the same direction. It follows that $i_L = I$, else we could reduce the cost of investment by lowering the initial scale I.

Eliminating t_{1j} using (2.30), and setting $t_{2H} = 0$ and $i_L = I$, we can rewrite program (2.28) through (2.31) as

$$\max_{\{I, i_H, t_{2L}\}} \{f_L t_{2L} + f_L (\rho_1 - \rho_0) I + f_H (\rho_1 - \rho_0) i_H\}, \tag{2.33}$$

subject to

$$f_L(\rho_0 - \rho_L)I - f_L t_{2L} - f_H(\rho_H - \rho_0)i_H = I - A, \tag{2.34}$$

$$t_{2L} + (\rho_1 - \rho_0)I = (\rho_1 - \rho_0)i_H + \xi(\rho_H - \rho_L)i_H, \tag{2.35}$$

$$t_{2L} \geq 0, \; 0 \leq i_H \leq I. \tag{2.36}$$

This is a linear program. Therefore one of the extreme points must be optimal. There are three candidate solutions:

Case I: $t_{2L} = 0$ and $i_H = \delta I < I$, where

$$\delta \equiv \frac{(\rho_1 - \rho_0)}{(\rho_1 - \rho_0) + \xi(\rho_H - \rho_L)} < 1 \quad \text{from (2.35)}.$$

Case II: $i_H = I$ and

$$t_{2L} = \xi(\rho_H - \rho_L)I > 0 \quad \text{from (2.35)}.$$

Case III: $t_{2L} = 0$ and $i_H = 0$.

We will shortly argue that case I always dominates case III. Looking at the incentive constraint (2.35), we see that cases I and II represent two extreme ways to prevent an L-firm from claiming that it has been hit by a high liquidity shock and diverting $(\rho_H - \rho_L)i_H$ for private consumption. In case I the incentive is established by reducing the scale of operations by a factor $1 - \delta$ when the firm reports a high liquidity shock. This corresponds to the investment distortion in a standard screening model. In case II, the firm is allowed to continue at full scale even if it claims a high shock, but a bribe $t_{2L} > 0$ is used to induce truth telling. The bribe corresponds to an information rent in a standard screening model. Normally we would both distort the investment and pay an information rent, but in our linear model one or the other is optimal. Note that $\xi < 1$ implies that a bribe is a more efficient way of paying the information rent than letting the firm consume the excess liquidity.

Case II can be interpreted as follows: Initially the entrepreneur keeps a fraction $\beta = t_{2L} / (\rho_0 I)$ of the "cash flow rights" of the firm. If the entrepreneur reports a high shock ρ_H, all initial shareholders as well as the entrepreneur lose their pledgeable shares through dilution. The missing amount $(\rho_H - \rho_0) I$ is paid by the investors according to the date-0 financial agreement (e.g., using a credit line). If the entrepreneur reports a low shock ρ_L, he retains his share β of the firm's pledgeable income, which pays t_{2L} at date 2 and receives $t_{1L} = \rho_L I$ to cover the liquidity shock. This incentive scheme wastes collateral relative to the case without diversion. The entrepreneur would rather hold just illiquid assets, but to prevent diversion, he also needs to have a stake in the pledgeable portion of the firm, which he can give up if he claims a high shock.

Let us compare cases I and II. Using the budget and incentive constraints, we can calculate the maximum investment scale I for the two cases. It is easy to see that $I_I > I^* > I_{II}$, where I^* is the second-best solution without diversion. Plugging these investment levels into the objective function, we obtain the maximum objective value in case I as

$$\max{}_I = \frac{A(\rho_1 - \rho_0)(f_L + f_H \delta)}{1 + f_H (\rho_H - \rho_0) \delta - f_L (\rho_0 - \rho_L)}. \tag{2.37}$$

In case II the maximum objective value is

$$\max{}_{II} = \frac{A[(\rho_1 - \rho_0) + f_L \xi (\rho_H - \rho_L)]}{1 - f_L (\rho_0 - \rho_L) + f_L \xi (\rho_H - \rho_L) + f_H (\rho_H - \rho_0)}. \tag{2.38}$$

At this point we can explain why case I always dominates case III. The value function $\max_I$ is the same as the value function without diversion, except that δ corresponds to a smaller scale in the H-state. Assumption (2.10), which assures us that it is optimal to continue in both states in the model without diversion, implies that $\max_I$ is increasing in δ and hence that we should raise i_H as high as constraint (2.29) permits.

The comparison between case I and case II is ambiguous. For $\xi = 0$, there is no temptation to divert funds and therefore no need to pay a bribe or distort the reinvestment scale. In this case both solutions coincide with the solution without diversion. For any value $0 < \xi \le 1$ numerical examples show that either case I or case II can be optimal depending on the choice of the other parameters. For instance, when the probability of a high shock is large (f_H is large) it is optimal to use a bribe (case II) rather than scale down the operations (case I), while the reverse is true for small values of f_H. This is intuitive, since the expected cost of reducing the scale of operations is higher when the probability of the H-state is higher, while the expected cost of forcing the entrepreneur to hold a piece of the pledgeable income (i.e., have him pay for the continuation ex post) is lower. Both effects work in the direction of making a bribe more desirable. In general, however, the difference $\max_I - \max_{II}$ may be nonmonotone as parameters are changed.

It is of interest to consider $\xi = 1$ when case II is optimal. We have

$$t_{2L} = \xi \, (\rho_H - \rho_L) \, I = (\rho_H - \rho_L) \, I. \tag{2.39}$$

Substituting this expression into the budget constraint (2.28), we see that the investors' payoff in the low state will now be

$$\rho_0 i_L - t_{1L} - t_{2L} = (\rho_0 - \rho_H) \, I < 0.$$

Investors end up paying the same amount $(\rho_H - \rho_0)I$ in both the high and the low state. Consequently there is no scope for insurance at all when $\xi = 1$. The firm is merely using investors to transfer some of its initial funds A to date 1 $(I < A)$ as if they were investing in a bond or some other storage technology. In effect, the best the firm can do is self-insure. We will study self-insurance in more detail in chapters 7 and 8.

To sum up, whether diversion is avoided by asking the entrepreneur to hold more than the minimum stake at the beginning (which he forgoes if he claims that the high shock has occurred) or by scaling down investment in response to a reported high shock, the solution is less efficient than when the shock is contractible. Sometimes the option to divert destroys all outside insurance opportunities and the firm is left to take care of itself, using market instruments that are not contingent on idiosyncratic shocks.

Appendix 2B: Relationship with Consumer Liquidity Demand

The Diamond–Dybvig model

To focus on corporate liquidity demand, our analysis has assumed that consumers are indifferent about the date of consumption (but see section 5.3.1). In reality, of course, consumers hoard substantial amounts of liquid assets in order to insure themselves against liquidity shocks. They are willing to sacrifice returns to ensure that they will have enough money for various expenditures such as buying a house or a car when the opportunity arises, to send their children to college, or to protect themselves against illness or unemployment. Thus consumers compete with corporations for the available stock of liquidity.

Consumer liquidity demand has been the focus of a large and interesting literature, starting with the seminal papers of Bryant (1980) and Diamond and Dybvig (1983). The purpose of this appendix is to compare the implications of the Diamond–Dybvig approach to consumer demand for liquidity (CDL) with our approach to producer demand for liquidity (PDL). To this end, we will first go over the Diamond–Dybvig model with our notation.

Timing   Like our model, the Diamond–Dybvig model has three periods, $t = 0, 1, 2$.

Consumer Preferences   Consumers are ex ante identical. For notational simplicity, let us assume that they have no demand for consumption at date 0, and therefore invest their entire date-0 endowment a (per consumer). They receive no additional endowments at dates 1 and 2. At date 1 consumers are revealed to be one of two types. A fraction $1 - \alpha$ are *impatient*: they only care about date-1 consumption. The remaining fraction α of consumers are *patient*: they are indifferent about date-1 and date-2 consumption. The consumer's state-contingent preference over consumption c_1 and c_2 is

$$\begin{cases} u(c_1) & \text{if impatient (probability } 1 - \alpha), \\ u(c_1 + c_2) & \text{if patient (probability } \alpha), \end{cases} \tag{2.40}$$

where the function u is increasing and *strictly* concave, and $u'(0) = \infty$. Consumers do not know at date 0 whether they will be impatient ("face a liquidity shock"). In the simplest version of this model (covered here), there is no aggregate uncertainty and exactly a fraction $(1 - \alpha)$ of consumers will want to consume at date 1.[14] In the CDL model, risk aversion creates a consumer demand for liquidity. In the PDL model, as we

---

14. As in the case of PDL, aggregate uncertainty raises the issue of how much of it can be insured by foreigners (ideally, all of it for a small economy). On this, see Allen and Gale (2000) and Castiglionesi et.al. (2010). In the absence of possibilities for international insurance, impatient and patient consumers must share the aggregate risk, and thus (safe) deposit contracts are not optimal; see Hellwig (1994). In chapter 6 we discuss international insurance in the context of the PDL model.

discussed, future credit rationing generates a form of risk aversion that creates a demand for liquidity by firms.

Technology   At date 0, consumers allocate their endowment a between (liquid) short-term projects and (illiquid) long-term projects. Investment in liquidity carries an opportunity cost, since long-term projects have a higher yield: Short-term projects yield 1 at date 1 (date 2) per unit of date-0 (date-1) investment, while long-term projects yield nothing at date 1 and r_2 at date 2 per unit of date-0 investment, with

$$r_2 > 1. \tag{2.41}$$

Let ℓ and i denote a consumer's investments in long- and short-term projects, respectively. The consumer budget constraint is

$$\ell + i = a. \tag{2.42}$$

There are two ways for the consumer to insure against liquidity risk: self-insurance and risk pooling.

• In *autarky*, each consumer is on her own. Self-insurance solves the problem:

$$\max_{\{\ell, i | \ell + i = a\}} \{(1 - \alpha)u(\ell) + \alpha u(\ell + r_2 i)\}. \tag{2.43}$$

The optimal solution is

$$\begin{aligned} \ell &= a \quad \text{if} \quad 1 - \alpha \ge \alpha(r_2 - 1), \\ (1 - \alpha)u'(\ell) &= \alpha(r_2 - 1)u'(\ell + r_2(a - \ell)) \quad \text{otherwise.} \end{aligned} \tag{2.44}$$

• In *pooling*, the consumer's use of liquidity is coordinated through some sort of intermediary, for instance, a bank. Consumers are better off with pooling. To see why, note that a consumer who turns out to be patient receives income ℓ from the low-yielding, short-term investment, which is wasteful as a patient consumer would rather enjoy the returns from the higher yielding long-term investment. In the autarky case patient (impatient) consumers "overconsume" ("underconsume") liquidity. In contrast, because there is no aggregate risk, it is optimal in a pooling solution to let the impatient consumers consume all the proceeds of the short-term assets and the patient consumers consume all the proceeds from the long-term assets. The optimal pooling solution maximizes the representative consumer's utility

$$(1 - \alpha)u(c_1) + \alpha u(c_2), \tag{2.45}$$

subject to the constraints

$$(1 - \alpha)c_1 = \ell,$$
$$\alpha c_2 = r_2 i, \tag{2.46}$$
$$\ell + i = a.$$

The optimal insurance-consumption policy is therefore

$$u'(c_1) = r_2 u'(c_2). \tag{2.47}$$

If the coefficient of relative risk aversion exceeds 1 (i.e., $u'(c)c$ decreasing), condition (2.47) implies that the ratio of the two levels of consumption is smaller than the marginal rate of transformation:

$$\frac{c_2}{c_1} < r_2.$$

The optimal policy does not call for equalization of the marginal utilities because of the difference in returns. However, it brings the marginal utilities in the two states of nature closer to each other in comparison with the marginal rate of transformation ($c_1 > a$ and $c_2 < r_2 a$) and thus involves insurance between consumers. The optimal insurance policy can be implemented by a deposit contract in which the consumers can withdraw c_1 at date 1, and if they have not done so, c_2 at date 2.

As in the PDL model to be studied in chapter 3, the CDL model stresses the superiority of liquidity pooling due to insurance across idiosyncratic consumer risks. Also long-term investments have higher returns than short-term ones, so liquidity ought to be hoarded sparingly and dispatched properly. In contrast, without coordination/planning, individuals will generally invest excessively in liquidity.

There are two well-known issues raised by the Diamond–Dybvig analysis worth highlighting. The first concerns bank runs and their prevention.

When the consumers' type cannot be verified at date 1, patient consumers may pretend that they are impatient and withdraw early. They have no incentive to do so as long as the other patient consumers do not withdraw early, since $c_2 > c_1$. However, there is also a bad equilibrium where patient consumers withdraw their money at date 1. Suppose that a fraction of consumers exceeding $(1 - \alpha)$ come to the liquidity pool to withdraw their money. Provided that liquidating long-term assets at date 1 generates a bit of income, the financial intermediary may liquidate these assets early in order to (partly) serve the withdrawing customers.

But this induces other patient consumers to run since their claim to date-2 income is depreciated. Indeed, if all run, then it is in the interest of each to run.[15]

Diamond and Dybvig have offered several ways out of such bad equilibria. The financial intermediary (perhaps with the assent of a prudential supervisor) can suspend convertibility of demand deposits when the fraction of withdrawers reaches $(1 - \alpha)$. Knowing that their long-term claim will not be jeopardized by early liquidation, patient consumers are better off waiting until date 2. Similarly the presence of a central bank acting as a lender of last resort, or international markets extending sufficient credit lines to intermediaries, can destroy the incentive for a run (we have more to say on the limits on international credit in chapter 6).

The second well-known point is that trading in financial markets can have an adverse impact on efficient liquidity provision. Jacklin (1987) showed that it is necessary to prevent consumer trading at date 1 in order for financial intermediaries to be able to provide efficient insurance. To see this, suppose that an entrepreneur uses his date-0 endowment a to set up a mutual fund that invests only in long-term assets at date 0. The entrepreneur does not issue shares in the mutual fund until date 1. Patient consumers are better off withdrawing their deposits c_1 and reinvesting the money in the mutual fund as long as the price of a share in the mutual fund does not exceed $(c_1/c_2)r_2$. Let the entrepreneur keep the shares of the mutual fund for himself if he turns out to be patient and sell them at price $c_1 r_2/c_2$ if he turns out to be impatient. This way the entrepreneur secures $r_2 a > c_2$ when patient and $(c_1 r_2/c_2)a > c_1$ when impatient.

In summary, consumer insurance against liquidity shocks involves a cross-subsidy that can be arbitraged by financial markets. The arbitrageurs free-ride on the liquidity (the investments in short-term assets) provided by the financial intermediaries. Trading must be prevented to maintain the optimal subsidy. More generally, Diamond (1997) shows that when some consumers do not have access to financial markets, there is still scope for insurance, but the social cost of financial markets increases as the number of consumers who have access to them increases.

Farhi et al. (2009) consider general preferences $u(c_1, c_2, \theta)$, where θ is a one-dimensional preference parameter learned by the consumer at

---

15. Recent theoretical contributions (Goldstein and Pauzner 2005; Morris and Shin 1998; Rochet and Vives 2004) have looked at asymmetric information environments in which the prediction is unique (either a panic or no panic).

date 1, and provide a general treatment of the Jacklin critique. They show that the inefficiency created by self-provision of liquidity paired with trading at date 1 can be entirely attributed to a failure to control the interest rate between dates 1 and 2. The interest rate here is technologically driven and, in general, does not coincide with the optimal interest rate, which involves cross-subsidies between patient and impatient consumers.[16]

More formally, let p denote the date-1 price of one unit of income at date 2. In equilibrium $p < 1$. The representative consumer solves

$$\max_{\{i,\ell\}} \left\{ (1 - \alpha)u(\ell + pr_2i) + \alpha u \left(r_2i + \frac{\ell}{p} \right) \right\},$$

subject to

$$\ell + i \leq a.$$

The market-clearing condition in the date-1 asset market is

$$(1 - \alpha)pr_2i = \alpha\ell.$$

The first-order conditions yield

$$(1 - \alpha)u'(c_1) + \frac{\alpha}{p}u'(c_2) = (1 - \alpha)pr_2u'(c_1) + \alpha r_2u'(c_2).$$

This equation is satisfied for the Jacklin price

$$p = \frac{1}{r_2}.$$

The term structure is driven by the technology alone.[17]

Farhi et al. demonstrate that the state can implement the efficient allocation by imposing on all financial intermediaries a liquidity

---

16. Their paper contains a useful discussion, for the separable case, of the difference between liquidity shocks à la Diamond–Dybvig, $\theta u(c_1) + u(c_2)$, and discount shocks of the type $u(c_1) + \theta u(c_2)$.

17. If the utility of impatient consumers were

$$u(c_1 + \underline{p}c_2) \quad \text{with} \quad \frac{1}{r_2} < \underline{p} < 1$$

instead of $u(c_1)$, however, the equilibrium allocation would involve an inefficient reallocation of liquidity ex post. We discuss such inefficient reallocations in more detail in chapters 7 and 8. More generally, the analysis of self-provision of liquidity in these chapters will provide the PDL analogue of Jacklin's CDL analysis.

requirement: a liquidity floor if the optimal cross-subsidy runs from patient to impatient consumers (the case where the coefficient of relative risk aversion exceeds 1) and a liquidity ceiling if the cross-subsidy runs the other way.

Reinterpreting Firms as Diamond–Dybvig Consumers

We introduce the analogue of consumer liquidity demand into our model simply by treating consumers as firms that are net lenders ($I > A$) with no pledgeable income ($\rho_0 = 0$). That is, we compare our approach to the extensive literature on consumer liquidity demand by making our firms similar to Diamond–Dybvig consumers.

To this end, consider an economy with ex ante identical firms of the following sort. The representative firm at date 0 has assets A and invests a variable amount $I < A$ in an illiquid project. Note that the initial investment is less than the firm's endowment in contrast to our earlier assumption. This assumption is essential since it makes firms save just as consumers do in the CDL model.

The representative firm faces a shock ρ per unit of investment

- either at date 1, with probability $1 - \alpha$, drawn from distribution $F^{ST}(\rho)$,
- or at date 2, with probability α, drawn from distribution $F^{LT}(\rho)$.

Provided that it meets the liquidity shock, the firm produces $\rho_1 I$ at date 2, all nonpledgeable ($\rho_0 = 0$). To draw the parallel with the Diamond–Dybvig analysis, we assume that there is no aggregate uncertainty, and we posit the existence of technologies that will help firms meet liquidity needs. At date 0 they can invest both in short-term projects that yield one per unit of investment at date 1 and in long-term projects that yield nothing at date 1 and r_2 at date 2 per unit of investment, with

$$r_2 > 1.$$

As before, we assume that investors are risk neutral and willing to invest at a zero rate of return, and that state-contingent policies can be used (there is monitoring of the use of liquidity). The representative firm maximizes the date-2 expected proceeds subject to the date-0 constraint on the allocation of savings. Letting $\bar{\rho}^{ST}$ and $\bar{\rho}^{LT}$ denote the cutoff levels, that is, the maximum shocks that the firm will meet, we solve the second-best program:

$$\max_{\{I,\,\bar{\rho}^{ST},\bar{\rho}^{LT}\}} \left\{ [(1-\alpha)F^{ST}(\bar{\rho}^{ST}) + \alpha F^{LT}(\bar{\rho}^{LT})]\rho_1 I \right\},$$

subject to the budget constraint

$$I + \left[(1 - \alpha) \int_0^{\bar{\rho}^{ST}} \rho f^{ST}(\rho) d\rho + \frac{\alpha}{r_2} \int_0^{\bar{\rho}^{LT}} \rho f^{LT}(\rho) d\rho \right] I \le A. \tag{2.48}$$

As in our earlier analyses, the solution to this program minimizes the expected cost of bringing one unit of investment to completion:

$$\min_{\{\bar{\rho}^{ST}, \bar{\rho}^{LT}\}} \left\{ c = \frac{1 + (1 - \alpha) \int_0^{\bar{\rho}^{ST}} \rho f^{ST}(\rho) d\rho + \frac{\alpha}{r_2} \int_0^{\bar{\rho}^{LT}} \rho f^{LT}(\rho) d\rho}{(1 - \alpha) F^{ST}(\bar{\rho}^{ST}) + \alpha F^{LT}(\bar{\rho}^{LT})} \right\}. \tag{2.49}$$

The optimal cutoffs are therefore determined by

$$\bar{\rho}^{ST} = \frac{\bar{\rho}^{LT}}{r_2} = c. \tag{2.50}$$

Let us now show how this analysis connects to that of Diamond and Dybvig. Because their results hinge on the stationarity of preferences (the utility function u is the same for impatient and patient consumers), a proper comparison requires that in the PDL model the distribution of shocks be identical:

$$f^{ST}(\rho) = f^{LT}(\rho) \equiv f(\rho) \qquad \text{for all } \rho.$$

For the optimal investment level I, let a denote net savings, and c_1 and c_2 the expected date-1 and date-2 consumptions of the good:

$$\begin{cases} a & \equiv & A - I, \\ c_1 & \equiv & [\int_0^{\bar{\rho}^{ST}} \rho f(\rho) d\rho] I, \\ c_2 & \equiv & [\int_0^{\bar{\rho}^{LT}} \rho f(\rho) d\rho] I. \end{cases}$$

With this notation, the representative firm's budget constraint (2.48) is

$$(1 - \alpha) c_1 + \frac{\alpha c_2}{r_2} \le a$$

as in the CDL model. The entrepreneur's payoff is

$$[(1 - \alpha) F(\bar{\rho}^{ST}) + \alpha F(\bar{\rho}^{LT})] \rho_1 I.$$

This suggests that we define a pseudo-utility function $u(\cdot)$ implicitly by

$$u(c(\bar{\rho})) \equiv F(\bar{\rho}) \rho_1 I, \tag{2.51}$$

where

$$c(\bar{\rho}) = \left[\int_0^{\bar{\rho}} \rho f(\rho) d\rho \right] I. \tag{2.52}$$

Recalling that nothing is pledgeable, we note that $u(c_t)$ is the expected surplus for expected consumption c_t when the liquidity need arises at date t. Differentiating (2.51) with respect to $\bar{\rho}$, we get

$$u'(c(\bar{\rho})) = \frac{\rho_1}{\bar{\rho}} > 0 \quad \text{and} \quad u''(c(\bar{\rho})) = \frac{-\rho_1}{\bar{\rho}^3 f(\bar{\rho}) I} < 0.$$

The entrepreneur exhibits risk aversion over consumption (expected liquidity demand) despite being risk neutral.

Next we investigate the existence of cross-subsidies and whether the analogue of the Jacklin critique holds in the PDL model. Cross-subsidies exist provided that

$$r_2 c_1 > c_2$$

or, from (2.52),

$$r_2 \left[\int_0^{\bar{\rho}^{ST}} \rho f(\rho) d\rho \right] > \int_0^{r_2 \bar{\rho}^{ST}} \rho f(\rho) d\rho.$$

Recall that cross-subsidies exist in the CDL model if the utility function exhibits a degree of relative risk aversion in excess of 1:

$$-\frac{u''(c)c}{u'(c)} > 1.$$

Using (2.51) and (2.52), we write the analogue of this condition for the PDL model as[18]

$$\frac{\int_0^{\bar{\rho}} \rho f(\rho) d\rho}{\bar{\rho}^2 f(\bar{\rho})} > 1. \tag{2.53}$$

Fixing $\bar{\rho}$, we consider the function

$$H(r_2) \equiv r_2 \int_0^{\bar{\rho}} \rho f(\rho) d\rho - \int_0^{r_2 \bar{\rho}} \rho f(\rho) d\rho.$$

---

18. Condition (2.53) is rather strong; in particular, it is not satisfied by uniform or increasing densities.

Clearly, $H(1) = 0$ and

$$H'(r_2) = \int_0^{\bar{\rho}} \rho f(\rho)d\rho - \bar{\rho}^2 r_2 f(r_2 \bar{\rho}).$$

To show that $H(r_2) > 0$ for $r_2 > 1$, it suffices to show that $H'(r_2) > 0$ whenever $H(r_2) = 0$, or

$$\int_0^{r_2 \bar{\rho}} \rho f(\rho)d\rho > r_2^2 \bar{\rho}^2 f(r_2 \bar{\rho}),$$

which is nothing but (2.53). There are cross-subsidies in the PDL model exactly under the same conditions as in the CDL model.

This completes the demonstration that when the firms are net lenders, the PDL model is isomorphic to the CDL model.

Does the Jacklin critique apply to the PDL model? Note that the cross-subsidy scheme studied above is an *average* cross-subsidy; given (2.53) this cross-subsidy takes the form

$$\int_0^{\bar{\rho}^{ST}} \rho f(\rho)d\rho > \frac{\int_0^{\bar{\rho}^{LT}} \rho f(\rho)d\rho}{r_2}.$$

In (2.50), by contrast, there is no subsidy at the margin:

$$\bar{\rho}^{ST} = \frac{\bar{\rho}^{LT}}{r_2}.$$

Suppose that the firm contracts with a bank for a credit line with the option of withdrawing up to $\bar{\rho}^{ST}I$ at date 1 or up to $\bar{\rho}^{LT}I$ at date 2. A firm that learns at date 1 that it will need liquidity only at date 2 cannot obtain more liquidity by withdrawing at date 1 and investing in a mutual fund at rate of return r_2. Thus, if the firm has no alternative investment opportunity (of the type considered in appendix 2A), Jacklin's critique does not apply.

Of course, the Jacklin critique of the CDL model rests on the idea that the consumer's balance sheet is not monitored by the liquidity provider. If, in the PDL model, the entrepreneur can claim that the firm has been hit by the highest permissible shock, so that he can draw down the full credit line, invest the balance in the market at rate r_2 and consume the proceeds (i.e., not return the money to investors) at date 2, then the credit-line scheme analyzed here is not immune to the Jacklin critique.

Firms' accounts, however, are probably more easily monitored than those of consumers. The extreme form of diversion considered in the previous paragraph is not the ordinary pattern of corporate behavior. But firms certainly have some leeway to make self-serving use of extra cash. It would be interesting in this context to consider imperfect opportunities for diversion, as we did in section 2.3 and appendix 2A.

II   Complete Markets

Much of the agency-based modeling of corporate finance focuses on the problem of raising funds for investment when investors worry that they may not get their money back. The model in chapter 2 is one such example, illustrating the constraints and distortions stemming from concerns over a firm's credibility. Much less attention has been paid to the converse credibility problem: ensuring that the suppliers of liquidity—the lenders, insurers and other investors who explicitly or implicitly commit to fund a firm in the future—will be able to deliver on their promises.[1]

This issue shows up starkly in the model in chapter 2 where investors are asked to commit to making date-1 investments that have a negative net present value. We suggested instruments that can be used to implement the optimal second-best policy, including credit lines, bonds and other financial vehicles such as credit default swaps (CDS). But sometimes banks are not able to honor credit lines, bonds may default and counterparty risks may materialize. The subprime crisis exposed the vulnerabilities of modern financial markets that rely on wholesale funding and complicated chains of derivative instruments. Investment banks failed, repo markets froze, and monoline insurers that were supposed to protect against subprime portfolio losses defaulted. The crisis has revealed that the determinants of liquidity (collateral) remain poorly understood.

In this part of the book we study the supply of inside liquidity, which is liquidity created within the corporate sector. Our main premise is that all financial commitments ultimately have to be backed up by claims on real assets that produce consumption or services of value to individuals and firms. Intermediaries and investors have to have enough capital, in that they must own (directly or indirectly) claims on real assets that will secure their pledges to fund firms in the future.

We show that the same factors that sometimes constrain firms from funding a project with a positive net present value also constrain the economy's supply of aggregate liquidity. Limited pledgeability is a problem for those demanding liquidity as well as those supplying liquidity; it puts a double wedge between investors and entrepreneurs. The

---

1. Of course, the availability of collateral has been the object of much attention in corporate finance. It has also been investigated in general equilibrium models; for example, Geanakoplos, in a series of papers starting with Geanakoplos et al. (1995), has emphasized the essential role of collateral in financial markets and studied the pricing and optimal assignment of collateral. The methods he uses and the questions he asks are different from ours; in particular, markets in collateral are not complete. See also Kilenthong and Townsent (2010).

smaller the share of pledgeable income, the lesser the base on which financial claims can be written. The much discussed "global savings glut" could be seen as a manifestation of these twin problems. Poorly developed financial markets and a booming economy in countries like China led to high savings chasing an inadequate supply of domestic financial assets.

The supply of liquidity can be analyzed in two steps. The first step is to determine the aggregate liquidity in each state of nature, that is, the total amount of pledgeable income that is available to back up promises of future funding. The second is to see whether the corporate sector can use aggregate liquidity efficiently.

The supply of aggregate liquidity influences but also depends on the investment plans of the firms. This creates a feedback loop running from limited demand of liquidity to limited supply of liquidity and back. The determination of aggregate liquidity presumes that the corporate sector understands this and can coordinate the use of liquidity perfectly. We model perfect coordination by assuming that markets for state-contingent claims on pledgeable income are complete. We leave out all institutional details that in reality enable coordination (banks, repo markets, money markets, etc.). As in general equilibrium theory, this level of abstraction is useful. It highlights general factors that affect the supply of liquidity and also provides a lower bound on the severity of liquidity supply problems.

In chapter 3 we study aggregate liquidity shortages in simple settings that illustrate how the demand and supply of liquidity are interlinked. A basic question we address is what determines whether there is enough aggregate inside liquidity to support the second-best policies described in chapter 2. We also show how liquidity shortages lead to liquidity premia and how the premia influence the firms' investment plans and the private production of liquidity. Chapter 4 goes on to develop a full-fledged general equilibrium analysis of asset pricing with heterogeneous firms. We use this framework to study the risk management of firms.

3   Aggregate Liquidity Shortages and Liquidity Premia

The key observation we made above is that the very problem that leads to a *demand* for liquidity, namely a wedge between pledgeable and non-pledgeable income, also limits the *supply* of inside liquidity. Insurance within the corporate sector depends on claims issued by the corporate sector. If firms have no pledgeable income, there are no corporate claims and therefore no inside liquidity to back up promises of funding or insurance. At the other extreme, if all corporate income is pledgeable (as in the Arrow–Debreu model), there is no need for insurance, since all continuation decisions are self-financing and therefore efficient.

We start by asking when the corporate sector will provide enough liquidity on its own, that is, when inside liquidity suffices to support second-best production plans. The demand and supply of inside liquidity are intertwined both through the amount of pledgeable income and the stochastic dependencies among firms. We show that if liquidity shocks are idiosyncratic and the corporate sector is a net borrower ($I - A > 0$), there will always be enough aggregate inside liquidity to meet corporate demand. Even so liquidity shortages can occur unless liquidity is coordinated in the right way, such as by intermediaries that offer credit lines to individual firms or by firms that hold shares in the market index and make commitments to pay back excess liquidity through dividends or other means.

At the other extreme, when all firms are hit by the same aggregate liquidity shock, inside liquidity will always be in short supply. With a shortage of aggregate liquidity some source of outside liquidity (e.g., government bonds) is necessary. Competition among firms will bid up the price of this liquidity, resulting in a liquidity premium. We provide a simple analysis of how the liquidity premium is determined and how it affects the investment decisions of firms when the outside liquidity is fixed. The supply–demand analysis is broadly consistent with the empirical evidence on the behavior of the liquidity premium of government bonds presented by Krishnamurthy and Vissing-Jorgensen (2010), as we discuss in section 3.2.3.[1]

In section 3.3 we analyze a model of consumer and producer demand for liquidity that merges the Diamond–Dybvig model of consumer liquidity with our model of producer liquidity. We end by discussing ways in which consumers can expand the supply of liquidity (section 3.4).

3.1   Inside Liquidity and Aggregate Shortages

Consider a three-period economy with a single good—"corn." Consumers are risk neutral and value consumption according to

$$c_0 + c_1 + c_2. \tag{3.1}$$

Consumers have large endowments of corn in each period but no way of storing corn from one period to the next. Equivalently, they have labor endowments that can be used to produce corn that must be eaten in the period it is produced. There is no outside liquidity in the economy for now; all liquidity is embedded in the returns of the corporate sector. In particular, consumers cannot promise to fund future investments without backing up their promises with claims on pledgeable corporate returns; the consumers' future endowments are not pledgeable.

3.1.1   Net Lending: The Case of Certainty
We begin with a very simple example that illustrates why there may be a shortage of liquidity. There is a continuum of ex ante identical firms of mass 1, endowed with technologies of the type described in chapter 2 and run by entrepreneurs each with a date-0 endowment A. The representative firm's initial investment I is variable, and we assume that it must be augmented with a *deterministic* date-1 continuation $\rho i(\rho)$, where $i(\rho) \leq I$ and $\rho > \rho_0$. (This is equivalent to assuming that in the model with two liquidity shocks, analyzed in section 2.2, we have $f_H = 1$ and $\rho_H = \rho$.) We suppose further $1 + \rho < \rho_1$, implying that the investment would always be worth undertaking from a net present-value point of view. If there are no liquidity problems, an entrepreneur with funds A invests as follows at date 0: He chooses I as the initial scale of the project and invests $(\rho - \rho_0)I > 0$ into a liquid asset or a credit line, where I is set

---

1. Chapter 4 on the liquidity asset pricing model (LAPM) provides a more general analysis of liquidity premia and their implications for asset pricing.

to exhaust the budget, $(1 + \rho - \rho_0)I = A$.[2] With these initial investments the entrepreneur is able to cover exactly the deterministic liquidity shock ρ at date 1. He can raise $\rho_0 I$ by issuing shares against his pledgeable date-2 income and add to it his investment in liquidity $(\rho - \rho_0)I$.

This investment plan presumes that there is a liquid asset, or a credit line backed by a liquid asset, that allows the entrepreneur to save $(\rho - \rho_0)I$ from date 0 to date 1. However, in the economy just described, the only available assets are claims on the continuation value of the very firms looking to save. Suppose, hypothetically, that all firms are able to meet the date-1 liquidity need ρI and therefore to continue at full scale. Then the date-1 continuation value of the corporate sector is $\rho_0 I$. But this is less than the liquidity needed, ρI. Since the *net* continuation value of the corporate sector, $(\rho_0 - \rho)I$, is negative, claims on the corporate sector written at date 0 are liabilities rather than assets. Consequently the corporate sector can neither act as a store of value nor provide collateral for future funding.

The problem here is that the corporate sector would like to be a *net lender*, but this is not possible because there are no external instruments (no outside liquidity) for transferring wealth from date 0 to date 1. The same problem was originally brought up by Woodford (1990) in his analysis of government debt as net wealth. Woodford studied an infinite-horizon model, described in figure 3.1, where two parties have the opportunity to invest in alternate periods and the investments pay off one period later in the form of a nonstorable consumption good. None of the output is pledgeable, and so a party's investment is bounded above by its available cash at the investment date. In the absence of outside stores of value, parties do not invest as their investment needs and cash flow receipts are completely asynchronized. The main point of Woodford's paper is that government bonds (the "liquid asset" in his model) are valuable as a way of transferring part of today's investment returns to tomorrow. This raises the overall welfare in the economy.

Apart from a finite rather than infinite horizon, the main difference between Woodford's model and our example is that we allow part of the project's income to be pledgeable ($\rho_0 > 0$). If enough of the income were pledgeable in Woodford's model, there would be no problem transferring wealth from one period to the next.[3] Investors whose firms

---

2. The constant returns to scale technology will allow the firm to invest up to

$$I = \frac{A}{1 + \rho - \rho_0} < A.$$

3. In the constant-returns-to-scale model, this requires capping the investment; otherwise, investment would be infinite.

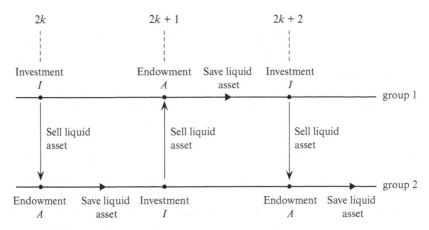

Figure 3.1
Net lending (Woodford's version)

pay off today could store the appropriate fraction of their income for reinvestment tomorrow by buying a financial stake in firms that invest today and pay off tomorrow; an equity market would be a perfect substitute for government bonds. But if the pledgeable income drops below the cost of investment ($\rho_0 < 1 < \rho_1$), there will again be a role for outside liquidity in Woodford's model; an equity market will not work if the pledgeable income is too small.

The general message here is that the problem of partial pledgeability, which limits the amount of funds that an entrepreneur can attract, also makes it harder for investors to supply liquidity. The specific observation that the corporate sector cannot provide sufficient aggregate liquidity whenever it is a *net lender* is very general. Even if the liquidity shocks were uncertain as in section 2.2, as long as $I - A < 0$ the budget constraint (2.4) implies that the expected date-1 net return of the corporate sector must be negative, and therefore that the corporate sector does not have sufficient assets to support the proposed plan.

3.1.2   Net Borrowing: Aggregate Shocks

Consider the same setup as above, but assume now that the corporate sector is a *net borrower*, $I - A > 0$, where A is the aggregate endowment of the entrepreneurs.[4] Further assume that there are only two liquidity

---

4. The corporate sector is typically a net borrower; see Mayer (1988). Recently, however, the corporate sector in a number of countries (United States, United Kingdom, and Japan in particular and a bit less in the euro area) have cut back on total borrowing causing them to run net financial surpluses several years in a row.

shocks, satisfying $\rho_L < \rho_0 < \rho_H$, with the additional property that the date-1 continuation investments should take place both when the liquidity shock is high and when it is low (condition (2.10) is satisfied). Because $I - A > 0$, the *expected* net return at date 1 must be strictly positive or else the budget constraint (2.4) would be violated. However, it is possible for the *realized* net return to be negative in some states, and therefore there could be states with insufficient inside liquidity. Whether this will be the case depends critically on the correlation of liquidity shocks across firms.

Consider first the extreme case where all firms are technologically identical and hit by the same shock—either all firms experience a high shock $\rho_H > \rho_0$ or all firms experience a low shock $\rho_L < \rho_0$. The high shock occurs with probability f_H and the low shock with probability f_L. Of course, when the aggregate shock is low, all firms continue at full scale because continuation investments are self-financing in that case. For instance, investors can contractually agree to let a firm in need of liquidity dilute the initial investors *pro rata* so that the amount $\rho_L I$ can be raised from new investors; alternatively firms may not contract for liquidity but rather negotiate with investors for fresh funds when the liquidity shock arises. By contrast, no firm can continue at full scale when the high shock hits; just as in the deterministic case discussed above, every firm now has a negative continuation value. There are no assets to back up investor promises to cover a high liquidity shock. The only option is then for all firms to close down.

3.1.3   Net Borrowing: Independent Shocks

Consider another extreme case, one where each firm is hit by an idiosyncratic liquidity shock at date 1. With a continuum of ex ante identical firms, the law of large numbers allows us to treat aggregate variables as deterministic. Assume tentatively that all firms are able to continue at full scale. The aggregate budget constraint for the corporate sector is then

$$f_L (\rho_0 - \rho_L) I + f_H (\rho_0 - \rho_H) I \geq I - A > 0,$$

implying that

$$f_H(\rho_H - \rho_0)I < f_L(\rho_0 - \rho_L)I. \tag{3.2}$$

The left-hand side represents the aggregate demand for liquidity by "distressed firms" (negative NPV firms), while the right-hand side is the aggregate supply of liquidity by "intact firms" (positive NPV firms).

Both terms are deterministic because shocks are independent. We conclude that with independent shocks and a continuum of firms that are net borrowers at date 0, the productive sector is self-sufficient with regard to liquidity.[5]

There are many institutional arrangements that support the efficient continuation of firms when shocks are independent. For instance, one could set up a financial intermediary that holds all the shares of the productive sector and then issues claims on this aggregate market portfolio to individual investors. The financial intermediary would provide liquidity to firms on a contingent basis: firms with a high shock would get $\rho_H I$, and firms with a low shock would get $\rho_L I$.

Another way of ensuring that the firms with a liquidity shortage (facing shock ρ_H) benefit from the liquidity provided by the other firms is to have each hold a sufficiently large share of the (stock) market portfolio.[6] At date 0, let each firm buy a fraction β of the market portfolio. Let the 100 percent date-0 value of the market portfolio be V_β. A firm could borrow $[I - A] + \beta V_\beta$ to finance its date-1 investments. Alternatively, a firm could issue equity and use the proceeds (equal to V_β because of unit mass) to pay both for the net investment $I - A$ and its purchase of a share β in the market portfolio.

At date 1 each firm sells its share in the market portfolio to the consumers, using the proceeds to cover its liquidity shock ρI. We need to show that β can be chosen so that the firm can always cover the high shock $\rho = \rho_H$. Any surplus from the sale of shares in the market portfolio is distributed as a dividend to the firm's shareholders at date 1. Adding the expected date-2 dividend $\rho_0 I$ to the contingent date-1 dividend provides date-0 investors with a total payout

$$\beta V_\beta - \rho I + \rho_0 I.$$

Averaging across firms, we get

$$V_\beta = \beta V_\beta - (f_H \rho_H + f_L \rho_L)I + \rho_0 I = \beta V_\beta + (I - A).$$

5. This conclusion also holds when firms are heterogeneous, as long as they are net borrowers at date 0 and face idiosyncratic shocks. However, if there is a finite number rather than a continuum of firms, there will always be a positive probability that the supply of liquidity is insufficient. For instance, with two firms, each facing a high shock with probability 1/2, there is an aggregate liquidity shortage if both experience a high shock simultaneously, which happens with probability 1/4.

6. In Holmström and Tirole (1998) we wrongly claimed that holding shares in the market portfolio does not always ensure sufficient liquidity for individual firms, since some of it would be wasted. We are very grateful to Ivan Werning for correcting this error.

The date-0 shares held by investors ($1 - \beta$ of the market portfolio) are therefore worth

$$(1 - \beta)V_\beta = I - A \tag{3.3}$$

per firm. The investors' initial investment is covered, so they are willing to get on board.

Finally note that (3.3) implies that V_β goes to infinity as β approaches 1.[7] Consequently we can always choose β so that the distressed firms can cover their liquidity shock:[8]

$$\beta V_\beta \geq \rho_H I.$$

This reasoning extends to the more general case where continuation is not second best for all shocks. For example, in the continuous version of the model, where the optimal cutoff ρ^* exceeds ρ_0, but is strictly less than ρ_1, some shocks will not be met. We encourage the reader to check that the reasoning above applies by having firms hold a share β of the market portfolio satisfying

$$\beta V_\beta = \rho^* I,$$

which allows them to cover all shocks up to ρ^*. This way firms with a shortage of liquidity ($\rho \in [\rho_0, \rho^*]$) benefit from the excess liquidity of those who either shut down ($\rho > \rho^*$) or are able to continue without using outside liquidity ($\rho \leq \rho_0$).

There are alternative ways to provide liquidity when there is no aggregate risk (shocks are independent). The key is to make sure that there is a mechanism whereby those firms that do not need all their date-1 liquidity (because of a low shock) will transfer their excess liquidity to those firms that do need it (because of a high shock). Intermediaries can

---

7. The smaller the outsiders' share per firm, $1 - \beta$, the larger is the 100 percent value of the firm V_β.

8. Equivalently, the entrepreneurs can buy a fraction β of the market portfolio such that they just have enough liquidity when facing a high shock, provided that they have secured the right to dilute initial investors:

$$(\rho_H - \rho_0)I = \beta V_\beta.$$

Then the date-1 stock market value corresponds to the payoff from intact entrepreneurs,

$$V_\beta = f_L \left[(\rho_0 - \rho_L)I + \beta V_\beta \right],$$

or equivalently,

$$V_\beta = f_L \left[(\rho_0 - \rho_L)I + \beta V_\beta \right] + f_H \left[(\rho_0 - \rho_H)I + \beta V_\beta \right]$$
$$= I - A + \beta V_\beta.$$

handle the job with credit lines, and equity markets can do it assuming that firms pay their dividends and sell their shares of the market portfolio in the right way.[9] By contrast, suppose that firms just borrow from consumers and do not secure a credit line nor invest in shares of other firms. Then distressed firms cannot continue, while the unused liquidity $(\rho_0 - \rho_L)I$ of the intact firms is wasted.

The smaller the pledgeable income ρ_0, the less there is inside liquidity and the more important it is to coordinate liquidity efficiently. The reverse may be more common in reality: the same problems that cause pledgeable income to be low (e.g., poor corporate governance and regulatory oversight over financial firms) tend to lead to poor coordination of liquidity (due to underdeveloped financial markets).[10]

3.2 Outside Liquidity and Liquidity Premia

3.2.1 Fixed Supply of Outside Liquidity

Let us return to the case of aggregate liquidity shocks discussed in section 3.1.2. All firms are identical, and each gets hit by the same liquidity shock that can be either high ($\rho_H > \rho_0$) or low ($\rho_L < \rho_0$). We concluded that all firms could continue in the low-shock state, but no firm could continue in the high-shock state because there was no inside liquidity in that state nor (by assumption) any outside liquidity.

Suppose now that there is an external, deterministic source of liquidity, an asset or a set of assets that produce L_S units of corn regardless of the state of nature (we let the aggregate payoff be deterministic for expositional purposes.) It will not matter whether the asset produces corn at date 1 or date 2, or some in both, because consumers are indifferent between consumption in the two states. In a more liberal interpretation of "corn," the asset could be anything that produces value for the consumer, such as real estate, land, or a natural resource like oil. As we have mentioned before, the outside liquidity here could also represent a fixed

9. Cross-holdings are a common way (e.g., in Europe and Asia) of maintaining control of companies with a smaller number of shares than cashflow rights, a practice that many consider bad corporate governance. Independent companies do not seem to hold shares for liquidity reasons, probably because the market portfolio is rather volatile. Indeed the stock index is likely to be low precisely when firms need cash.

10. There is a large literature linking financial development and growth (e.g., see Levine 1997; Pagano 1993; Rajan and Zingales 1998). Empirical work using various measures of financial development has attempted to capture the ease of access to funding liquidity.

amount of government bonds that are backed up by the government's ability to tax consumers.

With the help of outside liquidity, entrepreneurs can save some of their date-0 endowments to insure, at least partially, against a high liquidity shock at date 1. Let q be the price of a unit of liquidity; that is, the date-0 price of a unit of corn delivered in each of the two states at date 1. If the supply of outside liquidity, L_S, is so large that it can support the second-best plan described in chapter 2, q will equal 1. The price of liquidity can never go below 1 because consumers (who are assumed to have big aggregate endowments in each period) would then want to postpone all their consumption to date 1. This would drive the price of the liquid asset to its date-1 value, which is 1. By contrast, the date-0 price q can go above 1 because for firms the value of transferring wealth to date 1 may well be worth more than 1. The difference $q - 1 \geq 0$ is the *liquidity premium*. When the liquidity premium is strictly positive ($q > 1$), only firms will buy liquidity at date 0. Consumers do not have a demand for liquidity (but see section 3.3). The spot price of liquidity at date 1 is of course 1.

The budget constraint of a representative firm that buys ℓ units of liquidity at date 0 is

$$I - A + (q - 1)\ell \leq f_L (\rho_0 - \rho_L) I + f_H (\rho_0 - \rho_H) i_H. \tag{3.4}$$

The net cost of liquidity is $(q - 1)\ell$, since ℓ units of liquidity are worth ℓ at date 1. In the low-shock state, the firm will and can continue at full scale ($i_L = I$), regardless of ℓ, because continuation is self-financing. In the high-shock state, a firm needs outside liquidity to continue.

A firm that buys ℓ units of liquidity can in the H-state continue at a scale $i_H \leq I$ that satisfies the liquidity constraint

$$(\rho_H - \rho_0) i_H \leq \ell. \tag{3.5}$$

Constraint (3.5) assumes that, when necessary, the firm can raise up to $\rho_0 i_H$ at date 1 by diluting its initial stock (issuing claims that are senior to the initial claims; see section 2.3).

Let us determine the firm's demand for liquidity. Given the price of liquidity q, the firm simultaneously chooses its level of liquidity ℓ, the initial investment I, and the continuation scale $i_H \leq I$ subject to the budget constraint (3.4) and the liquidity constraint (3.5). Suppose that the firm decides not to continue in the high state ($i_H = 0$). Since it does not need any external liquidity in that case, the maximum initial investment-level is

$$I = \frac{A}{1 - f_L(\rho_0 - \rho_L)}. \tag{3.6}$$

This plan gives the entrepreneur a net payoff

$$U_0 = (\rho_1 - \rho_0)f_L I - A = \frac{[f_L(\rho_1 - \rho_L) - 1]}{1 - f_L(\rho_0 - \rho_L)} A. \tag{3.7}$$

Suppose instead that the firm in the high-shock state decides to continue at full scale $i_H = I$. To do so, it has to buy outside liquidity $\ell = (\rho_H - \rho_0)I$. Substituting ℓ into the budget constraint (3.4) gives the maximum initial investment

$$I(q) = \frac{A}{1 + (q-1)(\rho_H - \rho_0) - f_L(\rho_0 - \rho_L) - f_H(\rho_0 - \rho_H)}. \tag{3.8}$$

The entrepreneur's net payoff is then

$$U_1(q) = (\rho_1 - \rho_0)I(q) - A = \frac{\rho_1 - (1 + (q-1)(\rho_H - \rho_0) + \bar{\rho})}{(1 + (q-1)(\rho_H - \rho_0) + \bar{\rho}) - \rho_0} A. \tag{3.9}$$

Here $\bar{\rho} = f_L \rho_L + f_H \rho_H$ is the average liquidity shock at date 1.

The firm will continue in the high state as long as $U_1(q) > U_0$. Our earlier assumption $f_L(\rho_H - \rho_L) < 1$ implies that $U_1(1) > U_0$ (see (2.13)); if $q = 1$, it is optimal to continue. Note that $U_1(q)$ is a strictly decreasing function. Let q_{max} be the value at which the firm is indifferent between continuing and not continuing in the H-state:

$$U_1(q_{max}) = U_0. \tag{3.10}$$

Using the expressions for U_0 and $U_1(q)$, we can write this equality as

$$\frac{f_L}{f_H}(q_{max} - 1)(\rho_H - \rho_0) + f_L(\rho_H - \rho_L) = 1. \tag{3.11}$$

To interpret equation (3.11), we define again the *effective unit cost of investment* as the expected cost of bringing one unit of investment to completion; see (2.12). This value depends on the continuation policy. For a firm that continues in both states the effective unit cost is

$$c_1(q) \equiv 1 + (q-1)(\rho_H - \rho_0) + \bar{\rho}. \tag{3.12}$$

Because the firm always continues, $c_1(q)$ is the sum of the initial investment, the net cost of liquidity per continuation unit in the high state, and the expected reinvestment cost at date 1.

For a firm that does not continue in the H-state the effective unit cost is

$$c_0 \equiv \frac{1 + f_L \rho_L}{f_L}. \tag{3.13}$$

Since only a fraction f_L of projects are continued, the effective cost in this case is obtained by scaling the expected cost of a unit investment by the fraction f_L.

We see now that equation (3.11) equalizes the effective unit costs of investment under the two policies:

$$c_1(q_{max}) = c_0. \tag{3.14}$$

Since all firms are identical, the aggregate demand for liquidity is[11]

$$L_D(q) = \frac{(\rho_H - \rho_0) A}{1 + (q-1)(\rho_H - \rho_0) + \bar{\rho} - \rho_0} \quad \text{for } 1 \leq q < q_{max}. \tag{3.15}$$

If $q > q_{max}$, $L_D(q) = 0$. If $q = q_{max}$, the firms are indifferent about continuation investments $i_H \in [0, I]$ (because of the linear technology). Figure 3.2 graphs the supply and demand of liquidity.

The equilibrium value for liquidity q^* is found by setting the inelastic supply equal to the demand:

$$L_S = L_D(q^*). \tag{3.16}$$

For values L_S such that $1 < q < q_{max}$, the liquidity premium is

$$q^* - 1 = \frac{A}{L_S} - \frac{1 + \bar{\rho} - \rho_0}{\rho_H - \rho_0}. \tag{3.17}$$

The liquidity premium will be 0 if L_S exceeds the maximum demand for liquidity, $A(\rho_H - \rho_0)/(1 + \bar{\rho} - \rho_0)$.

3.2.2 Comparative Statics

Investment Scale in Response to q The firm's initial investment I is nonmonotone in the supply L_S. When there is plenty of outside liquidity the price is $q = 1$ and the firms continue in both states. As L_S decreases,

---

11. Note that the individual as well as the aggregate endowment of the entrepreneurs is A because there is a continuum of firms with unit mass.

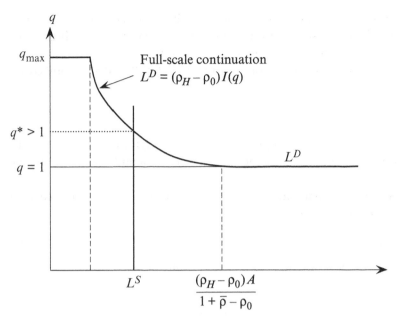

Figure 3.2
Equilibrium in the liquidity market

q increases, causing firms to spend more on buying liquidity and less on the date-0 investment I. At $q = q_{max}$ firms become indifferent about continuing in the H-state and the supply L_S determines the fraction of firms that continue. Funds no longer used to buy liquidity will instead be used to increase the initial scale of investment, leading to a nonmonotone relationship between L_S and the initial investment I.[12]

Entrepreneurial Wealth and Boom–Bust Cycles   The easy money that was available to the US corporate sector in the early 2000s seems to have paved the way for the subsequent liquidity crisis. Our framework suggests a reason why this may have been the case.

In practice, firms with more resources go for an expansion of scale or for more fragile investments. While both can easily be modeled in our framework, consider the case of expanded investment as analyzed

---

12. This nonmonotonicity disappears if the firm has two technologies that it can invest in at date 0: a liquidity producing short-term technology in addition to the long-term technology. In that case, as L_S decreases, more of the firm's initial investment will flow into the short-term technology, causing I to decrease.

in this section. Think of A as the date-0 free (noncollateralized) cash available to firms. From (3.15) we see that an increase in A creates a proportional shift in the demand for liquidity $L_D(q)$ (for $q < q_{max}$). Figure 3.2 then shows that the price of liquid assets q increases. When q reaches q_{max}, an increasing fraction of firms start to withdraw their demand for liquidity, implying that they will have to shut down operations in bad times. As a result a high supply of liquidity today leads to a liquidity shortage tomorrow. This can create recurring periods of booms and busts. (For more on the intertemporal links between liquidity and investment, see Farhi and Tirole 2009a, who show in an overlapping-generations model how firms that currently need stores of value can build on older firms' securities to create liquidity cushions.)

Likelihood of Liquidity Shortages   Let us look at what happens when the probability of the high shock, f_H, increases. Consider two separate cases. In one, the change in the probability of a high liquidity shock occurs before the investment I is made, so I will respond to the change. There is a long-term effect. In the other case, news about a change in f_H arrives after the investment I has already been made, so I stays fixed as does the purchase of liquidity. The only impact is on the changed (implicit) price of liquidity after the news.

1. *Long-term effects* (I variable)   Because

$$I(q) = \frac{A}{1 + (q - 1)(\rho_H - \rho_0) - (\rho_0 - \bar{\rho})},$$

an increase in f_H increases $\bar{\rho}$ ($= f_L \rho_L + f_H \rho_H$) and reduces investment. Intuitively the investment is less profitable, so there is less investment for a given q. Let us also examine how the maximal price q_{max} changes with f_H. Rewriting (3.11), we have

$$\frac{1 + f_L \rho_L}{f_L} = 1 + (q_{max} - 1)(\rho_H - \rho_0) + \bar{\rho},$$

implying that

$$\text{sign}\left(\frac{dq_{max}}{df_L}\right) = \text{sign}\left(\frac{d}{df_L}\left(\frac{1}{f_L} + f_L(\rho_H - \rho_L)\right)\right)$$

$$= \text{sign}\left(-\frac{1}{f_L^2} + (\rho_H - \rho_L)\right) < 0.$$

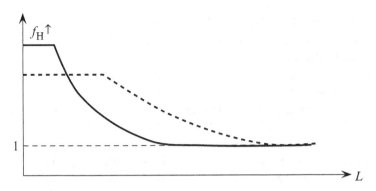

Figure 3.3
Long-term impact of growing concerns

This is because, by assumption, $f_L(\rho_H - \rho_L) < 1$; that is, there is a liquidity demand when $q = 1$. Therefore q_{max} increases as the likelihood of a high shock (f_H) increases.

The long-term impact on liquidity demand is depicted in figure 3.3. Bad news (f_H increases) increases q when there is little liquidity, and decreases it when there is much liquidity.

2. *Short-term effects* (*I* fixed)[13]   Suppose now that news about the likelihood of a high shock arrives after *I* has been chosen, but before the shock is revealed as depicted in the time line in figure 3.4.

Let q_0 be the price of liquidity at date 0, and $q(\omega)$ the price at date 1/2, contingent on news ω. At date 0, let the firm choose the initial scale *I*, a noncontingent amount of liquidity ℓ_0 and a contingent amount of liquidity $\ell(\omega)$, which can be construed as an adjustment to the initial amount of liquidity purchased, ℓ_0. In equilibrium, the contingent price of liquidity $q(\omega)$ delivered on date 1/2 in state ω will, of course, have to

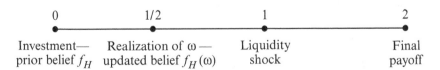

Figure 3.4
News accrual

---

13. This analysis is a special case of the analysis in Holmström and Tirole (2001).

be such that there is no actual adjustment in liquidity. This is because all firms are in identical position also at date $1/2$. Therefore in equilibrium it must be the case that

$$\begin{cases} \ell_0 = L_S, \\ \ell(\omega) = 0, & \text{for all } \omega. \end{cases}$$

To determine $q(\omega)$, consider an individual firm's choice of $\ell(\omega)$. The firm's budget constraint is

$$I - A + (q_0 - 1)\ell_0 + E\left[(q(\omega) - 1)\ell(\omega)\right]$$
$$= E\left[f_L(\omega)(\rho_0 - \rho_L)\right]I + E\left[f_H(\omega)(\rho_0 - \rho_H)i(\omega)\right].$$

Its liquidity constraint at date 1, if ω occurred at date $1/2$, is

$$\ell_0 + \ell(\omega) \geq (\rho_H - \rho_0)i(\omega) \qquad \text{for all } \omega.$$

The feasibility constraint is, as usual,

$$0 \leq i(\omega) \leq I \quad \text{for all } \omega.$$

Maximizing with respect to I, ℓ_0, $i(\omega)$, and $\ell(\omega)$,[14] the entrepreneur's utility

$$(\rho_1 - \rho_0)\left\{E\left[f_L(\omega)\right]I + E[f_H(\omega)i(\omega)]\right\},$$

subject to the liquidity, feasibility and budget constraints above, yields

$$\begin{cases} q_0 = E\left[q(\omega)\right], \\ q(\omega) - 1 = \dfrac{f_H(\omega)}{f_H}(q_0 - 1). \end{cases}$$

We see that the price follows a martingale. The date-0 price of date-$1/2$ liquidity, $q(\omega)$, goes up when the updated belief of a high liquidity shock $f_H(\omega)$ is higher than the initial belief f_H and down in the opposite case.

The interest rates r_0 from date 0 to date 1 and $r(\omega)$ from date $1/2$ to date 1 are defined by

$$q_0 - 1 = \frac{1}{1 + r_0} - 1 = \frac{-r_0}{1 + r_0} \quad \text{and} \tag{3.18}$$

---

14. In this program $\ell(\omega)$ is unconstrained even though the firm will not be able to pledge $\ell(\omega) > 0$ as it does not have collateral to do so. However, the solution to the subconstrained program, $\ell(\omega) = 0$, satisfies the omitted constraint, and so there is no loss of generality in looking at the subconstrained program.

$$q(\omega) - 1 = \frac{-r(\omega)}{1 + r(\omega)}, \tag{3.19}$$

respectively. Note that r_0 and $r(\omega)$ are negative. For small changes in the probability, hence small changes in the interest rates, we see from the equilibrium prices that

$$|r(\omega)| \simeq \frac{f_H(\omega)}{f_H} |r_0|.$$

The date-1/2 interest rate moves in proportion to the updated probability of an unfavorable liquidity shock.

3.2.3 Evidence of a Liquidity Premium in Corporate Bond Spreads

There is a lot of suggestive evidence consistent with a liquidity premium, but with so many factors affecting interest rates, it has been hard to make a strong case for a premium. Krishnamurthy and Vissing-Jorgensen (2010) try to get around this problem by analyzing how the spread of corporate bond yields over Treasury bond yields varies with the supply of Treasury bonds. Figure 3.5, imported from their paper, describes the main finding. The horizontal axis measures the ratio of US government debt to GDP. The vertical axis measures the spread between AAA-rated corporate bond yields and Treasury yields. The data points are September values from 1919 to 2005.

Using corporate bond spreads rather than absolute yields filters out common effects that influence all yields of AAA bonds. The ratio of debt to GDP is a good proxy of the amount of outstanding Treasury bonds (relative to the overall economic activity). The flat tail of observations with high debt/GDP ratios are from the 1940s and 1950s and evidently due to war spending. This suggests that an important part of the variation in the debt/GDP ratio is exogenous.

The resemblance between figures 3.2 and 3.5 is intriguing. Figure 3.2 may be interpreted as tracing out the demand for Treasury bonds in response to a liquidity premium. Much as in figure 3.5, there is an initial downward-sloping section as the increase in the supply of Treasuries brings down the premium. Then the demand curve turns flat suggesting that the liquidity premium has disappeared. Note, however, that the vertical axis in figure 3.5 measures yield spreads and not the liquidity premium as in figure 3.2. In the next chapter we will show that if corporate bonds default independently of the supply of Treasury bonds,

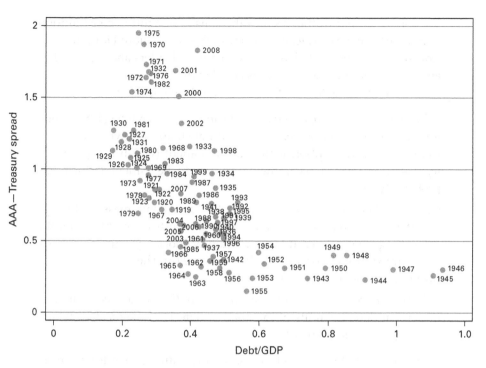

Figure 3.5
Liquidity premium in corporate bond spreads

the yield spread can be decomposed into two parts. It is the sum of a liquidity premium (determined by the supply of Treasuries) and a risk premium due to the difference in default risk between corporate bonds and Treasuries (which are essentially default free). Thus the fact that Treasuries have a zero liquidity premium in figure 3.2 when the supply is ample is fully consistent with a remaining baseline spread visible in the high debt/GDP observations of figure 3.5.

3.3 Competition for Liquidity between Consumers and Firms

Our workhorse model assumes that consumers are patient. Obviously consumers may also demand some liquidity. To consider this and see how our theory works with a mix of consumer and corporate liquidity demands, this section adds Diamond–Dybvig consumers (see appendix 2B) to the equilibrium analysis as follows. Because consumers save in the Diamond–Dybvig model, the corporate sector will be a net borrower.

The long-term return that secures the consumers' future consumption will come from the pledgeable income of the firms' illiquid investments. Consumers can be treated as firms that are net lenders and cannot offer any pledgeable income (their ρ_0 is equal to 0).

There are three dates: $t = 0, 1, 2$. The model comprises:

- *Consumers* They are exactly as in Diamond and Dybvig (1983). They invest their unit endowment ($a = 1$) at date 0 and receive utility $u(c_1)$ from date-1 consumption if they are impatient (which has probability $1 - \alpha$) and $u(c_1 + c_2)$ if they turn out to be patient (which has probability α).

- *Firms* There is a continuum of identical firms with mass 1. The representative firm has assets A at date 0 and invests a variable amount I in the long-term project. It faces a liquidity shock ρ per unit of investment, drawn from a continuous distribution $F(\rho)$. There is no aggregate uncertainty (the firms' shocks are i.i.d.).

- *Assets* Firms can also invest in short-term (liquid) assets. By investing $g(\ell)$ at date 0, ℓ units of the good at date 1 can be created, where $g' > 0, g'' > 0$, and $g'(0) = 1$.

Letting $\hat{\rho}$ denote the cutoff for continuing with the long-term project at date 1, the economy's resource constraints at dates 0, 1, and 2 are

$$I - A + g(\ell) \leq 1, \tag{3.20}$$

$$(1 - \alpha)c_1 + \left[\int_0^{\hat{\rho}} \rho f(\rho) d\rho \right] I \leq \ell, \tag{3.21}$$

$$\alpha c_2 \leq F(\hat{\rho})\rho_0 I. \tag{3.22}$$

Condition (3.20) reflects the fact that the economy's total endowment, $1 + A$, is invested in illiquid (I) and liquid ($g(\ell)$) assets. Condition (3.21) highlights how consumers and firms compete for liquidity at date 1. Finally (3.22) states that the consumers' long-term consumption comes from firms with limited pledgeable income (unlike the model in appendix 2B, where all income was pledgeable).

A Pareto optimum among consumers and entrepreneurs can be found by maximizing the representative entrepreneur's rent:

$$\max_{\{\ell, I, \hat{\rho}\}} \left\{ (\rho_1 - \rho_0)F(\hat{\rho})I \right\}, \tag{3.23}$$

subject to the resource constraints (3.20) through (3.22) and the representative consumer's expected utility exceeding some level $\bar{U}$:

$$(1 - \alpha)u(c_1) + \alpha u(c_2) \geq \bar{U}. \tag{3.24}$$

Let $\lambda_0, \lambda_1, \lambda_2,$ and λ_3 be nonnegative Lagrange multipliers corresponding to the constraints (3.20) through (3.22) and (3.24), respectively. The first-order conditions imply that

$$\frac{u'(c_1)}{u'(c_2)} = \frac{\lambda_1}{\lambda_2},$$

$$F(\rho^*) - \lambda_1 \left[\int_0^{\rho^*} \rho f(\rho) d\rho \right] + \lambda_2 F(\rho^*)\rho_0 - \frac{\lambda_1}{g'(\ell)} = 0, \tag{3.25}$$

$$1 - \lambda_1 \rho^* + \lambda_2 \rho_0 = 0.$$

The first condition shows that the consumer's marginal utilities of consumption may not be set equal, since the investment technologies allow only limited consumption smoothing while satisfying entrepreneurial objectives. The second condition determines the initial investment scale I, taking into account that ℓ is chosen so that the marginal cost $g'(\ell) = \lambda_1/\lambda_0$. The last condition determines the optimal $\hat{\rho} = \rho^*$.

Straightforward manipulations lead to the following condition for the optimal cutoff ρ^*:

$$g'(\ell)\rho^* = \frac{1 + g'(\ell) \int_0^{\rho^*} \rho f(\rho) d\rho}{F(\rho^*)}. \tag{3.26}$$

Condition (3.26) generalizes the standard optimal cutoff rule ($\rho^* = c$) to the case of costly liquidity hoarding. The average cost of bringing one unit of investment to completion for an arbitrary cutoff $\hat{\rho}$ becomes

$$c(\hat{\rho}, q) = \frac{1 + q \int_0^{\hat{\rho}} \rho f(\rho) d\rho}{F(\hat{\rho})},$$

which generalizes condition (2.22) to the case of costly liquidity ($q \geq 1$). Letting

$$q \equiv g'(\ell),$$

allows us to write condition (3.26) in a form analogous to the standard cutoff rule,

$$q\rho^* = c(\rho^*, q),$$

since $q\rho^*$ is the cost of raising the cutoff level marginally above ρ^*.

Patient consumers help firms "bridge" dates 1 and 2, as they do not demand cash at date 1. And so the discount factor $1/q$ between dates 0 and 1 is the only modification to the formula obtained in chapter 2.

The Pareto-optimal production plan can be decentralized in the following way. Let $Q = \lambda_2/\lambda_0$ be the consumer's marginal valuation of date-2 consumption relative to the marginal valuation of the date-0 endowment. The representative firm then solves:

$$\max_{\{\ell, I, \hat{\rho}\}} \left\{ (\rho_1 - \rho_0)F(\hat{\rho})I \right\},$$

subject to

$$I + q\ell \leq A + QF(\hat{\rho})\rho_0 I,$$

$$\left[\int_0^{\hat{\rho}} \rho f(\rho)d\rho \right] I \leq \ell,$$

which yields the same first-order conditions as in the Pareto program and therefore also (3.26).

A corresponding decentralization holds for consumers, but it requires that the demand for liquidity be intermediated by banking contracts of the Diamond–Dybvig type (i.e., contracts that provide limited insurance to consumers). The maximization of $(1 - \alpha)u(c_1) + \alpha u(c_2)$ subject to the budget constraint,

$$1 \geq (1 - \alpha)qc_1 + \alpha Q c_2,$$

yields

$$\frac{u'(c_1)}{u'(c_2)} = \frac{q}{Q},$$

which is consistent with the first condition in (3.25).

Our basic model is thus a special case of a model where

• consumers are always patient: $\alpha = 1$ (and so $\ell = I \int_0^{\rho^*} \rho f(\rho)d\rho$);

• consumers' marginal rate of substitution between dates 0 and 2 is normalized at $Q = 1$.

This framework could be extended to the case where only a fraction, $1 - \alpha$, of consumers face a liquidity shock, and the distribution of the corporate liquidity shocks are determined (i.e., driven) by a common factor. For instance, in the stylized model of section 5.2, workers become unemployed due to plant closings and so face liquidity needs at the same time as firms.

3.4 Endogenous Supply of Liquidity

So far we have mostly assumed that the supply of liquidity is exogenous. In reality, the private sector can produce liquidity through a variety of technologies, for instance, by investing in projects with safer and shorter term payoffs. As the liquidity premium rises with increased demand, the private sector will respond by shifting more resources toward supplying liquidity.

3.4.1 Producing Liquidity

To illustrate, let us consider a second sector, the S-sector (for short-term), consisting of a continuum of identical firms with unit mass. Assume that each entrepreneur in this sector has an individual endowment A_S and access to a linear storage technology that transforms one unit of corn at date 0 into $\rho_{0S} < 1$ units of corn at date 1. Also assume that the short-term project provides a private benefit to the entrepreneur, $\rho_{1S} - \rho_{0S}$, such that $\rho_{1S} > 1$. The budget constraint for each firm in this second sector is

$$l_S \leq A_S + q\rho_{0S}l_S. \tag{3.27}$$

The plan to invest ℓ_S at date 0 must be covered by the sum of the entrepreneur's own capital A_S and the date-1 return $\rho_{0S}\ell_S$ valued at unit price q. Because $\rho_{1S} > 1$, the entrepreneur will invest in the storage technology for all values $q \geq 1$. The maximum investment scale, implied by the budget constraint, gives the individual (and aggregate) supply function

$$\ell_S(q) = \frac{A_S}{1 - q\rho_{0S}}. \tag{3.28}$$

This supply function is strictly increasing and convex with $q = 1/\rho_{0S}$ as an asymptote. The higher is q, the more liquidity the S-sector will produce. The marginal cost of production is decreasing in q. At $q_{max} = 1/\rho_{0S}$, the S-sector becomes self-financing at which point it can supply an infinite amount of liquidity. For prices below this maximum, the supply is constrained by the initial capital A_S that the entrepreneurs have.

Note that the distribution of capital between the entrepreneurs in the two sectors matters for the amount of liquidity that will be produced as well as for the equilibrium price of liquidity. As the ratio of A_S/A decreases, the price of liquidity will rise and the leverage of A_S will grow while the leverage of A will decline.

By contrast, if all entrepreneurs have access to both technologies, the equilibrium price of liquidity will be such that each entrepreneur is indifferent between operating the storage technology and selling liquidity to others or operating the long-term technology and buying liquidity from others (or being self-sufficient by operating both technologies).

If liquidity-producing technologies have faster payoffs, something our model is silent about,[15] the logic above will have the simple prediction that tighter liquidity, as measured by a higher liquidity premium $q - 1$, will cause the private sector to reallocate funds from long-term to short-term investments.

3.4.2 Developing Financial Markets

There are other ways in which the private sector can expand liquidity supply in times of high liquidity demand. One way is to expand pledgeable income ρ_0, which we have so far taken as fixed. There are many ways in which the pledgeable income can be expanded. For instance, a bank, a venture capitalist, or some other intermediary may be able to monitor the firm, reduce the cost of moral hazard, and thereby reduce the illiquid stake that the entrepreneur needs to hold to keep him from cheating (see Holmström and Tirole 1997). Or a country may institute a better corporate governance system with regulatory changes that improve the firm's reporting and incentives more generally. Increased transparency and better regulatory mechanisms that protect investors make it easier for them to recover investments and therefore raises ρ_0 for most firms. In a dynamic model incentives are often strengthened by reputation effects, reducing the need for financial incentives. This too raises the pledgeable income.

Another important determinant of aggregate liquidity is the degree of financial market development and the extent to which corporate income and private wealth are turned into tradable assets. When a private firm goes public and its shares become liquid (in the traditional financial sense), the portfolio of tradable securities expands. Note that even if the pattern of returns from the new shares can be replicated with available securities on the market, a public offering can add value if the shares pay off in a state where liquidity is in short supply. This contrasts with standard financial models where there is no such effect.

---

15. It does not matter whether the units of corn produced by the firms in the second sector accrue at date 1 or date 2. The key property is that they are fully pledgeable (liquid).

One might conjecture, however, that short-term investments, either because they involve less uncertainty and therefore less asymmetric information, or because they offer less scope for diversion, have a higher pledgeability than longer term investments.

In the run-up to the subprime crisis, securitization of mortgages played a major role. Homeownership is by far the biggest component of household wealth (in the United States, 32.3 percent in 2000 and 41.2 percent in 2002; see Gottschalk 2008), and housing has for this reason always played a special role in the supply of liquidity. Traditionally liquidity was created through banks, which issued deposit contracts to finance investments in housing. Securitization, by making nontradable mortgages tradable, led to a dramatic growth in the US volume of mortgages, home equity loans, and mortgage-backed securities in 2000 to 2008, partly in response to increased global demand for savings instruments.

When a homeowner takes out a loan using her house as collateral, the gross supply of liquidity is increased because she has created an asset in which others can invest. How much the net supply of liquidity (and in which states) has increased depends on the structure of financial markets and its ability to utilize the mortgage assets efficiently. A major advantage of securitization is that collateral gets allocated in a state-contingent fashion. However, if the homeowner invests all of the proceeds from the loan into Treasury bonds or similar market instruments, the net increase in the supply of aggregate liquidity is much smaller than if she spends the proceeds on consumption or real investments. What the homeowner does with the borrowed money matters.

Similarly an IPO may have no consequences for net supply and prices of liquidity, nor production plans. Say the entrepreneur all along knew that he could issue equity to outsiders and therefore considered the shares of the company a future source of liquidity. If so, the value of the *potentially* pledgeable income would be part of his date-1 liquidity in our model. Taking the company public at date 0 would be a matter of indifference, if the entrepreneur were to hold equal amounts and an equal distribution of liquidity after the IPO as before it. If the IPO reduces the efficiency of the firm (e.g., because of moral hazard), the entrepreneur would do better to keep the firm private until some event forces an IPO.

The main point here is that the net addition to liquidity is typically smaller than the gross increase from the IPO, because even privately held assets provide liquidity. After the IPO, the entrepreneur will likely purchase liquidity to compensate for the loss of the liquidity embedded in the firm when it was private. But if the IPO has no direct payoff consequences, a public offering in the type of model we have studied never makes the liquidity supply worse and typically makes it better. Once the private returns are turned into publicly tradable claims, some of the liquidity will likely be used to support other projects than those of the entrepreneur. The market will make more efficient use of liquidity than if it is privately held.

3.5 Summary

In this chapter we illustrated, in the simplest setting, how a shortage of liquidity can naturally arise from limited pledgeability of income. We showed how the familiar limitations on the debt capacity of firms are directly linked to the much less discussed limitations on the funding capacity of investors. The supply problem arises because the production of goods also serves a collateral function.[16] The basic question to ask is whether the corporate sector generates enough collateral to support the second-best production plans, in other words, whether there is enough aggregate liquidity to meet corporate needs in each state of nature.

The chapter showed that when the productive sector is a net lender, there is always a shortage of aggregate liquidity. When the corporate sector is a net borrower, the presence of aggregate liquidity shortages depends on the stochastic structure of the firms' liquidity shocks. If all uncertainty is idiosyncratic and there is a continuum of firms, there is always sufficient aggregate liquidity. Then firms can meet their demand for liquidity simply by holding a fraction of the market portfolio. At the other extreme, when there is only aggregate uncertainty and all firms are hit by the same shock, there is always a shortage of aggregate liquidity. This creates a demand for outside liquidity, such as government bonds, that will command a liquidity premium. The liquidity premium declines as the supply of bonds increases in a manner broadly consistent with the evidence in Krishnamurthy and Vissing-Jorgensen (2010).

The government and international financial markets can alleviate liquidity shortages, as we discuss in chapters 5 and 6. There are also many ways in which the private sector can respond to liquidity shortages and high liquidity premia. Firms can change their production plans, private firms can go public, consumers can increase the leverage on their homes through home equity loans, and new pledgeable assets can be built. The subprime crisis may in part have been caused by global shortages of collateral that led to imaginative but, in the end, fragile ways to increase the aggregate supply of liquidity, a topic we will come back to in the epilogue.

---

16. Kiyotaki and Moore's (1997) model of credit cycles turns on this same dichotomy of capital, but in their model the dual use is within a single firm. Our emphasis is on collateral production for the rest of the economy.

4   A Liquidity Asset Pricing Model (LAPM)

In this chapter we extend the simple model from the previous chapter to a general liquidity asset pricing model (LAPM) with heterogeneous firms employing linear technologies of the sort we have been studying. Uncertainty can affect all the parameters of these technologies. The model shows how liquidity premia are determined in such a setting, how they affect bond yields and firm values, and how firms plan investments and optimally manage liquidity risks in light of such premia. We start with the case where there are two aggregate shocks, before moving on to the general model.

4.1   LAPM with Two Aggregate Shocks

4.1.1   Liquidity Premia and Bond Yields

For heterogeneous firms it is more convenient to work with state prices. All asset prices can readily be recovered from state prices, since markets for claims on date-1 liquidity (the pledgeable part of output) are complete.

Let $s_H f_H$ be the date-0 price of one unit of liquidity delivered only in the high-shock state, and let $s_L f_L$ be the corresponding price of liquidity delivered only in the low-shock state; here f_H and f_L are the probabilities of a high and a low liquidity shock, respectively ($f_L + f_H = 1$). Because consumers are indifferent about the timing of consumption, s_H and $s_L \geq 1$. If there is an aggregate shortage of liquidity in the high-shock state, we will have $s_H > 1$. We assume that there is no aggregate shortage of liquidity in the low-shock state, so the corporate sector is self-financing in that state, and hence $s_L = 1$. The date-0 price q of a unit of unconditional liquidity at date 1 (e.g., a risk-free unit bond, expiring at date 1) can then be written as

$$q = f_L \cdot 1 + f_H \cdot s_H, \tag{4.1}$$

and the liquidity premium as

$$q - 1 = f_H(s_H - 1). \tag{4.2}$$

The yield on a risk-free bond is

$$\kappa = \frac{1 - q}{q} = \frac{-f_H(s_H - 1)}{1 + f_H(s_H - 1)} \leq 0. \tag{4.3}$$

The yield is zero whenever the liquidity premium is zero; otherwise, it is negative since our risk neutral consumers do not discount the future. The yield on a bond that can default is strictly larger than κ. Take, for example, a bond, indexed by k, with face value 1 that in expectation pays $\theta_{kH} < 1$ in state H and $\theta_{kL} = 1$ in state L; that is, the bond partially defaults with probability f_H. Such a bond commands the date-0 price

$$q_k = f_L + f_H \theta_{kH} s_H. \tag{4.4}$$

The yield on the bond is

$$\kappa_k = \frac{f_L + f_H \theta_{kH} - q_k}{q_k} = \frac{f_H \theta_{kH}(1 - s_H)}{1 - f_H(1 - \theta_{kH} s_H)}. \tag{4.5}$$

Note that $\kappa_k - \kappa > 0$ because $\theta_{kH} < 1$.[1] Using this simple example we can interpret the spread between AAA-rated corporate bonds and Treasury bonds (Krishnamurthy and Vissing-Jorgensen 2010) described in figure 3.5. For bonds that may default, the average spread should stay strictly positive regardless of the liquidity premium. Variations in default risk would move the spread around for a given liquidity premium. The spread should decrease as the price of liquidity goes down, other things being equal, and reach a constant positive value when the liquidity premium is 0. This is the sense in which the theoretical figure 3.2 and the empirical figure 3.5 match, as suggested in section 3.2.3.

4.1.2 Asset Prices

Liquidity premia influence the pricing of firms. With two states, each firm, indexed by j, is characterized by four numbers $\{\rho_{j0}, \rho_{j1}, \rho_{jL}, \rho_{jH}\}$, where ρ_{j0} is the pledgeable payoff, ρ_{j1} is the total payoff, ρ_{jL} is the liquidity shock in the low aggregate state, and ρ_{jH} is the liquidity shock

---

1. We can write

$$\kappa_k - \kappa = \frac{f_H(1 - s_H)(\theta_{kH} - 1)(1 - f_H)}{[1 - f_H(1 - \theta_{kH} s_H)][1 - f_H(1 - s_H)]} > 0.$$

in the high aggregate state; all the numbers are per unit of investment. For simplicity, we assume that there are only two types of firms, "regular" firms and "contrarian" firms, and that $\rho_{jL} = 0$ for both types. Regular firms demand liquidity in the high aggregate state H:[2]

$$0 = \rho_{jL} < \rho_{j0} < \rho_{jH} < \rho_{j1}. \tag{4.6}$$

Contrarian firms, in contrast, supply liquidity in the high aggregate state (for them $\rho_{jH} < \rho_{j0}$). The fraction of contrarian firms is small enough that there still is a shortage of liquidity in the H-state.

At date 0, each firm j chooses an initial scale of investment I_j and the scale of date-1 continuation investments $i_{jL}, i_{jH} \leq I_j$. Since a regular firm is self-sufficient in state L, such a firm will choose $i_{jL} = I_j$. We assume, as before, that $(\rho_{jH} - \rho_{jL})f_L = \rho_{jH}f_L < 1$ holds for regular firms, so that continuation at full scale is optimal for them also when the high shock hits if the liquidity premium is zero (see (2.13)). For contrarian firms, $i_{jL} = i_{jH} = I_j$, since they never demand liquidity.

Define the *net (financial) payoff of firm j in state ω* as

$$y_{j\omega} \equiv (\rho_{j0} - \rho_{j\omega})i_{j\omega}, \quad \omega = L, H. \tag{4.7}$$

This is also the amount of liquidity that firm j supplies in state ω (if $y_{j\omega}$ is negative, the firm demands liquidity in state ω).

Firm j's budget constraint is

$$I_j - A_j \leq f_L y_{jL} + f_H y_{jH} s_H \equiv E_j(ys). \tag{4.8}$$

The right-hand side of the budget constraint, $E_j(ys)$, is the *date-0 market value of the firm*. The investor's expected date-1 payoff from firm j is

$$E_j(y) \equiv f_L y_{jL} + f_H y_{jH}. \tag{4.9}$$

The liquidity premium of firm j is

$$v_j \equiv f_H y_{jH}(s_H - 1). \tag{4.10}$$

The liquidity premium is negative for regular firms ($y_{jH} < 0$) and positive for contrarian firms ($y_{jH} > 0$). Since the budget constraint must bind, we have

$$I_j - A_j = E_j(ys) = E_j(y) + v_j, \tag{4.11}$$

---

2. Parameters must be such that investment is finite. A sufficient condition for that is $f_L(\rho_{j0} - \rho_{jL}) = f_L\rho_{j0} < 1$.

or equivalently

$$(I_j - A_j) - v_j = E_j(ys) - v_j = E_j(y).$$ (4.12)

The right-hand side of (4.12) is the investors' gross expected return at date 1. The left-hand side is their total investment, showing that for a regular firm, which demands liquidity in the high state, the total investment consists of two parts: the investors' contribution $I_j - A_j$ toward the initial investment plus the payment of the liquidity premium $-v_j > 0$ for securing the desired date-1 liquidity.

Define a *unit claim* on the firm as a claim that in expectation pays 1 at date 1. The date-0 value of a unit claim on the firm is

$$q_j = \frac{E_j(ys)}{E_j(y)} = \frac{f_L y_{jL} + f_H y_{jH} s_H}{f_L y_{jL} + f_H y_{jH}}.$$ (4.13)

When we compare firm values, q_j is the natural measure to use. It tells us how much investors are willing to pay for the asset per unit of return at date 1 net of the liquidity premium/discount.

Finally, we introduce *normalized net state payoffs for firm j*:

$$\bar{y}_{j\omega} \equiv \frac{y_{j\omega}}{E_j(y)}, \qquad \omega = L, H.$$ (4.14)

This normalization makes net state payoffs have unit expected values. The value of a unit claim on the firm can then be written as

$$q_j - 1 = f_H \bar{y}_{jH}(s_H - 1).$$ (4.15)

Regular firms demand liquidity in the high-shock state, so their unit claim features a liquidity discount ($q_j - 1 < 0$). For contrarian firms, the converse is true ($q_j - 1 > 0$).

The interpretation of the value of a unit claim as an asset price requires some elaboration. At first glance, it would appear that a unit claim cannot sell at a discount, since consumers (who have limitless wealth in our model) could compete for such claims until the discount would be driven to zero. So how can we make sense of (4.15)? The explanation is that for a regular firm the price q_j comes with the additional financial obligation to pay the firm the amount $-\bar{y}_{jH} > 0$ in state H at date 1. To secure this commitment, the investor needs to buy this much liquidity at date 0 at a liquidity premium $s_H - 1$. This just offsets the liquidity discount $q_j - 1$. The total cost of buying a unit claim of a regular firm is therefore 1. (Recall that consumer income is nonpledgeable, so commitments must be backed up by tradable assets.)

This interpretation somewhat resembles a venture capital deal with two stages of investment. At the initial stage, investors pay q_j, and at the second stage (date 1), they pay $-\bar{y}_{jH}$ if needed, which in expectation costs them $1 - q_j$.[3] An alternative arrangement is to have investors pay 1 per unit for a regular firm at date 0 with the firm investing q_j of it in productive assets and $1 - q_j$ in shares of contrarian firms (or other liquid assets). If the aggregate state turns out to be low, the firm turns the contrarian shares over to its investors (or sells the shares and pays out the proceeds as a date-1 dividend). If the state is high, it sells the contrarian shares and uses the proceeds to cover the liquidity shock. Either way, the expected return on the consumer-investor's total investment is zero. However, the price of a share per unit of investment scale at date 0 differs in the two cases. When everything is paid up front, the price paid at date 0 is 1. When there is a remaining investor liability, the price at date 0 is given by (4.15), reflecting a liquidity discount.

Kocherlakota (1996) has argued that in a world where a representative consumer holds equity either directly or indirectly (e.g., through mutual funds), prices will be determined by the consumers' marginal rate of substitution, which in our model always equals one. This conclusion need not hold when there is segmentation among investors, as illustrated here.[4] However, if investors pay the full cost of investment up front, letting regular firms arrange their own liquidity needs by buying shares of contrarian firms, say, the price of regular firms will equal the marginal rate of substitution of consumers, while the price of contrarian firms will feature a liquidity premium and consequently no consumer will buy these shares.

4.1.3 A Numerical Example

Before proceeding, it may be helpful to go through a numerical example that illustrates the definitions above. Let the net payoffs of a regular firm j be $y_{jL} = 2$, $y_{jH} = -1$, and assume that each state has equal probability, and therefore $E_j(y) = (0.5)$. Let the entrepreneur's date-0 endowment be $A = 10$. Without aggregate liquidity shortages, the maximum investment scale would be $I_j = A/[1 - (0.5)] = 20$, of which the investors would contribute 10.

---

3. For expositions of the staging of venture capital financing, see, for example, Gompers and Lerner (1999), Kaplan and Strömberg (2003), and Sahlman (1990).

4. He and Krishnamurthy (2009) present a model where only investment banks buy equity, and therefore asset prices do not reflect consumer rates of substitution. In empirical work, consumer segmentation has been used to reconcile equity premia with consumer marginal rates of substitution (see Vissing-Jorgensen 2002).

Assume further that there is a liquidity shortage in the H-state and that the liquidity premium in this state is $s_H - 1 = 0.2$. The liquidity premium adds $f_H(s_H - 1) = (0.5)(0.2) = 0.1$ to the cost of each unit of investment at date 0, reducing the maximum scale of investment to $I_j = 10/[(1 + 0.1) - (0.5)] = 16\frac{2}{3}$. The expected net financial return at date 1 is therefore $E_j(y) = (16\frac{2}{3}) \cdot (0.5) = 8\frac{1}{3}$. This equals the sum of what the investors contribute to the initial investment, $I_j - A = 16\frac{2}{3} - 10 = 6\frac{2}{3}$, and what they pay as a liquidity premium: $-v_j I_j = -(0.5)(-1)(0.2) \cdot 16\frac{2}{3} = 1\frac{2}{3}$.

Against a date-2 expected pledgeable return of $8\frac{1}{3}$, the firm is able to raise $6\frac{2}{3}$ units from investors at date 0 (all used for the initial investment) with the additional covenant that investors will promise to cover the liquidity shock at date 1. This covenant costs investors $8\frac{1}{3} - 6\frac{2}{3} = 1\frac{2}{3}$ because they have to buy liquid instruments (e.g., shares in contrarian firms) to secure their pledge. They could also pay in $8\frac{1}{3}$ at date 0 and let the firm buy the requisite liquidity. In either case, the date-0 value of the firm is $q_j = (6\frac{2}{3})/(8\frac{1}{3}) = 0.8$ per unit of expected date-1 return. The firm sells at a discount $q_j - 1 = -0.2$ because the purchase of liquidity costs 0.2 per unit of expected date-1 return.

4.1.4 The LAPM Formula with Two States

In the two-state economy, with a liquidity shortage only in the H-state, we find, using equation (4.15), the following simple relationship between the value of any pair (j, k) of assets:[5]

$$\frac{q_j - 1}{q_k - 1} = \frac{\bar{y}_{jH}}{\bar{y}_{kH}}. \tag{4.16}$$

This valuation formula shows that with a single liquidity shock, the ratio of the liquidity premia (or discounts as the case may be) of any two assets is independent of the probability of the state as well as the cost of liquidity and is simply the ratio of the payoffs in those two states. In particular, we can express the value of every asset in terms of the price q of a bond that pays one unit in each of the two states. From (4.16) we have

$$q_j = 1 + (q - 1)\bar{y}_{jH}. \tag{4.17}$$

4.1.5 Equilibrium Determination with Two States

In section 3.2.1 we described how the bond price q is established in equilibrium when firms are homogeneous and there are two states. The

---

5. This valuation formula can be found in Holmström and Tirole (2001).

equilibrium in the case of heterogeneous firms can be similarly found. Expressed as a function of s_H, the demand (or supply) function for state-contingent liquidity by each firm looks identical to the demand (or supply) function for the case of homogenous firms. As the price s_H rises, a regular firm, because it demands liquidity ($y_{jH} < 0$), will reduce its level of investment until it reaches the point of indifference between continuing in both states or continuing just in the L-state. A contrarian firm, because it supplies liquidity ($y_{jH} > 0$), will be able to expand its investment scale in response to an increase in s_H until s_H reaches a point where some firm becomes self-financing. This firm can then supply everyone with liquidity because of the constant-returns-to-scale technology.

We can ask which characteristics determine the order in which regular firms will drop out in the liquidity shortage state as the price of liquidity rises (i.e., the order in which firms switch from $i_{jH} = I_j$ to $i_{jH} = 0$ as s_H increases). We can also ask which contrarian firm will be the one that first becomes self-financing.[6]

To determine the critical value s_H at which a regular firm drops out in the H-state (contrarian firms never do), we equate the entrepreneur's net payoffs when the firm chooses $i_{jH} = I_j$ and when it chooses $i_{jH} = 0$. Recall that we assumed $\rho_{jL} = 0$ for all firms. It is easy to verify that a regular firm j will then continue in both states if and only if[7]

$$s_H \leq s_{jH}^{reg} \equiv \frac{1 - f_L \rho_{j0}}{f_L(\rho_{jH} - \rho_{j0})} \qquad \text{for all } j \text{ (regular).} \qquad (4.18)$$

Here s_{jH}^{reg} is the highest value of s_H such that regular firm j is willing to continue in state H. A regular firm drops out at a lower value s_H, the higher is ρ_{jH} and the lower is ρ_{j0}; a firm with a small pledgeable income, and/or a large demand for liquidity in the high state, will drop out early.[8] Note that neither the entrepreneur's wealth A_j nor his private benefit $\rho_{j1} - \rho_{j0}$ influence the point at which the firm's demand for liquidity drops to zero, because of the linear technology.

---

6. Note that these questions relate to comparisons across firms whose parameters are fixed. It is not a comparative statics exercise. The only things changing are the price s_H and the firm's investment policies in response to this price change.

7. The right-hand side of (4.18) can be derived from condition (3.11) by setting $\rho_{jL} = 0$, substituting $q_{max} = f_L + f_H s_H$, and solving for the maximum value of s_H such that firm j will continue in both states.

8. Recall that we must have $f_L \rho_{jH} < 1$; else it would not be worthwhile for the firm to continue in both states.

As long as a regular firm continues in both states (the inequality in (4.18) holds), the initial investment I_j decreases with s_H. Contrarian firms always continue in both states. They increase their initial investment as s_H increases, since the increased value of supplying liquidity relaxes their budget constraint. For a high enough liquidity premium, the budget constraint of a contrarian firm will no longer bind and the firm becomes self-financing. This occurs when $s_H = s_{jH}^{con}$ satisfies

$$f_L \rho_{j0} + f_H(\rho_{j0} - \rho_{jH})s_{jH}^{con} = 1. \tag{4.19}$$

As soon as one contrarian firm j becomes self-financing, it can supply all firms with liquidity in the H-state. This puts a second cap on the price of s_H:

$$s_H \leq s_{jH}^{con} \equiv \frac{1 - f_L \rho_{j0}}{f_H(\rho_{j0} - \rho_{jH})} > 0 \qquad \text{for all } j \text{ (contrarian).} \tag{4.20}$$

A contrarian firm becomes self-financing at a lower price s_H, the more it supplies liquidity in state H and the higher is ρ_{j0}.

4.2 LAPM—The General Case

In this main section we extend the two-state model to a general equilibrium model with a finite number of states and a finite number of heterogeneous firms whose linear technology parameters all may depend on the state of nature. The analysis highlights the close similarities of our model and the standard Arrow–Debreu general equilibrium model, as well as some key differences.[9]

Let ω be the state of nature revealed at date 1, $f(\omega)$ the probability of ω, and $s(\omega)f(\omega)$ the date-0 price of liquidity delivered in state ω (at date 1). As before, all agents are risk neutral and indifferent as to the timing of consumption, which implies $s(\omega) \geq 1$, since we use the value of a unit of consumption at date 0 as our numéraire. There are J firms indexed $j = 1, \ldots, J$ (or more precisely, J types of firms, each of

---

9. In Holmström and Tirole (2001), we study a liquidity asset pricing model using a different approach than in this section. We solve for an equilibrium by treating the corporate sector as a single entity that maximizes the aggregate entrepreneurial welfare. The technology is quite general, and the analysis richer, but the approach requires a particular distribution of entrepreneurial endowments for the maximization to match a competitive equilibrium.

Another model combining asset pricing with corporate finance is that of Dow et. al. (2005).

measure $1/J$, with j a representative firm). Firm j's investment plan is $\{I_j, i_j(\omega)\}$, where I_j is the initial investment, and $0 \leq i_j(\omega) \leq I_j$ is the continuation investment in state ω. Firm j's technology is fully described by the tuple $\{\rho_{j0}(\omega), \rho_{j1}(\omega), \rho_j(\omega)\}$, where $\rho_{j0}(\omega)$ is the pledgeable return at date 2, $\rho_{j1}(\omega)$ is the total return at date 2, and $\rho_j(\omega)$ is the reinvestment shock at date 1—all per unit of continuation investment $i_j(\omega)$. There is a strictly positive wedge between the firm's total output and what can be paid out to investors in each state, that is, $\rho_{j1}(\omega) > \rho_{j0}(\omega)$. For technical convenience, we assume that

$$\rho_{j0}(\omega) \neq \rho_j(\omega) \qquad \text{for all } j \text{ and } \omega. \tag{4.21}$$

We also assume that

$$0 < \sum_{\omega \in \Omega_j^+} [\rho_{j0}(\omega) - \rho_j(\omega)]f(\omega) < 1 < \sum_{\omega \in \Omega_j^+} [\rho_{j1}(\omega) - \rho_{j0}(\omega)]f(\omega) \quad \text{for all } j,$$
$$\tag{4.22}$$

where $\Omega_j^+ = \{\omega |\ \rho_{j0}(\omega) - \rho_j(\omega) > 0\}$ is the set of states in which firm j supplies liquidity. Assumption (4.22) guarantees that initial investments will be bounded and that the entrepreneur always prefers to invest his full endowment into the project.[10] To see this, consider an investment plan where firm j continues only in states where it supplies liquidity. Suppose that $s(\omega) = 1$ for all ω. Then the first term in (4.22) is the maximum share of the firm's investment that investors are willing to finance. The balance, which is strictly positive by (4.22), must be paid out of the endowment A_j. This limits the initial scale of the firm's investment, giving the entrepreneur the expected utility

$$\frac{\sum_{\omega \in \Omega_j^+} [\rho_{j1}(\omega) - \rho_{j0}(\omega)]f(\omega)}{1 - \sum_{\omega \in \Omega_j^+} [\rho_{j0}(\omega) - \rho_j(\omega)]f(\omega)} A_j > A_j. \tag{4.23}$$

We see that it is better for the entrepreneur to invest his full endowment in the firm, and continue in all states where the firm supplies liquidity, than to consume his endowment.

Now suppose that $s(\omega) > 1$ for some ω. In that case the entrepreneur's expected utility, using the same strategy as above, can be obtained by replacing $f(\omega)$ in the denominator with $s(\omega)f(\omega) > f(\omega)$. We see that the expected utility is higher than in (4.23). This is because investors are

---

10. Assumption (4.22) is much stronger than needed, but simplifies notation without sacrificing insights.

willing to pay a larger share of the initial investment if the firm only invests in states where it supplies liquidity and some such states carry a liquidity premium. It is not, in general, optimal for the firm to reinvest only in states where it supplies liquidity. Private benefits may be high enough to warrant continuation even in states where the firm demands liquidity. However, the entrepreneur will always invest his full endowment in the firm because of the linear technology.

Finally, let us introduce a source of outside liquidity in the form of assets $\{L_k\}, k = 1, \ldots, K$, each providing liquidity $L_k(\omega) \geq 0$ in state ω. For the equilibrium analysis we treat outside liquidity as exogenous, but later on, when we discuss government policy, the supply of outside liquidity is endogenous.

The *aggregate supply of liquidity in state* ω is

$$L_S(\omega) = \sum_j \rho_{j0}(\omega) i_j(\omega) + \sum_k L_k(\omega). \tag{4.24}$$

The *aggregate demand for liquidity in state* ω is

$$L_D(\omega) = \sum_j \rho_j(\omega) i_j(\omega). \tag{4.25}$$

Equilibrium is achieved when prices $s(\omega) \geq 1$, and the firms' plans $\{I_j, i_j(\omega)\}$ are such that the net aggregate demand for liquidity by the corporate sector is less than the supply of outside liquidity:

$$\sum_j [\rho_j(\omega) - \rho_{j0}(\omega)] i_j(\omega) \leq \sum_k L_k(\omega) \qquad \text{for all } \omega. \tag{4.26}$$

with an equality whenever $s(\omega) > 1$.

Given the prices $\{s(\omega)\}$, firm j solves the following problem:

$$\max_{\{I_j, i_j(\cdot)\}} \sum_\omega [\rho_{j1}(\omega) - \rho_j(\omega)] i_j(\omega) f(\omega), \tag{4.27}$$

subject to

$$\sum_\omega [\rho_{j0}(\omega) - \rho_j(\omega)] i_j(\omega) s(\omega) f(\omega) \geq I_j - A_j \tag{4.28}$$

$$0 \leq i_j(\omega) \leq I_j \qquad \text{for all } \omega.$$

The budget constraint (4.28) incorporates the purchase of sufficient liquidity to make the continuation plan $i_j(\omega)$ feasible in each state ω.

As long as the aggregate supply constraint is satisfied, as it will be in equilibrium according to (4.26), all the firms' demands for liquidity can be met. For this reason there is no need to include a date-1 liquidity constraint in the firm's program. We have written the objective function as the entrepreneur's expected payoff because it equals the social surplus when the budget constraint binds. Assumption (4.22) guarantees that this will be the case, as we discussed above.

Prices The date-0 price for a unit of the exogenous asset L_k, where the unit is defined as the amount of asset that in expectation delivers one unit of liquidity at date 1, is given by

$$q_k = \frac{\sum_\omega L_k(\omega)s(\omega)f(\omega)}{\sum_\omega L_k(\omega)f(\omega)}. \qquad (4.29)$$

Because $s(\omega) \geq 1$ and outside sources of liquidity, by assumption, deliver nonnegative liquidity in each state of nature, the price of the exogenous asset k will be such that $q_k - 1 \geq 0$, with a strict liquidity premium whenever the asset supplies a strictly positive amount of liquidity in some liquidity-constrained state.

We define the date-0 price q_j of a unit claim on firm j's equity as the amount that the firm can raise for investment purposes at date 0 per unit of expected return at date 1:

$$q_j = \frac{\sum_\omega [\rho_{j0}(\omega) - \rho_j(\omega)]i_j(\omega)s(\omega)f(\omega)}{\sum_\omega [\rho_{j0}(\omega) - \rho_j(\omega)]i_j(\omega)f(\omega)} = \frac{I_j - A_j}{\sum_\omega [\rho_{j0}(\omega) - \rho_j(\omega)]i_j(\omega)f(\omega)}.$$

$$(4.30)$$

As described in the two-state case, the logic behind this definition can be understood as follows. Take the case where a firm always demands liquidity in the states in which there is an aggregate liquidity shortage ($s(\omega) > 1$). In that case $q_j < 1$. Of the funds that the firm raises from outside investors at date 0, it spends $I_j - A_j > 0$ on the initial scale of the investment and $\sum_\omega [(\rho_j(\omega) - \rho_{j0}(\omega))i_j(\omega)(s(\omega) - 1)f(\omega)] > 0$ on state-contingent claims that provide date-1 liquidity for continuation investments. The price q_j only reflects the return on the investment in scale. An alternative implementation has the investors (or their representatives, such as banks) promise to supply the liquidity that the firm needs at date 1. To back up that promise, investors must go out and buy the necessary amounts of state-contingent claims at date 0. The firm sets the date-0 issue price sufficiently below 1 so that investors are able to recoup their additional investment in state-contingent liquidity. In both of these implementations, the investors' net return is 0, despite the fact that $q_j < 1$.

Suppose now that firm j supplies liquidity in every state where there is an aggregate shortage and hence $q_j > 1$. The firm benefits from supplying liquidity by being able to raise more funds for investment than it would in a world where there are no liquidity shortages. The firm could issue separate claims on its date-1 return and the liquidity service that its assets provide. Or it could have investors invest in both claims and deal with the allocation of liquidity through contracts with other firms. Nevertheless, investors do not invest in assets that command a liquidity premium for their own sake. Investors earn a zero net return, while the liquidity premium is determined by the intertemporal marginal rate of transformation of firms.

Equilibrium   The special structure of the model allows us to recast the equilibrium analysis in terms of an exchange economy without production. This is useful for understanding the underlying structure and convenient for proving existence and efficiency.

The key idea is simple. Instead of viewing the firm as choosing a continuation scale $i_j(\omega)$ in state ω, we can think of it as choosing its demand for liquidity $\ell_j(\omega)$ in that state, as defined by

$$\ell_j(\omega) \equiv [\rho_j(\omega) - \rho_{j0}(\omega)]i_j(\omega). \tag{4.31}$$

In states where $\rho_j(\omega) - \rho_{j0}(\omega) < 0$, the firm supplies liquidity.

Recall that for technical convenience we assumed $\rho_j(\omega) - \rho_{j0}(\omega) \neq 0$ (see (4.21)). With the change of variables (4.31), the constraint $0 \leq i_j(\omega) \leq I_j$ can then be expressed as

$$0 \leq \frac{\ell_j(\omega)}{\rho_j(\omega) - \rho_{j0}(\omega)} \leq I_j. \tag{4.32}$$

Note that this constraint forces $\ell_j(\omega)$ to have the same sign as $\rho_j(\omega) - \rho_{j0}(\omega)$ as required by (4.31).

Firm j's payoff in state ω becomes

$$U_j(I_j, \ell_j(\omega), \omega) = [\rho_{j1}(\omega) - \rho_{j0}(\omega)]i_j(\omega) = \frac{\rho_{j1}(\omega) - \rho_{j0}(\omega)}{\rho_j(\omega) - \rho_{j0}(\omega)}\ell_j(\omega). \tag{4.33}$$

For every firm j we assume that there is an upper bound $\bar{I}_j$ on the initial investment level. This assumption guarantees the compactness of the set of feasible investments. In the appendix we show that $\bar{I}_j$ can be chosen so that it does not constrain investments in equilibrium. We define firm j's investment set as

$$\Phi_j \equiv \left\{ I_j, \ell_j(\cdot) \mid 0 \leq I_j \leq \bar{I}_j, \quad 0 \leq \frac{\ell_j(\omega)}{\rho_j(\omega) - \rho_{j0}(\omega)} \leq I_j \quad \text{for every } \omega \right\}.$$

(4.34)

Note that Φ_j is determined by primitives alone (which includes $\bar{I}_j$ as defined later).

The exogenously given liquid assets $L_k(\omega) \geq 0$ could be owned by the government and hence indirectly by the consumers and entrepreneurs. For simplicity, we assume that all of the outside liquidity is owned by the consumers and that the total amount of outside liquidity is strictly positive in each state ω:

$$L(\omega) \equiv \sum_k L_k(\omega) > 0 \quad \text{for all } \omega.$$

(4.35)

Firm j's choice problem is

$$\max_{\{I_j, \ell_j(\cdot)\}} \left\{ \sum_\omega U_j(I_j, \ell_j(\omega), \omega) f(\omega) \right\},$$

(4.36)

subject to

$$I_j + \sum_\omega \ell_j(\omega) s(\omega) f(\omega) \leq A_j$$

(4.37)

and

$$\{I_j, \ell_j(\cdot)\} \in \Phi_j.$$

(4.38)

With all consumers identical, the representative consumer solves

$$\max_{\{c_0, c_1(\cdot)\}} \left\{ c_0 + \sum_\omega [c_1(\omega) + c_2(\omega)] f(\omega) \right\},$$

(4.39)

subject to

$$c_0 + \sum_\omega [c_1(\omega) + c_2(\omega)] f(\omega) \leq A^0 + A^1 + A^2 + \sum_\omega L(\omega)(s(\omega) - 1) f(\omega),$$

(4.40)

$$c_0, c_1(\omega), c_2(\omega) \geq 0.$$

(4.41)

Here (A^0, A^1, A^2) are the representative consumer's endowed incomes in the three periods. These endowments are sufficiently large so that the price of consumption at each date is equal to 1 (the normalized price of date-0 consumption). The endowed incomes are nonpledgeable. By contrast, the liquidity $L(\omega)$ that consumers own earns rents by securing commitments to fund reinvestments. The value of the rent in the budget constraint is $(s(\omega) - 1)f(\omega)$ per unit. This assumes that $L(\omega)$ is not consumed (or rather, it is capital with a predetermined allocation of consumption benefits that cannot be reallocated). The reason we use this formulation is that consumption out of $L(\omega)$, which also can act as collateral, would have to be treated separately from consumption out of nonpledgeable endowed income. This would add notation, without changing anything materially.

The economy's resource constraints are as follows:

At date 0,

$$c_0 + \sum_j (I_j - A_j) \le A^0. \tag{4.42}$$

At date 1,

$$c_1(\omega) + \sum_j \rho_j(\omega) i_j(\omega) \equiv c_1(\omega) + \sum_j \rho_j(\omega) \frac{\ell_j(\omega)}{\rho_j(\omega) - \rho_{j0}(\omega)} \le A^1$$

$$\text{for every } \omega. \tag{4.43}$$

At date 2,

$$c_2(\omega) - \sum_j \rho_{j0}(\omega) i_j(\omega) \equiv c_2(\omega) - \sum_j \rho_{j0}(\omega) \frac{\ell_j(\omega)}{\rho_j(\omega) - \rho_{j0}(\omega)} \le A^2$$

$$\text{for every } \omega. \tag{4.44}$$

All resource constraints will bind, of course.

The consumers' date-0 endowment is allocated between consumption and the firms' initial investments. The consumers' date-1 endowment is allocated between consumption and the firms' reinvestments. Finally, at date 2, the consumers consume their date-2 endowment and the pledgeable income of firms. We have not included in these constraints the entrepreneurs' consumption, since it is a private benefit that cannot be reallocated.

In addition to the standard resource constraints, there is a constraint on the amount of aggregate liquidity (collateral) that is available in the economy in each state:

$$\sum_j \ell_j(\omega) \le L(\omega) \qquad \text{for every } \omega. \tag{4.45}$$

The liquidity constraints limit date-1 reinvestments, which have to be backed up by collateral.

We have transformed our original economy with production into a relatively standard exchange economy, in which firms solve the program (4.36) through (4.38), the representative consumer solves the program (4.39) through (4.41) and the economy's aggregate resource constraints are (4.42) through (4.45).

Because the prices of consumption at dates 0, 1, and 2 are all equal to 1, the only nontrivial equilibrium prices, $s(\omega)$, are associated with the aggregate liquidity constraints (4.45). An equilibrium is achieved when complementary slackness holds: For every ω, (1) $s(\omega) = 1$ if constraint (4.45) is slack, and (2) $s(\omega) > 1$ if constraint (4.45) binds. We can solve for the equilibrium prices $\{s(\omega)\}$ without explicitly considering consumer decisions, since consumers do not care about the timing of consumption. Their consumption is simply determined by the resource constraints (4.42) through (4.44) once we know $\{s(\omega)\}$.

The existence of equilibrium is proved in the appendix. The main step in the existence proof is to show that prices and investments are bounded. On the one hand, we have $s(\omega) \ge 1$, because of the particular consumer preferences and our choice of units (date-0 unit of consumption has value 1). On the other hand, for each ω there is a price $\bar{s}(\omega)$ such that whenever $s(\omega) > \bar{s}(\omega)$, all firms stop demanding liquidity in state ω (they set $\ell_j(\omega) \le 0$) *regardless of the other prices* $s(\omega')$, $\omega' \ne \omega$. We also show that the initial investments I_j are bounded by the amount that could be invested by firm j if all of the economy's resources were devoted to maximizing I_j. This amount is finite because we have assumed that every unit invested in a firm requires some amount of entrepreneurial endowment (see (4.22)).

In the appendix we also show that the equilibrium is *constrained efficient* in the sense that there does not exist a plan of consumption and investment that satisfies the aggregate resource constraints (4.42) through (4.45), such that every entrepreneur and the representative consumer are as well off as in the price equilibrium, with at least one of them strictly better off. Notice that even the social planner's allocations have to satisfy the aggregate liquidity constraint (4.45); the social planner cannot circumvent the fact that contingent reinvestment decisions must be backed by collateral.

Remark It is straightforward to extend the model and proofs of existence and efficiency to the case where each firm has access to more than
one linear technology. A firm would then have to solve a more complicated linear program to determine how it should allocate its funds
among the available technologies. Because the optimization takes place
against a single resource constraint—the budget constraint—the solution will generically allocate all the capital to a single technology. The
active technology will vary as the price vector $s(\cdot)$ varies. Since each
technology will be associated with its own private benefit, private benefits as well as the resource costs will determine how much liquidity
a firm demands or supplies. In response to an increased liquidity premium in a state ω, a firm will switch toward a technology that produces
more liquidity in that state, giving up private benefits for the value of
liquidity. Technologies with a smaller wedge between pledgeable and
private income—for instance, technologies with more established (or
earlier) cash flows or tangible assets—would be favored.

4.3   Risk Management

Traditional models of asset pricing, such as the CAPM, cannot explain
why firms buy insurance against fires or other casualties, nor can these
models provide much guidance on how firms should manage risk in
general. The basic problem is that risk can just as well be managed by
individual investors. Of course, there might be some scale advantages
from having a firm deal with some of the risks it faces, but it is not
plausible that these advantages would warrant the extensive attention
to risk management that firms devote. Firms do not buy only casualty
insurance, they also spend large amounts of time and money on hedging
against adverse financial risks like defaults, exchange rate shocks, and
other price fluctuations. Decisions on how much cash to keep on hand
to cover unexpected liquidity needs and how to deal with fluctuations
in the stock of cash are matters that the management agonizes over a
lot. In the traditional theory they need not do that.

The liquidity asset pricing model developed in this chapter is a small
step away from complete markets, but big enough to explain why firms
care about liquidity and to give some insights into the way risk should
be managed. However, as will become clear below, a full account of
hedging and other risk management strategies must necessarily address

implementation problems that depart even further from the standard model.

The perspective underlying LAPM is that firms should consider risk management a part of liquidity management. This means that risk should be managed jointly with the firm's investment decisions so that sufficient liquidity is assured throughout the planning horizon in the most cost-effective way, and so that the cost of capital in future states guides the firm's investment plan. This perspective is not new. Froot et al. (1993) have also analyzed the joint determination of financing and investment using an explicit agency model. One element that is new in our approach is that LAPM places the discussion in an equilibrium context where the price of liquidity influences risk management and conversely. Also much of the Froot et al. (1993) analysis is devoted to imperfect implementation of optimal risk management strategies rather than to fully contingent policies as discussed here.[11]

Before looking at the analytics, let us first consider a concrete question faced by many firms: Should a firm insure its production facilities against fire or other damage, and if so, how extensively? The answer presumably depends on the cost of insurance. Let us assume that insurance is provided competitively at market determined prices. Given that firms are effectively risk averse, one might think that full coverage is optimal. Then again, one could embrace risk, given that a mean preserving spread in the date-1 liquidity shock increases welfare (as shown in section 2.4).

In practice, risk management policies typically recommend that "external" risks like a fire hazard be fully insured or hedged. However, when one cannot find instruments that are perfectly correlated with the risk, hedging should be partial.[12]

The message from LAPM is different. The amount of hedging depends on whether risk affects the productivity of the firm or just the liquidity constraint.[13] Events that only influence the date-1 income of the firm, and not continuation investments, should be fully insured provided

---

11. Holmström and Tirole (2000) address related implementation issues in the same setup as here.

12. For a list of reasons why hedging should be partial rather than complete, see chapter 5 in Tirole (2006).

13. We are assuming here that firms have access to insurance in every state, albeit at a potentially high price.

that current income is uncorrelated with future income.[14] However, an event that affects the productivity of the firm's date-1 investment will in general be partially rather than fully insured. A fire may fall in either category as discussed below.

To explain these conclusions let us return to the model with general shocks described in section 2.5.[15] We start by adding state-contingent liquidity prices to this model and after that introduce shocks to productivity. The basic problem is, as before, to decide the level of the date-0 investment I and the date-1 continuation scale $i(\omega)$ in all states ω. These decisions are solved by the program

$$\max_{\{I,i(\omega)\}} \int b(\omega)i(\omega)dF(\omega), \tag{4.46}$$

subject to

$$\int [(\rho_0(\omega) - \rho(\omega))i(\omega) + w(\omega)(I - i(\omega))]s(\omega)dF(\omega)$$
$$+ \int [r(\omega)I + y(\omega)]s(\omega)dF(\omega) \geq I - A, \tag{4.47}$$

$$0 \leq i(\omega) \leq I \qquad \text{for every } \omega. \tag{4.48}$$

As in section 2.5 we write the entrepreneur's private benefit $b(\omega) = \rho_1(\omega) - \rho_0(\omega)$, to separate the effect that $\rho_0(\omega)$ has on the objective function from its effect on the budget constraint. Recall that the variable $w(\omega)$ is the liquidation value of a unit of initial investment at date 1, $r(\omega)$ is the date-1 income per unit of investment, and $y(\omega)$ is the income from old assets in place, which therefore does not depend on the initial investment.

Let $1 + \hat{\lambda} \geq 1$ be the shadow price of the budget constraint. The continuation investment $i(\omega)$ is then determined by the sign of

$$\hat{\Psi}(\omega) = b(\omega) - (1 + \hat{\lambda})s(\omega)[\rho(\omega) + w(\omega) - \rho_0(\omega)] \tag{4.49}$$

---

14. Suppose that a high profit at date 1 is good news about the date-2 profit (as in DeMarzo et al. 2009, or Tirole 2006, pp. 217–18). Then date-1 reinvestment is more desirable when date-1 profit is high. This pattern may be implemented in a variety of ways. A natural one is to partially hedge at date 0 the date-1 profit so as to provide the firm with more liquidity when its profits are high. Alternatively, the date-1 profit shock may be neutralized (fully hedged), provided that the firm receives a credit line that is indexed to the realization of profit.

15. Note that the model in section 2.5 is more general than the formulation in section 4.2, as it includes date-1 income of two kinds and also a positive value of liquidation. The proof in the appendix can be extended to cover existence of equilibrium and constrained efficiency in this more general setup.

as follows:

$$i(\omega) = 0, \qquad \text{if } \hat{\Psi}(\omega) < 0,$$

$$i(\omega) = I, \qquad \text{if } \hat{\Psi}(\omega) > 0,$$

$$i(\omega) \in [0, I], \quad \text{if } \hat{\Psi}(\omega) = 0.$$

Shocks to income at date-1 take the form $r(\omega)I + y(\omega)$. Since income shocks only affect the budget, they do not directly affect the continuation rule $i(\omega)$. There is an indirect effect through the budget and the investment I, but these effects only depend on the expected values $E[s(\omega)r(\omega)]$ and $E[s(\omega)y(\omega)]$. All income shocks with the same *weighted* expected costs will lead to the same investment decisions and continuation rules. We interpret this as a case where income shocks are treated as if they are fully hedged, that is, as if income were constant.

Compared with a situation where there is ample liquidity in all states ($s(\omega) = 1$ for all ω), the full distribution of the income shock, including its correlation with prices $s(\omega)$ will matter for the firm's decisions because it affects the multiplier $\hat{\lambda}$. However—and this is the key point—the change in $\hat{\lambda}$ will affect every contingent decision, not just the decision in state ω. There is no direct link between the continuation decision in a state and the total income in that state. Continuation decisions are determined by $\hat{\Psi}(\omega)$, which depends on the incomes in all states.

The continuation index $\hat{\Psi}(\omega)$ measures the entrepreneurial value of continuing in state ω. The only change in the continuation rule compared to the case where there are no liquidity shortages comes from a positive liquidity premium $s(\omega) - 1 > 0$. The cost of capital now varies with the state ω, whereas before it was constant. Liquidity premia are, of course, economically important. They influence the firm's investments as well as repayment plans and therefore what kinds of securities the firm should issue to the investors. Other things equal, firms want to repay investors in states where liquidity premia are high and continue investments in states where they are low.[16] As before, only the sum of the liquidity shock and the liquidation value, less the pledgeable income $\rho(\omega) + w(\omega) - \rho_0(\omega)$, matters for the continuation decision, but now the importance of this sum relative to the private benefit depends on $s(\omega)$ with the weight on the private benefit $b(\omega)$ reduced in states with

---

16. In Froot et al. (1993) a firm's optimal state-contingent plan is set up to manage liquidity so that the marginal value of future investments (in our model, continuation investments) are equalized across states.

liquidity premia. The liquidation value is an opportunity cost exactly on par with the liquidity shock or a shock to pledgeable income.

Let us return to the fire insurance question, looking at it through the lens of (4.49). If a fire destroys some property, a building say, it is different from a shock to income, since an alternative option to repairing the building is to abandon it. The financial impact of a fire could take many forms, each affecting differently the decision to continue. Suppose that the building is essential for production and that the cost of repairing it is proportional to the scale of reinvestment. In that case there would be an additional liquidity shock per unit of investment $\tilde{\rho}(\omega)$ so that the total per-unit cost of continuing would become $\rho(\omega) + \tilde{\rho}(\omega)$. In states where there is no fire, we would have $\tilde{\rho}(\omega) = 0$. Assuming, for simplicity, that the cost of abandoning the building is zero, this case is then equivalent to a change in the distribution of the liquidity shock. The structure of the continuation rule would be as in (4.49) but with a change in $\hat{\lambda}$ due to the expected cost of covering the fire in some of the states. Even when the cost of the fire is constant $(\tilde{\rho}(\omega) = c_{\text{fire}} > 0$ if there is a fire), there may be states in which the building will be abandoned after a fire if in that state there is a high cost of capital. In short, unlike income shocks, productivity shocks are not, in general, fully insured.

These insights into risk management and insurance also suggest that risk management is linked fundamentally to implementation problems of the sort discussed in section 2.3.2. When investors cannot observe the shocks experienced by firms, insurance against exchange rate fluctuations and related "external" shocks may become more desirable as a way to control the amount of liquidity the firm has available for reinvestments at date 1. To illustrate the point, let us go back to our basic model with a continuum of liquidity shocks (section 2.4), where there never was a shortage of liquidity (so $s(\omega) = 1$ for all ω), where liquidation was worth zero, where there was no kind of date-1 income, and where the only uncertainty concerned the cost of reinvestment $\rho(\omega)$. In this basic model the second-best reinvestment was characterized by a cutoff rule ρ^* $(\rho_0 < \rho^* < \rho_1)$ such that the firm continued at full scale if and only if $\rho \leq \rho^*$.[17] Even if the investors did not observe the liquidity shock, the second best could be implemented by providing the firm with a credit line up to ρ^*; since the firm had no alternative use for funds, it

---

17. The continuum of states assumption is inconsequential for the point we want to make. Even with a finite number of states, as we have in this chapter, the second-best solution is characterized by a cutoff rule if the other assumptions of the basic model in section 2.4 hold.

would only use the credit line up to the amount needed to continue at full scale. Now introduce an income shock $y(\omega)$ to this setup. A cutoff rule ρ^* will still be optimal (though not necessarily the same cutoff as without $y(\omega)$) because the optimal decision rule fully insures against variations in the income $y(\omega)$, as we saw earlier in this section. However, if investors cannot contract on $y(\omega)$, the entrepreneur would invest $\rho(\omega)i(\omega) = \max\{(\rho^*I + y(\omega), \rho(\omega)I\}$ at date 1, since he always wants to continue at the maximum feasible scale (constrained either by the available funds or the initial investment). He would invest a positive amount at $\rho(\omega) > \rho^*$ if $y(\omega) > 0$, and he would be unable to go ahead at full scale at $\rho(\omega) < \rho^*$ if $y(\omega) < 0$, both decisions being inefficient.

4.4 Concluding Remarks

Our approach to liquidity is based on the two essential assumptions that (1) there is a wedge between total income and pledgeable income and (2) fully state-contingent contracts can be written on the pledgeable part of the income. In this chapter we showed how these two assumptions make an asset pricing analysis both natural and relatively straightforward to carry out in an economy that closely parallels an Arrow–Debreu economy. Nevertheless, a LAPM equilibrium differs from an Arrow–Debreu equilibrium in interesting ways. Notably, asset prices can exhibit liquidity premia. Because we assumed that consumers are risk neutral and indifferent about the timing of their consumption, our liquidity premia are entirely driven by the corporate demand for liquidity. This segments investors into two: corporate entrepreneurs, who are willing to pay a premium, and investors-consumers, who are not.[18]

Liquidity premia affect the way corporations hedge risks and plan their investments, as discussed in the section on risk management. The important lesson here is that when income shocks are serially uncorrelated and independent of a firm's actions—when there is no moral hazard at date 0[19]—income shocks should be fully hedged. This is so because for the budget only the expected value of income matters. By contrast, shocks to productivity are not fully neutralized.

---

18. This claim needs a qualification. As we discussed in this chapter, there are implementations of a firm's investment plan, where investors-consumers buy liquidity at a premium in order to back up promises of future payments. But this is not driven by a consumption demand for liquidity, rather by the firm's demand for liquidity, that is, by segmentation.

19. See Rochet and Tirole (1996a) for an extension of our model to one with date-0 moral hazard affecting date-1 profitability.

Low-productivity states rather than low-income states determine whether investments should be discontinued. As we noted, these conclusions are critically dependent on fully contingent contracting. If markets are incomplete, then hedging will typically be incomplete also for income shocks.[20]

Liquidity premia and the way they influence corporate investment and funding decisions (the issuing of securities) will take on more importance as we go on to study the optimal use of outside liquidity both by the government and by international investors.

Appendix: Existence and Efficiency of Equilibrium

We prove existence without consumers, because consumers have no material role in determining equilibrium prices. The consumer is only relevant for proving constrained efficiency because of the rents enjoyed from owning $L(\omega)$.

Existence[21]
Our approach to existence is standard. We first define compact, convex choice sets, then a mapping from the product space of choices and prices into itself, which has a fixed point by Kakutani's theorem. Finally we show that the fixed point is an equilibrium.

Define the price space $S = \{s(\cdot)|1 \leq s(\omega) \leq \bar{s}(\omega)$, for every $\omega\}$, where the upper bound $\bar{s}(\omega)$ is chosen so that

$$\bar{s}(\omega) > \max_j \frac{\rho_{j1}(\omega) - \rho_{j0}(\omega)}{\rho_j(\omega) - \rho_{j0}(\omega)}. \tag{4.50}$$

Note that S only includes the state-contingent prices at date 0, since the price of the date-0 good was normalized to 1. The upper bound $\bar{s}(\omega)$ ensures that aggregate demand for liquidity in state ω will be zero if $s(\omega) = \bar{s}(\omega)$, regardless of the other components of $s(\cdot)$. To see this, suppose that firm j demands a positive amount of liquidity $\ell_j(\omega) > 0$ when $s(\omega) = \bar{s}(\omega)$. Consider an alternative plan where (1) the firm reduces the demand for liquidity in state ω to 0, and (2) the entrepreneur reduces his investment in the firm by the amount $\ell_j(\omega)\bar{s}(\omega)f(\omega)$ and consumes it instead. With these changes the budget will continue to balance, since the amount the entrepreneur has withdrawn is exactly the date-0 cost of the amount that investors were expected to invest in state ω in the

---

20. For more on this, see Froot et al. (1993) and Holmström and Tirole (2000).

21. We are grateful to Philip Reny for advice on this section.

original plan. Having the entrepreneur consume at date 0 is not optimal, of course, but it gives a lower bound on the value of an alternative plan. The benefit of the alternative plan is the entrepreneur's date-0 consumption value $\ell_j(\omega)\bar{s}(\omega)f(\omega)$. The cost of the alternative plan is the entrepreneur's loss of the private benefit in state ω. The expected net benefit of the alternative plan is therefore

$$\ell_j(\omega)\bar{s}(\omega)f(\omega) - \frac{[\rho_{j1}(\omega) - \rho_{j0}(\omega)]\ell_j(\omega)f(\omega)}{\rho_j(\omega) - \rho_{j0}(\omega)} > 0, \tag{4.51}$$

where the inequality comes from (4.50) and the assumption that $\ell_j(\omega) > 0$. We conclude that a strictly positive liquidity demand by firm j (hence any firm) cannot be optimal if $s(\omega) = \bar{s}(\omega)$.

Let the set $\mathcal{I} = \Phi_1 \times \cdots \times \Phi_J$ be the space of investments and liquidity demands by firms, where, as before,

$$\Phi_j \equiv \left\{ I_j, \ell_j(\cdot) \mid 0 \le I_j \le \bar{I}_j, \ 0 \le \frac{\ell_j(\omega)}{\rho_j(\omega) - \rho_{j0}(\omega)} \le I_j \quad \text{for every } \omega \right\}.$$

We can now define the upper bounds $\bar{I}_j$ on initial investments that were left unspecified earlier. For firm k, let $\bar{I}_k$ be the highest level of investment that it can achieve if all of the economy's resources are devoted to maximize I_k. That is, let $\tilde{I}_k$ solve

$$\max_{\{I_j, \ell_j(\cdot)\}} I_k, \tag{4.52}$$

subject to

$$-\sum_j \sum_\omega \ell_j(\omega)f(\omega) \ge \sum_j (I_j - A_j), \tag{4.53}$$

$$0 \le \frac{\ell_j(\omega)}{\rho_j(\omega) - \rho_{j0}(\omega)} \le I_j \quad \text{for all } j. \tag{4.54}$$

Notice that this program does not impose any liquidity constraints, just the *aggregate budget constraint* for the corporate sector (4.53) and the technological restrictions on continuation investments $i_j(\cdot)$. The aggregate budget constraint for the corporate sector does not include $L(\omega)$, which the consumers own. By assumption (4.22), this program has a maximum. In fact no firm other than k will be assigned a positive level of investment in the program. The optimal plan will devote all of the aggregate endowment to firm k's investment, because any investment into a firm $j \ne k$ consumes some of the aggregate endowment, reducing resources for I_k.

We will see that the aggregate budget constraint cannot be violated in equilibrium, guaranteeing an interior solution if we choose the upper bounds so that for all j $\bar{I}_j > \tilde{I}_j$, the maximum in value of (4.52).

Define the mapping $\varphi : \mathcal{S} \times \mathcal{I} \to \mathcal{S} \times \mathcal{I}$ in the standard way. For every selection of prices $s(\cdot)$ in $\mathcal{S}$, firms solve program (4.36) through (4.38), which determines the range of φ in $\mathcal{I}$. And for every selection of investment decisions $\{(I_j, \ell_j(\cdot)) \in \Phi_j\}$ in $\mathcal{I}$, the range of φ in $\mathcal{S}$ is defined by the set of prices $s(\cdot)$ that maximize the value of the excess demand for liquidity $[\sum_j \ell_j(\omega) - L(\omega)]s(\omega)$. This mapping is upper hemi-continuous, since firms solve a linear program with choices from a compact, convex set.

Let $s^*(\cdot), \{I_j^*, \ell_j^*(\cdot)\}$ be a fixed point of φ. Such a point exists according to Kakutani's theorem. As we argued earlier, if $s^*(\omega) = \bar{s}(\omega)$ for some ω, then aggregate demand for liquidity will be zero in state ω. Zero demand implies that there is an excess supply of liquidity, given that $L(\omega) > 0$. By the definition of φ, excess supply is inconsistent with $s^*(\omega) = \bar{s}(\omega)$ being part of a fixed point. While prices at the fixed point cannot be at their upper bound, some or all prices can be at their lower bound 1. The definition of φ guarantees that $s(\omega) = 1$ whenever there is an excess supply of liquidity in state ω. Only if the demand for liquidity equals the supply of liquidity can we have an interior price $s^*(\omega) > 1$. We conclude that at a fixed point, complementary slackness holds, as required by an equilibrium:

$$\left[\sum_j \ell_j(\omega) - L(\omega)\right][s(\omega) - 1] = 0 \qquad \text{for every } \omega. \qquad (4.55)$$

Finally we need to verify that for each firm j, the initial investment I_j is strictly below the upper bound $\bar{I}_j$, when the firm chooses an optimal plan given prices $s^*(\cdot)$. We do so by checking that the firms' optimal plans at the fixed point satisfy the aggregate budget constraint (4.53). We multiply the complementary slackness condition (4.55) by $f(\omega)$ and sum over ω. This gives

$$\sum_\omega \left[\sum_j \ell_j(\omega) - L(\omega)\right][s(\omega) - 1]f(\omega) = 0. \qquad (4.56)$$

We have then

$$-\sum_j \sum_\omega \ell_j(\omega)f(\omega) = -\sum_j \sum_\omega \ell_j(\omega)s(\omega)f(\omega) + \sum_\omega [s(\omega) - 1]L(\omega)f(\omega).$$

$$\geq \sum_j (I_j - A_j). \qquad (4.57)$$

The last inequality follows because the first term in the middle expression is the sum of each firm's budget constraint in (4.37) and therefore greater than or equal to $\sum_j (I_j - A_j)$, while the second term in the middle expression is nonnegative. The economic intuition is that when $s(\omega) > 1$, some of the budget will be spent on paying for liquidity and therefore the aggregate budget constraint will be slack (the liquidity premium will go to the consumers).

Because the firms' investment plans at the fixed point satisfy the aggregate budget constraint, we must have $I_j < \bar{I}_j$ for every j. Therefore firms will choose the same optimal plans without the imposed upper bound on I_j in the feasible set Φ_j. This concludes the proof of existence.

Constrained Efficiency

For constrained efficiency we need to show that a plan that strictly Pareto improves on an equilibrium plan $\{I_j^*, \ell_j^*(\cdot)|j = 1, \ldots, J\}$, $\{c_0^*, c_1^*(\cdot), c_2^*(\cdot)\}$, cannot be a feasible plan; it must violate some of the economy's four resource constraints (4.42) through (4.45). Consider an alternative plan in which the representative consumer consumes $\{\hat{c}_0, \hat{c}_1(\cdot), \hat{c}_2(\cdot)\}$ and the firms invest $\{\hat{I}_j, \hat{\ell}_j(\cdot)|j = 1, \ldots, J\}$. Suppose that the alternative plan Pareto improves on the equilibrium plan. In the equilibrium plan the budget constraint for each firm must bind, else the entrepreneur could do better by increasing the initial scale along with some continuation investments. The budget constraints for consumers must also bind; otherwise, consumers would do better by increasing their date-0 consumption. Since the alternative plan makes everyone as well off and some better off, it must violate the sum of the producer and the consumer budget constraints at the equilibrium prices $s^*(\cdot)$. Formally

$$\sum_j (\hat{I}_j - A_j) + \sum_j \sum_\omega \hat{\ell}_j(\omega)s^*(\omega)f(\omega) + \hat{c}_0 + \sum_\omega (\hat{c}_1(\omega) + \hat{c}_2(\omega))f(\omega)$$

(4.58)

$$> A^0 + A^1 + A^2 + \sum_\omega L(\omega)[s^*(\omega) - 1]f(\omega).$$

Consider now the economy's resource constraints (4.42) through (4.45). Suppose that all the resource constraints are satisfied in the alternative plan. Multiply each constraint by the corresponding equilibrium price—which is 1 for all constraints except the liquidity constraint (4.45), for which it is $s^*(\omega)$—and add up the constraints. The result is an expression that is identical to (4.58), except that the inequality runs in the opposite direction. The assumption that the alternative plan satisfies all the economy's resource constraints is inconsistent with the plan being Pareto improving. We conclude that the equilibrium allocation must be constrained efficient. A planner who must satisfy the economy's resource constraints, including the liquidity constraints, could not find an allocation that is a Pareto improvement on an equilibrium allocation.

III   Public Provision of Liquidity

Chapter 3 demonstrated that the wedge between total returns and pledgeable returns on investments can create a shortage of instruments for transferring wealth from one period to the next and thereby make it more costly, or even impossible, for firms to insure against future liquidity shocks through credit lines or other forms of advance funding. In the language of the book's title, there may be a shortage of inside liquidity (corporate-backed claims) in some states of nature. This impairs the insurance market between consumers and entrepreneurs. While the consumers have the income needed to make insurance payments at date 1, some will not be able to buy the collateral that is necessary to back up their promises of funding at date 0. There is a potential waste of liquidity whenever firms are not generating enough pledgeable income to support insurance contracts.

A shortage of inside liquidity creates a demand for outside liquidity. In chapter 5 we study the role of government as the sole source of outside liquidity. The government's policy can, at an abstract level, be viewed as remedying the waste of liquidity or, equivalently, as making up for the missing contracts between consumers and firms.

The government supplies liquidity in a variety of forms. Treasury bonds are the most obvious example. Consumers, firms, and especially financial intermediaries use bonds as savings instruments, as risk-sharing instruments and as collateral for complex state-contingent contracts such as credit swaps and repurchase agreements. Less direct, but equally important, are all the ways in which the government provides consumer insurance such as social security, health, and unemployment insurance. The government also takes an active role in securing the functioning of financial markets. Deposit insurance, the discount window, and various refinancing facilities are examples of ongoing forms of liquidity supply. The subprime crisis shows that the government is prepared to provide substantial amounts of contingent liquidity, not just by lowering interest rates and easing monetary policy but also by creating new, temporary credit facilities in an attempt to alleviate systemic disturbances in financial markets. These interventions can be interpreted as implicit forms of insurance. Our aim is to show that they can be rationalized within the logic of our model.

As always, one has to ask what enables the government to do more than the private sector can do on its own. In our view, the key feature that sets the government apart is its exclusive right to certain decisions, most important the right to tax its citizens. As a result the government can make commitments on behalf of consumers, including generations that are not yet born or active participants in the market. Put simply, the government is an insurance broker between consumers and firms, transferring funds from consumers to producers in states where the net returns from such transfers are high and making the corporate sector pay for this insurance either ex ante through liquidity premia on government securities or ex post with corporate taxes. Of course, if there is a fear that the government may default on its debt or inflate it away, it may be in a poor position to issue debt, or the debt may end up carrying an unreasonably high price, making the government's supply of outside liquidity unreliable or very costly. We assume that the government is credible but that taxation is costly.[1]

Another way to see this is to note that consumers are like firms without pledgeable income ("their ρ_0 is equal to 0") because they are unable to borrow against future income. The state then acts like an intermediary. Through its regalian taxation power, it is able to transform some of the future income of consumers into pledgeable income ("make their ρ_0 positive").[2] Many government interventions can be broadly construed as transfers from consumers to corporations in states of nature in which inside liquidity proves insufficient. This precept comprises not only loose monetary policy or recapitalizations of the banking sector but also and more surprisingly policy interventions such as the stabilization of asset prices under fire sales conditions. We show that state interventions are particularly desirable in low-probability events.

Chapter 6 asks whether the precepts unveiled in chapter 5 carry over to a financially open economy. One might conjecture that provided that a country's shocks do not coincide with worldwide shocks, domestic shortages of inside liquidity could be remedied either by arranging some form of credit line with consortia of foreign banks or a multilateral organization such as the IMF, or by holding foreign assets that the domestic private sector can resell when necessary. This conjecture, however, misses the point that countries themselves have limited pledgeable

---

1. Kocherlakota (2001) takes exception with the view that the government has special contracting powers that private parties could not replicate. Instead, he analyzes a model, in some ways similar to ours, where the government can improve social welfare by insuring, not the firm, but the financiers of the firm (they are all depositors because debt is optimal due to private information). He views this as a rationale for bailouts, using the banking crisis in Japan as an example.

2. This is reminiscent of the way in which banks raise the pledgeability of borrowers' income in Holmström and Tirole (1997).

income. Foreigners must be reimbursed in goods and services that they can consume (tradable goods). The ability of a country to make up for shortages of domestic inside liquidity therefore hinges on its ability to generate a sufficient volume of export income and credibly pledge it to foreign investors. Chapter 6 builds on this idea and studies optimal government policy in a financially open economy. We derive a "pecking order" for the use of the three alternative sources of liquidity: first inside liquidity, then government-provided liquidity, and last international liquidity.

5   Public Provision of Liquidity in a Closed Economy

As we discussed in the introduction above, consumers' future labor income by and large cannot be pledged to the corporate sector. Yet firms do face shortages of pledgeable income in bad states of nature, and transfers to the corporate sector can therefore be Pareto improving (provided that opposite transfers are made in good states of nature). When there is a missing insurance contract between consumers and firms, the state, through its power to tax, can in part make up for this missing contract. This is the very rationale behind countercyclical policies.

This chapter studies the nature of the missing insurance contract, and thereby of countercyclical policies. It stresses the state's comparative advantage in implementing transfers in low-probability events.

When and how much funds should be transferred from consumers to producers also depends on the consumers' liquidity needs. Current generations of consumers may need liquidity precisely in the states that firms need liquidity. A case in point is unemployment insurance, which in most countries is taken up by governments and belongs to the set of automatic stabilizers; were unemployment insurance provided by firms, the (direct plus indirect) corporate liquidity demand in recessions would be even larger. For the most part, we will assume that consumer liquidity demand is unrelated to corporate liquidity demand (or that consumers represent future generations), and leave consumer demand for liquidity out of the picture because it complicates the analysis. (The exception is section 5.2.)

The chapter is divided into three parts. Section 5.1 focuses on government bonds and how they should be structured, viewing the issue purely from a liquidity point of view (the supply of government bonds is, of course, in the first instance determined by public finance considerations). Section 5.2 studies optimal risk sharing between firms and risk averse consumers, mediated by government taxes and subsidies. Section 5.3 gives two examples of indirect supply of government liquidity—in the first example through unemployment insurance, in the second example by supporting collateral values to avert a bad equilibrium with fire sales.

5.1 Public Supply of Liquidity

5.1.1 Government Bonds

The analysis of government supply of liquidity follows closely our analysis of private supply of liquidity in chapter 3. We continue to use the two-state, variable investment-scale model of section 2.2, focusing on the case of pure aggregate uncertainty. All firms are identical and hit by the same shock ρ, which can be high or low with $\rho_L < \rho_0 < \rho_H$. We assume, for simplicity, that there are no additional private stores of value. When the high shock ρ_H occurs, it hits all firms and no firm can continue without outside liquidity. Firms will nevertheless invest provided that the benefits from continuing in the low-shock state are sufficiently valuable (recall that continuation is always feasible and desirable in the low-shock state because it is Pareto optimal and therefore self-financing).

We start with the case where the government issues noncontingent bonds at date 0. The face value of the bond is one unit of the good paid at date 1 regardless of the state of nature. To be specific, we assume that when the government sells a bond at date 0, the bond is acquired by a firm using the funds available to the entrepreneur at date 0 (this includes his own funds A and what can be raised from the market). At date 1, if the liquidity shock is low, the bond goes unused and its value is returned to the investors, who hold the rights to all pledgeable income. This will allow the entrepreneur to maximize the initial investment and thus his private benefit. If the liquidity shock is high, the entrepreneur uses the proceeds from selling the bond to cover the liquidity shock.[1] Regardless of the shock, the government will redeem the bond at date 1 by taxing the consumers and paying the bond holders the face value of their bonds. At date 0, when the bond is issued, the government receives $q \geq 1$ per bond and distributes the proceeds to the consumers. The net effect of these transactions is that consumers will transfer goods to firms in the

---

1. An alternative interpretation with the same net outcome has consumers either directly or through intermediaries buy up bonds to back up pledges to cover a firm's high liquidity shock.

high-shock state, but not in the low-shock state. There will also be a net loss of goods due to the deadweight loss of taxation.

How is the price of the bond determined, and how many bonds should the government issue? The answers to these questions depend on what objective function the government uses. Credit rationing models raise well-known conceptual problems for welfare analysis. Even though parties are risk neutral and have identical time preferences over consumption, Pareto optimal allocations cannot simply be determined by total surplus maximization. We assume that the government maximizes producer surplus subject to the constraint that consumers are not made worse off than they would be without the bond issue. This means that the deadweight cost of taxation will in the end be borne by the corporate sector and therefore the supply function of the government is determined by the marginal deadweight cost of carrying out a bond transaction.

Let $g(L) > L$ be the government's total cost of redeeming L bonds at date 1. One should think of the marginal deadweight loss, $g' - 1$, as the marginal cost of public funds due to the cost of distortions embodied in taxation. For now, assume that the marginal cost g' is constant and denote it $1 + \lambda$. Since the government's objective is to keep the consumers' welfare unchanged, the price of government bonds is set at $q = 1 + \lambda$.[2] At this price, firms can buy as many bonds as they wish. The outcome will be as in figure 3.2, but with the equilibrium price fixed by q and the equilibrium quantity purchased by firms determined by the intersection between the government's horizontal supply curve and the firms' aggregate demand curve.

To avoid general equilibrium effects, we assume that the deadweight loss is associated with date-1 household production that is discouraged by government taxes. At date 0, when the government distributes the proceeds from the bond issue to consumers, there are no distortionary effects because there is no production at that date. This makes the deadweight loss of taxation increase from date 0 to date 1. There is no reason why it should. Furthermore it is unlikely to be optimal to shift the full burden to date-1 taxpayers. In general, it will be better to spread the cost of providing liquidity over many periods and across states of nature (for more on this, see section 5.2). The broad picture, however, remains the same: when the economy experiences major adverse liquidity shocks,

---

2. In the general case, with convex $g(L)$, the government will run a surplus when setting the price q equal to the marginal cost g'. This surplus would have to be distributed back to the firms in some manner.

it may be desirable to transfer funds from the consumers to the corporate sector. These transfers operate through coercive and distortionary recourse to taxpayer money. While the government must consider the overall deadweight loss in its fiscal and debt policy, it can create liquidity for the private sector that may improve welfare.

5.1.2 State-Contingent Bonds

If we were to reintroduce a storage technology, or some other short-term private-sector technology, it would appear from the previous discussion that private and public supply of liquidity would be qualitatively very similar. The two would generally coexist and the equilibrium price would be determined by the intersection of the aggregate supply and demand curves of liquidity. The composition of the aggregate supply would be determined by the marginal cost of public and private supply, respectively.

This view is misleadingly simple. The government's actions will naturally influence state prices as determined in the equilibrium model of chapter 4. Our arguments do not take into account these general equilibrium effects. They only reflect the value of marginal changes.

The view also overlooks a potentially significant advantage that government-supplied liquidity has over privately supplied liquidity. When the private sector invests in a storage technology that yields a lower composite return than the long-term technology (taking into account both pledgeable and nonpledgeable income), the value of that liquidity will be wasted if the liquidity shock at date 1 turns out to be low. The problem is that the private sector often has to decide on the supply of liquidity before the state is known, whereas the government can wait and see whether the aggregate shock is high or low before taxing consumers. Only if the aggregate shock is high does the government need to step in and offer liquidity. This reduces the cost of providing liquidity without losing any of its insurance benefits. For this reason the public sector may be able to produce liquidity more efficiently than the private sector.[3]

Superiority of Contingent over Noncontingent Bonds   Recall that λ is the constant deadweight loss per unit of tax raised. We show that the most effective way for the government to supply liquidity is to issue a *state-contingent bond* that pays

---

3. In this chapter we set aside commitment, incentive, political economy, and other organizational problems associated with government.

1 if the aggregate shock is high, $\rho = \rho_H$, and

0 if the aggregate shock is low, $\rho = \rho_L$.

To make consumers as well-off as in the absence of a bond, the date-0 price of the contingent bond should be

$$q^c = f_H(1 + \lambda). \tag{5.1}$$

Firms will demand contingent bonds as long as the state-contingent price of liquidity in the bad state in the absence of such bonds satisfies $s_H > 1 + \lambda$ (see chapter 4).

Compare this with the case of a noncontingent bond. Consumers' constant welfare condition requires that the price of the noncontingent bond is

$$q^{nc} = 1 + \lambda. \tag{5.2}$$

Let $\ell \equiv (\rho_H - \rho_0)I$ denote the amount of liquidity needed in state H (firms do not need any liquidity in state L). The net cost of liquidity for the firms is $f_H(1 + \lambda)\ell$ with a contingent bond and $(1 + \lambda)\ell - f_L\ell$ with a noncontingent bond.[4] Thus contingent bonds allow firms to save

$$f_L\lambda\ell. \tag{5.3}$$

More generally, if λ_L is the marginal deadweight loss of taxation in the L-state, noncontingent bonds add an extra cost $f_L\lambda_L\ell$ to the firms. It is only when taxation is nondistortionary in the low state (relative to date 0; see the discussion in section 5.1.1) that noncontingent bonds have no advantage over contingent ones.

Government's Comparative Advantage in Providing Contingent Liquidity With these preliminaries in place, let us get back to the question whether the government can provide liquidity more efficiently than the private sector. Suppose that additional liquidity in the private sector requires a physical investment, a silo for corn, say. Then the private sector's marginal cost of supplying liquidity will be determined by the cost of building additional silos, a cost analogous to the noncontingent bond. Let the private cost of building a unit of storage be c^{silo} and assume, for the sake of argument, that $1 + c^{silo} < q^{nc} = 1 + \lambda$; if the government

---

4. The net cost refers to the cost of the liquidity used less the value of unused liquidity. With a contingent bond, all of the liquidity is used. With a noncontingent bond, liquidity is unused in the L-state, but the marginal deadweight cost λ is still incurred.

could issue only noncontingent bonds, it would be more efficient for the private sector to build silos than to use government supplied liquidity. Now assume that the government can issue state-contingent bonds. The public sector's cost of supplying liquidity is then $q^c = f_H(1 + \lambda)$. This cost is proportional to the likelihood of the high state occurring. Assuming that the value of government supplied liquidity is strictly positive in the high-shock state $(1 + \lambda < s_H)$, the government will be able to supply liquidity more efficiently than the private sector whenever

$$f_H < \frac{c^{silo}}{\lambda}. \tag{5.4}$$

We see that the government has a comparative advantage in supplying liquidity in sufficiently rare states of liquidity shortage.

This conclusion rests on the assumption that the private sector cannot offer state-contingent liquidity.[5] Why should that be the case? There are two reasons. First, and as we already noted, if there is too little pledge-able income in some state of nature, the corporate sector has to generate additional income in a manner that typically involves an ex ante, real investment, which like the metaphorical silo will deliver liquidity not just in the desired state but in a broad range of states. Liquidity will likely be wasted in a number of these states. The government, by contrast, can act ex post rather than ex ante and therefore does not waste liquidity. Second, because the government can act ex post, it can avoid the diffi-culty of having to identify the state in advance. It can call a recession when it sees it. Note that even if the private sector is much more efficient than the government in building silos ($c^{silo} \ll \lambda$), the fact that the gov-ernment can step in, even at a high cost, only when liquidity is needed, can give it a substantial advantage (see (5.4)). Below we will give some illustrations of ex post interventions by the government.

The logic of the two-state case carries over to many states. In general, the government's cost of delivering liquidity will vary with the state. One reason is that consumers may also have a demand for liquidity, resulting in a state-contingent deadweight loss of taxation. The relevant

---

5. In the wake of the 2008 financial crisis, Kayshap et al. (2008) recommended that financial intermediaries should be required to carry private insurance against adverse events. To be credible, such insurance should be backed by Treasury bonds held in escrow by the insurer. This proposal can be viewed as a private market variant of our government insurance scheme (see Rochet 2008a). Note, however, that our equilibrium (see chapter 4) already employs this form of private insurance to the fullest. Our interest here is in the case where Treasury bonds are scarce, as the high liquidity premia experienced during the subprime crisis suggest they were.

comparison will then be between the consumers' marginal cost of taxation (or marginal value of liquidity) $1 + \lambda(\omega)$ versus the firms' value of liquidity $s(\omega)$. The government should provide liquidity in state ω if and only if $s(\omega) > 1 + \lambda(\omega)$.[6] On the one hand, with no deadweight losses from taxation and no consumer demand for liquidity, the government should provide liquidity in all states with a liquidity shortage (more on this in section 5.2). On the other hand, if the marginal cost of a tax dollar is already so high that it exceeds the private cost of supplying liquidity in a state, then the government should not provide any additional liquidity.

5.1.3 Ex post Public Liquidity Provision—Some Examples

In reality we rarely observe the government issuing explicit, state-contingent bonds. An interesting exception occurred at the end of the millennium when the Federal Reserve Bank of New York issued call options on the right to access the discount window (see Sundaresan and Wang 2004). The Fed decided to offer state-contingent liquidity due to the so-called Y2K fear that computer systems would break down at the start of the new millennium and wreak havoc in the financial markets. Indeed the liquidity premia for dates shortly after January 1, 2000, were exceptionally high (about 150 basis points before the government intervened). The Fed's response to the elevated liquidity premia in the market is consistent with the logic of state-contingent delivery of liquidity, as discussed above. Optimal risk sharing (subject to budget and liquidity constraints) suggests that the Fed probably was right in using taxpayers' funds to provide insurance against exceptional aggregate liquidity shortages. Of course, we never got to observe how well the provision of liquidity would have worked had there been a major crisis, but the significant reduction in liquidity premia suggests that market participants thought the problem was alleviated by the Fed's intervention.

One reason government bonds are not state contingent as the model prescribes is that it is hard to identify the right contingencies in advance. The government instead manages liquidity by following state-contingent policies that one can view as emulating a state-contingent bond.

Consider, for instance, monetary policy in the face of an adverse shock to the productive sector. A looser monetary policy drives bond prices

---

6. We should note again that the government's actions will naturally influence state prices as determined in the equilibrium model of chapter 4. Our arguments do not take into account these general equilibrium effects. They merely show the value of marginal changes.

up (interest rates down) helping entrepreneurs that bought government bonds weather the shock. A loose monetary policy also reduces the
cost of capital, especially for those firms and financial institutions with
a substantial maturity mismatch (a very short average maturity of liabilities), and therefore with a higher need for refinancing.[7] Consumers
holding bank deposits and comparable assets are worse off. In effect
a loose monetary policy represents a transfer of wealth from the consumers to the producers, an outcome that is broadly consistent with
what our analysis suggests the government should do.

The primary application of our analysis is to large tail risks such
as those realized in the subprime crisis. This crisis is an example of
an exceptional state where the government was in a unique position to
deal with the tail risk (ex post) by supplying badly needed collateral.
But the analysis also provides foundations for a fine-tuned, continu-
ously adjusting liquidity management policy by the government. The
magnitude of government intervention should be commensurate with
the liquidity shortage. The latter may not be directly measurable, but a
good indicator is the liquidity premium observed in markets.

The Federal Reserve Bank's attempt to deal with the potential Y2K
problem as well as major financial crises, are fairly transparent examples of how the government engages in contingent liquidity supply.
There are many other government programs with significant, indirect
liquidity effects: the social security system, mandated or government-
run unemployment insurance, use of deposit insurance premia that are
not indexed to the banking industry's solvency, industry bailouts, and
a host of welfare programs. We will come back to discuss two examples of these kinds of liquidity schemes in more depth after the next
section. But first we show that the date-0 contingent-bond intervention
studied earlier has a counterpart in terms of a date-1 ex post liquidity
support/bailout.

Suppose, as earlier, that the corporate sector's shortfall is $(\rho_H - \rho_0)I$ in
the bad state of nature and that the marginal deadweight cost of public
funds in that state of nature is λ. Let the government

• levy a tax $T = (\rho_H - \rho_0)I$ at date 1 on consumers in the bad state of
nature and transfer it to corporations, possibly by taking a negative
NPV stake in them;

---

7. To capture this in our framework, suppose that consumers demand a return R—
normalized to 1 in this book—between dates 1 and 2; then for continuation investment i
at date 1, the firm can raise up to $\rho_0 i/R$ at that date by issuing securities. Refinancing is
thus easier, the lower the rate of interest.

• demand a "deposit insurance" premium $\tau \equiv f_H(1 + \lambda)(\rho_H - \rho_0)$ per unit of investment at date 0. Note that τ exactly compensates the consumers for their date-1 expected cost of insurance.

The firms' budget constraint is then

$$(1 + \tau)I - A = f_L(\rho_0 - \rho_L)I,$$

which, given the choice of τ, amounts to

$$I - A + f_H s_H(\rho_H - \rho_0)I = f_L(\rho_0 - \rho_L)I,$$

where $s_H = 1 + \lambda$. Letting q be defined by $q - 1 \equiv f_H(s_H - 1)$ returns us to equation (3.4):

$$I - A + q(\rho_H - \rho_0)I = f_L(\rho_H - \rho_L)I.$$

This demonstrates the formal equivalence between a contingent bond and an ex post bailout in our stylized description of government provision of liquidity.[8]

5.2 Optimal Supply with Risk Averse Consumers

Our assumption that consumers are risk neutral allowed the cost of government-supplied liquidity to be determined by the deadweight loss of taxation. In this section we show that if consumers are risk averse, then even without a deadweight loss of taxation, the supply of government liquidity is limited.

The starting point is an economy where the corporate sector supplies its own liquidity and in the high state H, there is a shortage of liquidity. We assume that the state takes the liquidity premium determined in the private market, $s_H - 1$, as given. This assumption is fine provided that either public liquidity supply is small, or that the liquidity premium is fixed by a private, constant-returns-to-scale, short-term savings technology.

The setting is as follows. There are two types of noncorporate agents:

• *Investors* are, as before, risk neutral with preferences $c_0 + c_1 + c_2$ over consumption. Their endowments can be hidden away (e.g., abroad) and therefore cannot be taxed. By contrast, their investments in and returns

---

8. Many economists have criticized the Federal Reserve for engaging in ex post redistribution (e.g., see Meltzer 2009). This criticism either overlooks or disagrees with the feasibility of government-provided implicit insurance as described here.

from the firms can be taxed or subsidized. Taxation takes place at the firm level by way of lump-sum taxes. Let τ_0, τ_L, and τ_H denote the lump-sum taxes (subsidies if negative) at date 0 and at date 1, in states L and H, respectively. The firm is protected by limited liability. The entrepreneur distributes all pledgeable income net of taxes. The firm's budget constraint is then

$$I - A + f_H s_H (\rho_H - \rho_0) i_H + \tau_0 \leq f_L [(\rho_0 - \rho_L) I - \tau_L] - f_H s_H \tau_H, \tag{5.5}$$

where $f_H s_H$ is the date-0 state price for date-1 liquidity and $i_H \leq I$ is the continuation scale in the bad state of nature. Because of the firm's limited liability we have

$$\tau_L \leq (\rho_0 - \rho_L) I \tag{5.6}$$

and

$$\tau_H \leq 0. \tag{5.7}$$

In the low-shock state the tax on capital is bounded above by the return on capital; similarly in the high-shock state, investors receive no return and only capital subsidies are feasible.

• *Consumers* are risk averse and do not invest. For example, they could be successive generations, each living for a single period. Let T_0, T_L, and T_H denote the taxes (subsidies if negative) that they pay. The government's budget constraint is

$$[T_0 + \tau_0] + f_L[T_L + \tau_L) + f_H s_H[T_H + \tau_H] \geq 0.$$

The consumers have expected utility

$$U_0(-T_0) + f_L U_L(-T_L) + f_H U_H(-T_H),$$

where U_k ($k = 0, L, H$) is increasing and concave.

We look for a Pareto optimum whereby the state maximizes the consumer's welfare subject to a given level of utility for the representative entrepreneur.[9] For a given s_H, keeping the entrepreneurs' utility constant requires keeping the total corporate tax $\tau_0 + f_L \tau_L + s_H f_H \tau_H$ constant. We can therefore rewrite the government's budget constraint as

$$T_0 + f_L T_L + s_H f_H T_H \geq \bar{T}_0. \tag{5.8}$$

---

9. Alternatively, as in section 5.1 we could maximize the entrepreneurs' utility subject to consumers being as well off as before government intervention (i.e., solve the dual program). The results would be the same.

The maximization of the consumers' utility

$$\max_{\{T_0, T_L, T_H\}} \{U_0(-T_0) + f_L U_L(-T_L) + f_H U_H(-T_H)\},$$

subject to the constraints (5.5) through (5.8), yields

$$U_0' = U_L' < U_H' = s_H U_0' = s_H U_L'. \tag{5.9}$$

Assuming that utility functions are not date- or state-contingent and $\bar{T}_0 = 0$, (5.9) implies that

$$(1 + f_L)T_0 + s_H f_H T_H = 0,$$

and so

$$T_0 < 0 < T_H.$$

In the optimal insurance arrangement, consumers are asked to contribute in case of an adverse macroeconomic shock. More generally, if the consumer's utility is state-dependent (which is reasonable since workers may be laid off in bad times; see the next section), a sacrifice in the sense of a lower marginal utility is demanded from consumers in bad times. Even with a state-dependent utility function, consumers end up sharing macroeconomic risks.

The extent to which consumers participate in supplying contingent liquidity depends on the cost of liquidity in the private sector. The optimal risk-sharing solution indicates that the higher is the corporate sector's value from liquidity, as measured by the liquidity premium $s_H - 1$, the higher will be the participation by the consumers; that is, the more the government will supply liquidity.

Finally, we note that as long as corporate taxes (τ_0, τ_L, τ_H) are lump sum and therefore do not distort the firm's behavior, their allocation is irrelevant, since the investors care only about the total pledgeable income net of taxes.

5.3 Other Forms of Government-Supplied Liquidity

5.3.1 Short-Term Savings: Unemployment Insurance as Liquidity

We keep assuming that the corporate sector makes efficient use of liquidity, but question the premise that it does not influence the aggregate supply of liquidity. This premise is reasonable for assets such as Treasuries whose supply and state-contingent payoffs can be considered exogenous from the point of view of the corporate sector. But, as we will show by means of simple examples, the corporate sector's date-1 policy may affect aggregate liquidity and do so in ways that are quite relevant for policy making. In the first example, analyzed in this subsection, the aggregate supply of liquidity depends on the labor contracts agreed on in the corporate sector. In the second example, considered in the next subsection, asset prices depend on how heavily corporations sell assets to meet liquidity shocks. In both cases coordination failures may occur and justify government intervention.

For the first example only, consumers whose mass is 1 must consume at least a "subsistence level" $\underline{c}_1$ (of food, education, housing, etc.) at date 1. That is, we replace the utility

$$c_0 + c_1 + c_2$$

from consumption flow (c_0, c_1, c_2) by the utility

$$c_0 + u(c_1) + c_2,$$

where

$$u(c_1) = \begin{cases} c_1 & \text{if } c_1 \geq \underline{c}_1 > 0, \\ -\infty & \text{otherwise.} \end{cases} \tag{5.10}$$

Consumers thus care about the timing of their consumption as well as its overall level.

Firms, whose mass is also 1, have each a fixed-sized investment opportunity at date 0 that costs I. They have no assets ($A = 0$). As before, we assume that consumers have enough of the nonstorable good at date 0 to help finance the initial investment I. The representative firm's income at date 1 has two possible values: a high income y_H with probability α (the good state), and a low income y_L with probability $1 - \alpha$ (the bad state), where[10]

$$y_H > y_L = \underline{c}_1. \tag{5.11}$$

Continuation at date 1 requires, in addition to the entrepreneur, one worker/consumer per unit of investment.[11] A worker must be paid an efficiency wage w, where[12]

$$w > \underline{c}_1. \tag{5.12}$$

---

10. That y_L is exactly equal to $\underline{c}_1$ facilitates the analysis, but is not crucial: y_L could be (at least a bit) above $\underline{c}_1$.

11. Since the measure of workers-consumers is the same as the measure of firms, there is full employment when all firms continue.

12. We can invoke a standard efficiency wage argument where the worker can "steal" w. Suppose the worker's decision is verifiable ex post, that the worker is protected by limited

Assumptions (5.10) and (5.12) imply that consumers do not value liquidity at date 1 provided that they know that they will have a job at date 1. Notice also that the liquidity shock is here a random date-1 income rather than a random reinvestment need (the "reinvestment" here is the nonstochastic wage w that the firm has to pay). There is, of course, no significant difference between the two approaches. Because we assume that there are no stores of value in this economy, liquidity shocks must be met through retained earnings.

Continuation yields a private benefit $\rho_1 - \rho_0$ to the entrepreneur, and a pledgeable income ρ_0. Assume $\rho_1 > w$ so that continuation is efficient from the point of view of the entrepreneur. Further assume that

$$\rho_0 - w < 0, \tag{5.13}$$

$$y_L + \rho_0 - w \geq 0, \tag{5.14}$$

and

$$-I + \alpha(y_H + \rho_0 - w) \geq 0. \tag{5.15}$$

These conditions can be interpreted as follows: continuation is not self-financing ($\rho_0 < w$), but retained earnings combined with pledgeable income/dilution always enables continuation ($y_L + \rho_0 > w$). Finally, condition (5.15) implies that investors are willing to finance the initial investment as their return in the good state can cover the initial investment outlay. With these parameter restrictions there is a feedback effect between aggregate liquidity and the maturity of savings such that multiple equilibria can arise:

• *A long-maturity, high-liquidity, high-employment equilibrium* In the best of possible worlds all firms continue at date 1 in both states of nature. All consumers then have a job at date 1 and receive a wage w. By (5.10) and (5.12) they have no demand for liquidity and are thus willing to defer all payments on their date-0 investment to date 2. Since the corporate sector need not meet any short-term payment obligations, it always has enough liquidity to pay the date-1 wage w, as $y_L + \rho_0 \geq w$ from (5.14). That is, even in the bad state of nature (state L), the firms can use their retained earnings and dilute somewhat their investors in order to cover the wage bill. By condition (5.15), the firms can repay date-0 investors out of the pledgeable income ρ_0, since $-I + [\alpha y_H + (1 - \alpha)y_L] + \rho_0 -$

---

liability and that stealing has disastrous consequences for production so that it is optimal to prevent it. Then a firm must pay its worker at least w.

$w \geq 0$. In this efficient equilibrium, the corporate sector issues long-term claims and does not lay off workers.

• *A short-maturity, low-liquidity, low-employment equilibrium*   In this equilibrium firms are unable to continue in the bad state of nature. Consumers become unemployed, and because they have to consume $\underline{c}_1$, they insist on receiving at least $\underline{c}_1$ in the bad state of nature. Therefore they want to hold short-term claims on firms. Condition (5.11) guarantees that this is feasible, whereas (5.13) implies that given that investors are paid $\underline{c}_1$, firms no longer have any cash to finance the reinvestment. Firms continue only in the good state of nature, and equation (5.15) ensures that such a plan can be financed at date 0.

The coordination failure and inefficiency[13] in the short-maturity equilibrium illustrates that the liquidity available to the corporate sector depends on the liability side as well as the asset side. Interestingly, public decision makers occasionally call for "well-oriented savings," meaning a switch from short-term market investments by the households toward long-term equity investments that will benefit the productive sector.[14]

Further the *government can create aggregate liquidity by offering unemployment insurance*. Unemployment insurance (at or above $\underline{c}_1$) eliminates the consumers' demand for liquidity and restores the efficient equilibrium. However, unemployment insurance raises the issue of where the money for it comes from. If unemployment insurance is financed through a levy on corporations, it may not eliminate the bad equilibrium. Suppose that all firms lay off their employees in the bad state and that the only source of cash for the government is a tax on firms. Then each firm must pay a tax equal to (at least) $\underline{c}_1$, and so in state

---

13. One may wonder whether this coordination failure could be avoided if workers invested solely in their own firm at date 0 and signed a contract with their employer, specifying that no cash be withdrawn at date 1 as long as they are not laid off. But this arrangement is not robust to minor perturbations of the model such as job mobility or idiosyncratic liquidity shocks. Suppose, for example, that with a small probability each firm receives no income at all at date 1. Then the workers, who want to secure $\underline{c}_1$, must diversify their portfolio (have claims at least worth $\underline{c}_1$ in other firms), and the coordination failure may still occur. (Technically one must assume that y_L exceeds $\underline{c}_1$ slightly so as to offset the absence of income in this small number of firms and allow all consumers to "survive" in the bad state of nature.)

14. At the January 14, 1997, French parliamentary hearings on savings, former finance minister Jean Arthuis suggested some ways of encouraging equity investments, such as the creation of pension funds and the reform of the tax system (at the time, equity investments in France were taxed at the personal income rate, an overall tax rate of 61.7 percent for the highest tax bracket. In contrast, money market funds were taxed in a lump sum, with withholdings ordinarily not exceeding 20 percent).

L is unable to cover the efficiency wage plus the tax by issuing securities and using its short-term income. For deposit insurance to be effective, the cash must come from an external source such as a tax on future consumers (or of current consumers not affected by liquidity needs).

5.3.2 Prevention of Fire Sales

Events such as the recessions of the late 1980s and early 1990s or the subprime crisis often leave the financial institutions burdened with depreciated real estate. While banks, badly in need of liquidity, would like to divest their real estate holdings, simultaneous dumping of real estate assets on the market can have a disastrous effect on prices in a state of low demand for real estate. Cartel-like restraints on the sale of real estate or government support to stabilize real estate prices may prevent prices from falling too far.[15] In the eyes of an industrial organization economist, such price-fixing would appear wrong and in need of corrective measures. This section argues that there is more to it than just collusion.

Soft Pricing and Multiple Equilibria   We return to our basic paradigm in which preferences are linear on the consumer side: $c_0 + c_1 + c_2$ (consumers have no liquidity needs). As in section 5.3.1, continuation at date 1 requires paying for an input, but this time let the input be commercial real estate rather than labor. In case of continuation, one unit of commercial real estate is needed. The date-0 investment yields each firm a date-1 income $y_L = 0$ (the bad state) with probability $(1 - \alpha)$ and $y_H > 0$ (the good state) with probability α. Income shocks across firms are perfectly correlated. As in section 5.3.1, reinvestment yields a private benefit $\rho_1 - \rho_0$ at date 2, but no pledgeable income ($\rho_0 = 0$). The reinvestment cost is $\rho + \upsilon_j$, where $\rho > 0$ is a fixed cost and υ_j is the price of commercial real estate and depends on the state $j = L, H$, and the particular equilibrium. We assume that $\rho < y_H$. Commercial real estate construction is part of the initial investment. Each firm builds one unit of real estate per unit of investment. Firms invest in commercial real estate at date 0 because they want to be able to produce at least in the good state. Real estate fully depreciates at the end of date 1. The overall liquidity need is

ρ in the bad state (probability $1 - \alpha$)

---

15. Such cartels are sometimes organized by the central bank.

and

$$\rho - y_H < 0 \qquad \text{in the good state (probability } \alpha\text{).}$$

Divested commercial real estate is costlessly converted into residential real estate at date 1 on a one-to-one basis. To make our main point sharply, suppose that there is a fixed (residual) demand for residential real estate at the price υ, with the total demand for residential real estate $\zeta < 1$. If less than ζ units of commercial real estate is converted, the price on the residential real estate market is υ; if more than ζ is converted, there is excess supply and the price on that market drops to 0 (or, to be precise, some small ε so that the sale of assets is a strictly preferred option). Assume that

$$\upsilon > (1 - \zeta)(\rho + \upsilon). \qquad (5.16)$$

Again, there are two possible equilibria, which differ in the low-income state. In the high-income state firms can cover the reinvestment cost ρ without selling real estate.

• *Low-price, low-production equilibrium* In the bad state, the corporate sector dumps all its commercial real estate onto the residential market. The price drops to 0, and since there is no other liquid asset besides real estate, and pledgeable income ($\rho_0 = 0$) is smaller than the reinvestment cost (ρ), all firms are liquidated. Even though the commercial real estate is now free, firms are unable to continue.

• *High-price, high-production equilibrium* Suppose instead that only a fraction $\hat{\zeta}$ of the assets are liquidated in the bad state, where

$$\upsilon = (1 - \hat{\zeta})(\rho + \upsilon). \qquad (5.17)$$

Conditions (5.16) and (5.17) imply that $\hat{\zeta} < \zeta$, and so the market price of real estate is $\upsilon_L = \upsilon$. The proceeds of the sale of a fraction $\hat{\zeta}$ of the firms' assets yield $\hat{\zeta}\upsilon$, which must be high enough to cover the firms' cost of reinvestment $(1 - \hat{\zeta})\rho$ corresponding to the real estate that they retain, $(1 - \hat{\zeta})$. (The firms own their real estate, so part of this liquidity need is already provided.) From (5.17),

$$\hat{\zeta}\upsilon = (1 - \hat{\zeta})\rho.$$

In this equilibrium, consumers (involuntarily) provide liquidity to the corporate sector by paying a higher date-1 price for residential real estate, and the restraint on sales provides insurance to the corporate

Price

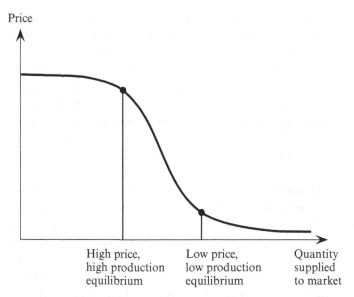

| | High price, high production equilibrium | Low price, low production equilibrium | Quantity supplied to market |

Figure 5.1
Soft pricing

sector against a complete price collapse and total credit rationing at date 1.[16] This implicit insurance raises the ex ante social surplus.

To conclude (and as illustrated in figure 5.1), if dumping real estate on the market provokes a steep fall in real estate prices, there may be multiple equilibria. Measures that prevent a fire sale of assets can then be ex ante Pareto improving provided that the consumers are appropriately compensated.

Remark Early analyses of fire sales in the context of the Diamond–Dybvig model of consumer liquidity demand as reviewed in appendix 2B are due to Allen and Gale (e.g., 1994, 1998; see also 2007). In those papers investors invest in an uncoordinated fashion in liquid (short-term) assets, which yield a safe return at the intermediate date, and in higher yield illiquid (long-term) assets. A fraction of consumers, the "impatients," want to consume at the intermediate date; they use the returns on the short-term assets and also resell their long-term assets. How

---

16. This example is in the spirit of Kiyotaki and Moore's (1997) analysis of the dual role of assets as stores of value and inputs into production. Our analysis differs both in the key drivers (our treatment relies on the existence of aggregate shocks while theirs does not) and in the emphasis (they stress the possibility of business cycles, whereas we emphasize market power and liquidity creation through price support policies).

much these long-term assets fetch in the secondary market depends on the realized number of consumers who desire to consume early, so there is aggregate uncertainty. Consumers who desire to consume late use the proceeds of their short-term assets to purchase the long-term assets not wanted by the consumers who desire to consume early. The former— the buyers—have limited cash on hand, and so the asset price decreases when more consumers—the sellers—want to dispose of their long-term assets in the market. This phenomenon is called "cash-in-the-market pricing" by Allen and Gale (1994, 1998).[17]

Soft Pricing and Price Stabilization   Finally, we turn to a brief analysis of price stabilization using restricted trade. Assume that the representative firm invests a fixed amount I at date 0, and faces a random shock ρ per unit of continuation investment at date 1, where ρ is drawn from the distribution $F(\rho)$. It can then reinvest $i(\rho) \in [0, I]$. The shock is the same for all firms, so there is only aggregate uncertainty. Each identical entrepreneur has endowment $A \geq I$ at date 0 and no endowment thereafter.

The only store of value in the economy is the investment itself, which can be sold to consumers (liquidated) at date 1 at a market determined price p. When facing a shock $\rho > \rho_0$, firms must sell a fraction of their initial investment if they wish to continue. Let m be the amount of assets placed on the market at date 1. The consumers' demand for assets at date 1 is described by a downward-sloping demand curve $p(m)$, which is derived from the marginal gross consumer surplus $S'(m)$. The revenue collected by the representative firm is $R(m) \equiv p(m)m$. For purposes of illustration, we will focus on the *linear demand case* $p(m) = 1 - m$.

Free Market   Provided that the value ρ_1 is "large enough" (see below), firms choose to reinvest as much as they can by selling in the secondary market. Given the state of nature ρ and the market price $p(m)$, the maximum scale of investment i is given by

$$i = \frac{p(m)I}{(\rho - \rho_0) + p(m)}.$$

17. Allen and Gale then allow intermediaries to pool liquidity, while still offering non-contingent deposit contracts. The lower the resale price, the more long-term assets the intermediary needs to sell in order to honor its commitment toward depositors. This, together with the intermediaries' limited liability, adds a discontinuity in the resale price of the secondary asset. If the resale price is too low, the intermediary goes bankrupt and then its entire holdings of long-term assets are dumped on the market, creating a "crisis." Related work on fire sales has recently been done by Diamond and Rajan (2009).

Equivalently, expressed in terms of m, we must have in equilibrium

$$(\rho - \rho_0)(I - m) = p(m)m = R(m).$$

This equation defines the equilibrium amount of assets put on the market $m = m^*(\rho)$, or equivalently the continuation investment $i^*(\rho)$, since $i^*(\rho) = I - m^*(\rho)$. In general, the equilibrium will not be unique; in the linear case there is either one or two equilibria.

Continuing with the investment at date 1 has a positive net present value provided that $\rho_1 \geq p + \rho$. For example, with $I = 1$, we have $(\rho - \rho_0)$ $(1 - m) = m(1 - m) \Longrightarrow m^*(\rho) = \rho - \rho_0$ (a unique equilibrium). In this case the net present value will be positive if $\rho_1 \geq 1 + \rho_0$.

Price Stabilization   Let us now show that a state-contingent cap on sales m can sometimes increase total surplus, which together with a date-0 transfer from entrepreneurs to consumers results in a Pareto improvement. To this end, imagine that consumers and entrepreneurs agree at date 0 on a transfer $T \leq A - I$ and date-1 policies $i(\rho)$ and $m(\rho)$. Given the consumers' gross surplus $S(m)$ from acquiring m units of assets at date 1, the optimal insurance contract solves:

$$\max_{\{T, i(\cdot), m(\cdot)\}} \{-T + E[(\rho_1 - \rho_0)i(\rho)]\},$$

subject to

$$T + E[(\rho_0 - \rho)i(\rho) + S(m(\rho))] \geq \underline{U},$$

$$(\rho - \rho_0)i(\rho) \leq R(m(\rho)), \qquad \text{for all } \rho,$$

$$i(\rho) + m(\rho) \leq I,$$

$$I + T \leq A.$$

In this Pareto program, the representative entrepreneur's expected utility is maximized subject to consumers being guaranteed some level of utility $\underline{U}$. The reinvestment $i(\rho)$ may be constrained either by the date-1 liquidity constraint $(\rho - \rho_0)i \leq R(m)$ or by the technological constraint $i + m \leq I$.

Rather than solve the entire program, we will investigate whether reducing m slightly by capping sales below the market level can improve welfare. To simplify matters, we assume that the entrepreneurs' endowment A is so large that the shadow value of the consumers' budget constraint is 1. In that case we can substitute the budget constraint into the objective function to obtain the maximand $E[(\rho_1 - \rho)i(\rho) + S(m(\rho))]$.

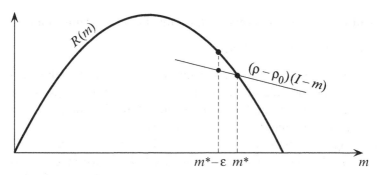

Case 1: Technology constraint binds when m is capped

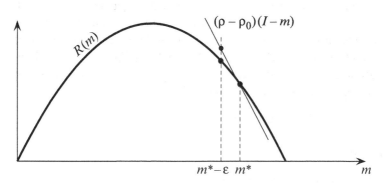

Case 2: Liquidity constraint binds when m is capped

Figure 5.2
Price stabilization

Note that if the market equilibrium $m^*(\rho)$ lies below the monopoly level (i.e., $R'(m^*(\rho)) \geq 0$), it cannot be improved by capping m because a decrease in m reduces the revenue $R(m)$ and, through the liquidity constraint, the reinvestment i. Therefore we are only interested in levels of m beyond the monopoly level.

Two cases, depicted in figure 5.2, need to be considered. In case 1, the revenue curve $R(m)$ has a higher slope at the selected market equilibrium (lying to the right of the monopoly price) than the liquidity demand $(\rho - \rho_0)(I - m)$. Notice that a cap at $m^* - \varepsilon$ increases revenue by more than enough to finance an additional reinvestment ε as permitted by the technology constraint $i(\rho) + m(\rho) \leq I$; the technology constraint will bind while the liquidity constraint will be slack with the cap.

The increase in total surplus (the objective in the Pareto program) is $(\rho_1 - \rho - S'(m^*(\rho)))\varepsilon = (\rho_1 - \rho - p(m^*(\rho)))\varepsilon$, which is strictly positive. A cap improves welfare, provided that consumers are compensated through an increase in T.

In case 2, a restraint on sales generates little income and, as the figure indicates, the liquidity constraint will be binding, $(\rho - \rho_0)i = R(m)$, while the technology constraint stays slack, $i < I - m$. This means that some of the initial investment will be completely wasted. Nonetheless, the cap *may* generate an increase in surplus. This occurs when

$$(\rho_1 - \rho)di + pdm = \left[(\rho_1 - \rho)\left(-\frac{R'}{\rho - \rho_0}\right) - p\right]\varepsilon > 0.$$

For example, when $I = 1$ (and $p(m) = 1 - m$), this condition becomes $\rho_1 > \rho_0 + [m^2/(2m - 1)]$. Near the monopoly price, very little extra revenue is generated when m is reduced, implying that i cannot be increased much and instead most of the reduction in m goes to waste. More generally, an equilibrium that is close to the monopoly price cannot be improved upon using a cap.

We conclude that efforts to stabilize the market price (perhaps with the help of government) by reducing the amount of asset sales when liquidity is scarce can be beneficial. Of course, price stabilization is only one instrument to transfer income from consumers to firms. For policy purposes, the relative merits/inefficiencies of the various instruments need to be compared, but we have not attempted to do that.

Remark   Lorenzoni (2008) motivates the consumers' downward sloping demand for second-hand corporate assets in a different way (consumers are endowed at date 1 with an alternative, decreasing-returns-to-scale storage technology), but this is inconsequential. He also shows that there is overborrowing (I is too high).

5.4   Concluding Remarks

The main message of this chapter is that the government can play an important role in supplying and managing liquidity. When there is a wedge between total and pledgeable income, privately supplied liquidity may not be sufficient for supporting second-best production plans. Put differently, optimal risk sharing between producers and consumers, when all contracts have to be backed up by claims on real output, may fall short of second best because of a shortage of aggregate liquidity.

Consumers, directly or through intermediaries, would be willing to provide insurance that firms want, but there are not enough claims to back up such promises. We take the view that the government is in a position to back up such promises because of its unique right to tax. We showed that granted this ability, government intervention, especially in rare states of nature where liquidity is exceptionally short, is warranted. We also showed that the basic logic behind the optimal supply of government liquidity follows the logic of state-contingent pricing of the kind seen in traditional general equilibrium models.

One of the many open issues that deserve serious attention is the optimal channel for the government to use in distributing liquidity. It is reasonable to consider banks and related intermediaries as the natural channels to use because they have the expertise to know which entrepreneurs are deserving of more liquidity. Another important issue is what price signals the central bank or the government might use to decide when and how to intervene. The central bank is in a unique position to signal or certify states of liquidity shortage by making announcements or, more convincingly, by acting.[18] The Y2K intervention as well as the interventions triggered by the subprime crisis were based on price signals such as liquidity premia and unusual spreads. It is likely that other signals such as the rapid growth of credit could have proved useful too. Also the government should be, and seems to be, letting the shape of the yield curve determine the duration of bond issues. The optimal use of the yield curve could be approached from the point of view of aggregate liquidity shortages as well (see Holmström and Tirole 2001).

We also hinted at the possibility that liquidity depends in complex ways on equilibria in the labor and asset markets. Again, this suggests some scope for government intervention. Viewed more broadly, the government can either create some "general purpose liquidity" in the form of stores of value that any economic agent in the economy can make use of. Or it can provide more "directed liquidity" that aims at resolving a particular source of liquidity shortage. Unemployment insurance makes consumers more willing to invest their savings in long-term securities, thereby creating more liquidity for the corporate sector. Asset price stabilization makes the corporate sector less dependent on outside stores of value. In a similar vein, the state often targets its provision of liquidity to the banking sector, which then dispatches the liquidity to the nonfinancial sector. We know very little about the optimal

---

18. For more on such a proposal, see Caballero and Kuralt (2009).

structure of liquidity provision, and this is definitely a key subject for future investigation.

Throughout this chapter we assumed that the government can costlessly commit to actions, such as state-contingent interventions. We did so to highlight the potential benefits of government interventions. In reality, problems of commitment are serious and will constrain what types of interventions are worthwhile. The political economy issues related to government interventions are another large and fruitful area of research.

6 Liquidity Provision with Access to Global Capital Markets

In this chapter we study an economy with free access to global financial and goods markets. We have two objectives in mind with this extension. The first is to suggest that the model we have developed, appropriately extended to an international context, can offer a useful perspective on worldwide events such as the 1990s financial crises in Thailand and Mexico and the current concerns about global imbalances. Our second, closely related objective is to address a conceptual question of great relevance for our study: How can a shortage of savings/insurance instruments in a small country like Thailand play a significant role given the enormous depth, scope, and liquidity of today's global financial markets? Why would Thai companies, banks, and the Thai government not be able to meet their liquidity needs on international financial markets using foreign exchange swaps, dollar or euro loans and lines of credit, and foreign bond and equity investments? Our theory rests on a shortage of aggregate liquidity within a country. If a national shortage of liquidity could easily be overcome through international financing, our theory would be of little relevance.

There is a simple reason why international markets cannot meet a country's liquidity needs despite an abundance of international financial instruments for saving and insurance. Foreign investments and foreign debts have to be paid with (or be backed up by) the country's pledgeable income internationally, namely its net production of tradable goods. Therefore the amount of foreign liquidity that a country can access—the amount of international insurance that it can buy—is constrained by the amount of pledgeable *tradable* income that it has. The problem is not that international markets have limited instruments for transporting wealth from one period to the next or for securing insurance across states of nature, but rather that the country that seeks insurance may not produce enough tradable goods to pay for them.

The theory of aggregate liquidity shortages has interesting applications in international finance. Following Caballero and Krishnamurthy (2001, 2002, 2003a, b), we distinguish between a country's international collateral and its domestic collateral. International collateral consists of claims backed up by tradable goods, while domestic collateral consists of claims backed up by nontradable goods.[1] Our objective is to indicate, through two simple examples, how the implications of aggregate liquidity shortages get enriched and modified when firms have access to international financial markets.

We show that if international collateral is scarce, the need for domestic collateral and government liquidity provision remains relevant as in our earlier analysis without international financial markets, but the prescriptions are somewhat different. We analyze how the task of liquidity supply is ideally shared between the three providers of liquidity: (1) the corporate sector, (2) the domestic government, and (3) the international financial markets. We conclude with some thoughts on the role of multilateral organizations such as the IMF in dealing with national liquidity shortages.

6.1 A Model with Domestic and International Liquidity

We extend our basic model to a small open economy facing aggregate shocks that on the international financial markets can be considered idiosyncratic and therefore carry no risk premium. We are interested in how the corporate sector makes optimal use of international insurance and how the government supplies and manages liquidity in this situation, assuming that arbitrarily rich contracts contingent on liquidity shocks can be written both in domestic and international markets.

Goods and Preferences   There are two kinds of goods:

• *Tradable goods*, which are consumed by foreigners as well as domestic residents. These goods will at times be called *dollar goods* or simply dollars.

• *Nontradable goods*, which only domestic residents consume. These goods are called *peso goods* or pesos.

---

1. Domestic consumers will be indifferent between consuming tradable and nontradable goods. For this reason we could alternatively have defined domestic liquidity as the value of all pledgeable goods.

All variables referring to dollars are indexed by a $-sign, while those referring to pesos are non-indexed.

There are three periods, $t = 0, 1, 2$. Economic agents only care about the sum of their consumption at the three dates, and therefore demand a zero expected rate of return on investments. We further assume, mainly for convenience, that domestic residents view tradables and non-tradables as perfect substitutes. Thus a foreigner's utility from the consumption stream $\{c_t^\$\}_{t=0,1,2}$ is

$$\sum_{t=0}^{2} c_t^\$,$$

while a domestic resident's utility from the consumption stream $\{(c_t^\$, c_t)\}_{t=0,1,2}$ is

$$\sum_{t=0}^{2} \left[c_t^\$ + c_t \right].$$

We use date-0 pesos as our numéraire.

All uncertainty is realized at date 1. Let ω be the realized state of nature, with ex ante density $f(\omega)$. In line with the general model in chapter 4, we let $s(\omega)f(\omega)$ be the date-0 price of a peso delivered in state ω at date 1 (or date 2—it does not matter) and $s^\$(\omega)f(\omega)$ the corresponding date-0 peso price of a date-1 dollar.

The model has a real exchange rate, defined as the relative price of tradables over nontradables. The date-0 exchange rate, denoted e_0, is the peso price of a dollar at date 0. The date-0 forward exchange rate for dollars at date 1 in state ω is denoted $e_1(\omega) = s^\$(\omega)/s(\omega)$. In equilibrium, $e_0, e_1(\omega) \geq 1$ because domestic consumers are indifferent between pesos and dollars delivered in state of nature ω.

Technologies and Timing   There is a continuum of ex ante identical domestic firms with mass 1, each run by an entrepreneur. The representative firm has a peso endowment A and a dollar endowment $A^\$$. With little loss of generality, we assume that domestic consumers have no dollar endowments, but they have, as before, nonbinding amounts of peso goods at all dates. In addition there is an external supply of date-1 liquidity in the form of tradable claims on peso goods L and dollar goods $L^\$$.[2] We need not specify the source of the external liquidity yet,

---

2. Alternatively, we could assume that there are storable goods at date 0 in the amounts L and $L^\$$.

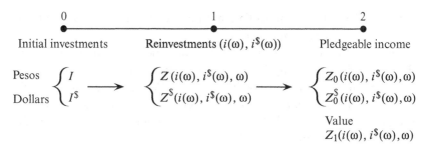

Figure 6.1
Technology

but later on assume that they are government bonds that can be used to affect the overall level of external liquidity.

We will use technologies of the following generic form (see figure 6.1):

Date 0:   Firms invest I, $I^\$$.

Date 1:   Conditional on the realized state of nature ω firms make reinvestments $i(\omega)$ and $i^\$(\omega)$. The total cost of reinvestment in state ω is $Z(i(\omega), i^\$(\omega), \omega)$ pesos and $Z^\$(i(\omega), i^\$(\omega), \omega)$ dollars. Reinvestments $(i(\omega), i^\$(\omega))$ are constrained by the initial investments and the state ω, described abstractly at this point by a compact set $D(I, I^\$, \omega)$, that is, $(i(\omega), i^\$(\omega)) \in D(I, I^\$, \omega)$.

Date 2:   The pledgeable peso and dollar payoffs $Z_0(i(\omega), i^\$(\omega), \omega)$ and $Z_0^\$(i(\omega), i^\$(\omega), \omega)$ as well as the total payoff $Z_1(i(\omega), i^\$(\omega), \omega)$, are realized. We assume that the nonpledgeable private benefit $Z_1 - Z_0 - Z_0^\$$ is always strictly positive. Notice that we write the total payoff without a \$-sign, because it makes no difference whether private benefits derive from peso or dollar goods.

Because international investors only consume tradables, all promises to international investors have to be backed up by claims on dollar goods. The amount of *international collateral* produced by the corporate sector is $Z_0^\$(i(\omega), i^\$(\omega), \omega)$. Since domestic investors are indifferent between consuming tradable and nontradable goods, the total amount of collateral available for transactions on the domestic market is $Z_0(i(\omega), i^\$(\omega), \omega) + Z_0^\$(i(\omega), i^\$(\omega), \omega)$, the sum of *domestic collateral* and international collateral.

The Firm's Decision Problem   The representative firm has to decide on the level of initial investments I and $I^\$$ and the date-1 choice $(i(\omega), i^\$(\omega))$. The firm also has to make sure it has enough liquidity to implement this investment plan. For this purpose the firm buys at date 0 domestic and international liquidity $\ell(\omega)$ and $\ell^\$(\omega)$ at the going prices $s(\omega)f(\omega)$ and $s^\$(\omega)f(\omega)$. These variables are negative if the firm sells liquidity (i.e., promises net payments to investors). When buying liquidity, the firm takes into account that international liquidity can substitute for domestic liquidity, but not the other way around. Let $t^\$(\omega) \geq 0$ denote the amount of international liquidity that the firm decides to "transform" into domestic liquidity—that is, the amount of dollar goods that will be paid domestic agents. This variable is constrained to be nonnegative, because domestic investors accept one-for-one dollar goods for peso goods in consumption, while international investors do not accept any peso goods.

The firm's decision problem is the following:

$$\max_{\{I, I^\$, i(\cdot), i^\$(\cdot), \ell(\cdot), \ell^\$(\cdot), t^\$(\cdot)\}} E_\omega\{Z_1(i(\omega), i^\$(\omega), \omega) - Z_0(i(\omega), i^\$(\omega), \omega)$$

$$- Z_0^\$(i(\omega), i^\$(\omega), \omega)\}, \tag{6.1}$$

subject to

(i) $(I - A) + e_0(I^\$ - A^\$) + E_\omega[\ell(\omega)s(\omega) + \ell^\$(\omega)s^\$(\omega)] \leq 0,$

(ii) $Z_0(i(\omega), i^\$(\omega), \omega) - Z(i(\omega), i^\$(\omega), \omega) + \ell(\omega) + t^\$(\omega) \geq 0,$ for every $\omega,$

(iii) $Z_0^\$(i(\omega), i^\$(\omega), \omega) - Z^\$(i(\omega), i^\$(\omega), \omega) + \ell^\$(\omega) - t^\$(\omega) \geq 0,$ for every $\omega,$

(iv) $t^\$(\omega) \geq 0$ and $(i(\omega), i^\$(\omega)) \in D(I, I^\$, \omega),$ for every $\omega.$

Constraints (ii) and (iii) define the firm's demand for peso and dollar liquidity, respectively, in each state. These constraints are always binding, else the budget constraint could be relaxed by reducing the levels of liquidity. Given this, we see that the budget constraint (i) presumes that all of the pledgeable income, domestic $(Z_0(i(\omega), i^\$(\omega), \omega))$ and international $(Z_0^\$(i(\omega), i^\$(\omega), \omega))$, is paid to investors. This is optimal, since the rate of return on entrepreneurial capital is higher than the market rate (normalized to 0). With (i) binding, the total surplus equals the entrepreneur's expected private benefit, which is the objective function that is being maximized. The auxiliary transfer variable $t^\$(\omega)$ is strictly positive whenever it is desirable to augment domestic liquidity with international liquidity and nonnegative, because internationational investors will not accept pesos.

Equilibrium Prices   The prices for contingent peso liquidity, $s(\omega) \geq 1,$ have to be such that the exogenous date-1 supply of peso liquidity $L(\omega)$

in state ω covers the representative firm's demand $\ell(\omega)$:

$$\ell(\omega) \le L(\omega) \quad \text{for every } \omega, \text{ with } s(\omega) = 1 \text{ if the constraint is slack.}$$
$$(6.2)$$

There is no corresponding condition for dollar liquidity because foreign investors are not collateral constrained. By assumption, the international markets are deep enough to back up any dollar pledges that international investors make. The relevant constraint is instead the availability of domestic dollars. Foreign investors need to get paid the expected dollar return required in international markets (0, because we assumed that domestic risk is independent of international risk). This gives the equilibrium condition for the date-0 exchange rate e_0:

$$I^{\$} + E_{\omega}\ell^{\$}(\omega) \le A^{\$} + E_{\omega}L^{\$}(\omega), \tag{6.3}$$

with $e_0 = 1$ if the constraint is slack.

What about prices $s^{\$}(\omega)$? Contingent date-1 dollars must cost the same as date-0 dollars, so

$$e_0 = s^{\$}(\omega) \ge 1 \quad \text{for every } \omega. \tag{6.4}$$

To see why, recall that the price $s^{\$}(\omega)$ is the *peso* price for contingent dollars. Also date-1 contingent dollars can be bought at a zero premium in international markets using dollars. Now, if $1 \le e_0 < s^{\$}(\omega)$, a firm could buy date-0 dollars in the domestic market for the price e_0 and exchange these dollars for contingent dollars in the international market. This would be cheaper than buying contingent dollars using pesos in the domestic market eliminating the price premium $s^{\$}(\omega) > e_0$. In the reverse case ($e_0 > s^{\$}(\omega) \ge 1$) the arbitrage runs in the opposite direction. A firm could buy contingent dollars in the domestic market and sell them in the international market in exchange for date-0 dollars that would cost less than e_0. There would be no demand for domestic date-0 dollars to sustain a price differential.

Finally, because dollar goods—either consumed or used as collateral—are perfect substitutes for peso goods, their value has to be at least as high as that of peso goods. We conclude that

$$e_0 = s^{\$}(\omega) \ge s(\omega) \ge 1 \quad \text{for every } \omega. \tag{6.5}$$

International investors do not earn any rents. Rents (in addition to the nonpledgeable income) go to entrepreneurs with pledgeable income in states where liquidity is scarce as well as to domestic agents who have date-0 dollar endowments.

Rather than analyzing the general model, we highlight its key features with two illustrative examples.

6.2   All Output Tradable

We start with a useful benchmark: all pledgeable output is tradable. When all pledgeable output is tradable, international markets can meet the firms' liquidity demands at zero cost. Consequently there is no need for domestic liquidity supply; the solution is the same as when domestic liquidity is so plentiful that it commands a zero liquidity premium.

It will not matter in the end, but for now, let us assume that all inputs as well as the endowment of the representative firm are in peso goods ($A^\$ = I^\$ = Z^\$ \equiv 0$). To simplify further, consider our standard constant returns-to-scale technology. Firms initiate projects at date 0 by choosing an initial investment scale I measured in pesos. At date 1, an additional amount of pesos ρI is needed to continue the project at full scale, where ρ is the liquidity shock, which we assume has a continuous distribution. The date-1 shock ρ represents the state ω, so we use ρ instead of ω to denote the state of nature. The date-1 decision concerns the extent of downsizing from I to i. A smaller continuation scale $i(\rho) \leq I$ can be chosen by reinvesting $Z = \rho i(\rho)$, since $Z^\$ = 0$. At date 2, projects produce no pledgeable peso goods ($Z_0 = 0$), a pledgeable amount of dollar goods $Z_0^\$ = \rho_0^\$ i(\rho)$ and a private benefit $(\rho_1 - \rho_0^\$)i(\rho)$, consumed by the entrepreneur.

Assume tentatively that there is no shortage of liquidity at date 1. This is equivalent to positing equilibrium prices

$$e_0 = s^\$(\rho) = s(\rho) = 1 \qquad \text{for all } \rho. \tag{6.6}$$

With these prices the representative firm chooses the optimal investment I and the optimal continuation rule $\{i(\rho)\}$ by solving

$$\max_{\{I, i(\cdot)\}} E_\rho[(\rho_1 - \rho_0^\$)i(\rho)], \tag{6.7}$$

subject to

(i) $I - A \leq E_\rho[(\rho_0^\$ - \rho)i(\rho)]$,

(ii) $0 \leq i(\rho) \leq I$ for all ρ.

This is the same program as we analyzed in section 2.4. The optimal continuation rule takes the form $i(\rho) = I$ if $\rho \leq \rho^*$, and $i(\rho) = 0$ otherwise, where the optimal cutoff level ρ^* satisfies

$$\rho_0^\$ < \rho^* < \rho_1. \tag{6.8}$$

Is there enough liquidity to implement this second-best plan at a zero premium as posited in (6.6)? The answer is yes. We have assumed that international financial markets are willing to offer domestic firms insurance at a zero premium up to their pledgeable dollar income. Since all the firm's pledgeable income is in dollars and dollars are as good collateral as pesos, the only constraint on the firm's access to liquidity is the budget constraint (i) in program (6.7). This confirms that (6.6) is indeed an equilibrium.

The simple but important point here is that when all the pledgeable output is in dollars, there is no role for government supplied domestic liquidity. If a small open economy has enough export income, international markets can in principle eliminate any domestic liquidity shortages. This conclusion holds quite generally. It holds for the model we described in section 6.1 with the added restriction that pledgeable output is in dollars.

In the example firms choose incomplete insurance ($\rho^* < \rho_1$), even though international investors offer insurance on actuarially fair terms. This is the key implication of optimal risk management with limited pledgeability: both initial investments and continuation investments will be credit rationed. Placed in an international context, such credit rationing suggests that a country, even if it could do otherwise, will leave its corporate sector exposed to extreme liquidity shocks. Put a bit provocatively, financial crises can be part of an optimal insurance plan even in the most favorable of circumstances (when all collateral is acceptable to international investors). With our linear specification, output drops to zero when ρ is above the cutoff ρ^*, making a "crisis" appear very dramatic. It would look less dramatic with a concave date-1 production function. However, as shown in Rampini and Viswanathan (2010), if there are decreasing returns to scale at the initial investment stage, then the amount of insurance bought will depend on entrepeneurial endowments. If these endowments are small, firms (and the nation) will choose to buy very little or even no insurance due to the same trade-off that drives our cutoff ρ^*. The implication is that poor countries will have to choose plans that make them prone to crises.

6.3 Tradable and Nontradable Outputs

In the previous section there was no role for government supplied domestic liquidity. We now show that when a country produces limited amounts of tradable goods so that its international collateral is scarce,

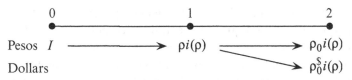

Figure 6.2
Domestic inputs, scarce international collateral

there is a role for government supplied domestic liquidity. This addresses the important concern we raised earlier that because international markets are so deep, these markets might resolve a small country's liquidity problems.

6.3.1 The Setup

We continue to use a constant-returns-to-scale technology and assume that both the initial investment and the date-1 (per unit) liquidity shock ρ, are in peso goods. As in the previous section, the date-1 decision concerns the scale $i(\rho)$ of the continuation investment, all paid in pesos ($Z = \rho i(\rho)$, $Z^\$ = 0$). But now, in addition to the pledgeable dollar output $Z_0^\$ = \rho_0^\$ i(\rho)$, there is a pledgeable peso output $Z_0 = \rho_0 i(\rho)$. The maximum amount of income that can be pledged to foreign investors is therefore $\rho_0^\$ i(\rho)$, while the maximum amount of income that can be pledged to domestic investors is $(\rho_0^\$ + \rho_0)i(\rho)$. The representative entrepreneur has a date-0 endowment A of peso goods and $A^\$$ dollar goods. Figure 6.2 illustrates the setup.

Let the government supply L units of one-period, noncontingent peso bonds and $L^\$$ units of one-period, noncontingent dollar bonds (we will discuss state-contingent supply of liquidity at the end). The representative firm chooses its initial investment I, its net demands for liquidity $\ell(\rho)$ and $\ell^\$(\rho)$, the amount of dollar liquidity, $t^\$(\rho)$ that it transforms into domestic liquidity, and its planned continuation investments $i(\rho)$, to solve the following program:

$$\max_{\{I, i(\cdot), \ell(\cdot), \ell^\$(\cdot), t^\$(\cdot)\}} \{E_\rho[(\rho_1 - \rho_0 - \rho_0^\$)i(\rho)]\}, \tag{6.9}$$

subject to

(i) $I - A - e_0 A^\$ + E_\rho[\ell(\rho)s(\rho) + \ell^\$(\rho)s^\$(\rho)] \leq 0$,

(ii) $(\rho_0 - \rho)i(\rho) + \ell(\rho) + t^\$(\rho) \geq 0$ for all ρ,

(iii) $\rho_0^\$ i(\rho) + \ell^\$(\rho) - t^\$(\rho) \geq 0$ for all ρ,

(iv) $t^\$(\rho) \geq 0$ and $0 \leq i(\rho) \leq I$ for all ρ.

This program is also a special case of the general program (6.1). Constraints (ii) and (iii) are the liquidity constraints for pesos and dollars at date 1. These constraints ensure that the demand for peso liquidity $\ell(\rho)$ and dollar liquidity $\ell^\$(\rho)$ are consistent with the investment plan $(I, i(\rho))$ and the planned transfer $t^\$(\rho)$ of dollar liquidity into peso liquidity. These constraints always bind. Negative values for $\ell(\rho)$ and $\ell^\$(\rho)$ imply that the firm supplies liquidity. The auxiliary variable $t^\$(\rho)$ is constrained to be nonnegative because international liquidity cannot be augmented with the help of peso liquidity. Constraint (i) is the date-0 peso budget constraint. There is no date-0 dollar budget, since dollar goods can be exchanged into peso goods at date 0 using the date-0 peso prices $\{e_0, s^\$(\rho)\}$.

It bears emphasizing that the sole purpose of international liquidity is to alleviate the *domestic* shortage of liquidity (or collateral). To isolate the role of international markets in supplying stores of value, we designed the example so that *dollars are not needed for production* (there is no international liquidity shock $\rho^\$$). Equilibrium prices are determined by equalizing the supply and demand of domestic liquidity in each state (see (6.2)) and dollars at date 0 (see (6.3)). In this example the equilibrium is characterized by

$$\ell(\rho) \leq L \qquad \text{for every } \rho,$$

with equality whenever $s(\rho) > 1$, and

$$E_\rho[\ell^\$(\rho)] \leq A^\$ + L^\$,$$

with equality whenever $e_0 > 1$.

We know that $e_0 = s^\$(\rho) \geq s(\rho) \geq 1$ for all ρ. The key difference between this example and the previous one is that prices are not necessarily unity. We can have $e_0 > 1$ because dollar liquidity can be scarce, and we can have $s^\$(\rho) > s(\rho)$ in some states because dollars are potentially more valuable than pesos: they are as good as pesos in consumption, but unlike peso liquidity, dollar liquidity can be distributed across states through $t^\$(\rho)$.

6.3.2 The Planning Problem

Given that all firms are identical, it is easiest to find an equilibrium by solving the central planner's problem, which maximizes the representative firm's utility. In doing so, we assume, for simplicity, that the available peso liquidity L and the dollar liquidity $L^\$$ have been distributed equally across firms by the government. The representative firm's program is

$$\max_{\{I, i(\cdot), t^\$(\cdot)\}} E_\rho[(\rho_1 - \rho_0 - \rho_0^\$)i(\rho)], \tag{6.10}$$

subject to

(i) $I - A + E_\rho[(\rho - \rho_0)i(\rho) - t^\$(\rho)] \leq 0,$

(ii) $A^\$ + E_\rho[(\rho_0^\$ i(\rho) + L^\$)] \geq E_\rho[t^\$(\rho)],$

(iii) $(\rho - \rho_0)i(\rho) - t^\$(\rho) \leq L$ for all ρ,

(iv) $t^\$(\rho) \geq 0$ and $0 \leq i(\rho) \leq I$ for all ρ.

Constraint (i) is the peso budget constraint. The dollar–peso exchange constraint (ii) will always hold as an equality. As we have (re)formulated the problem here, the expected value of the pledgeable dollar income is transferred into the peso budget constraint. The cost of reinvestments is explicitly accounted for in the budget. The dollar liquidity can be used to relax the peso liquidity constraints (iii) in an arbitrary state-contingent manner. This highlights the insurance role of the international investors. They only care about the expected repayment, not about the states in which repayments are made (see (ii)). Without access to international markets, there would be no insurance at all across states ρ, since all firms are hit by the same shock ρ. In each state ρ, the domestic market would have to make do with the outside domestic liquidity supply $L + L^\$$ plus the net inside liquidity $(\rho_0 - \rho)i(\rho)$. For small shocks ρ there would be excess liquidity, and for high shocks ρ there would be a shortage of liquidity. This inefficiency is reduced by the presence of international investors who can provide insurance across states.

The extent to which international markets can provide insurance depends on the amount of pledgeable dollar income that firms generate. We are, of course, interested in the case where there is a limited amount of dollar income so that even with insurance through the international market, the liquidity constraint (iii) will be constrained by available dollars for high enough liquidity shocks ρ. The main questions of interest are how the foreign and domestic liquidity will optimally be used and how the state prices will behave.

Let λ_i, λ_{ii} and λ_{iii}, be nonnegative Lagrangian multipliers for the first three constraints. The first-order conditions for $i(\rho)$ are

$$\rho_1 - \rho_0 - \rho_0^\$ - (\lambda_i + \lambda_{iii}(\rho))(\rho - \rho_0) + \lambda_{ii}\rho_0^\$ \geq 0 \qquad \text{whenever } i(\rho) = I.$$
(6.11)

When $0 < i(\rho) < I$, this constraint holds as an equality. The first-order conditions for $t^\$(\rho)$ are

$$\lambda_i - \lambda_{ii} + \lambda_{iii}(\rho) \leq 0.$$
(6.12)

with (6.12) an equality whenever $t^\$(\rho) > 0$. When $t^\$(\rho) = 0$, the value of additional liquidity is zero, so $\lambda_{iii}(\rho) = 0$.

From these first-order conditions we can deduce that the solution to the representative firm's program has four regions, described graphically in figure 6.3.

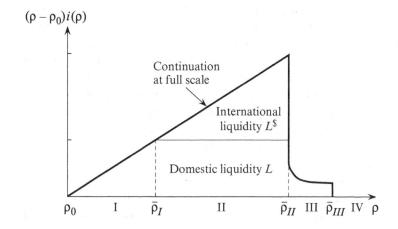

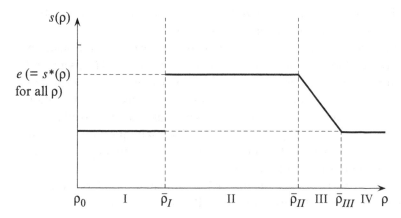

Figure 6.3
Demand for liquidity

Formally, the regions are defined as follows:

Region I: If $\rho \le \bar{\rho}_I$, where $(\bar{\rho}_I - \rho_0)I = L$, then $i(\rho) = I$ and $t^\$(\rho) = 0$.

Region II: If $\bar{\rho}_I < \rho \le \bar{\rho}_{II}$, where $\int_{\bar{\rho}_I}^{\bar{\rho}_{II}} [(\rho - \rho_0)I - L]f(\rho)d\rho = \rho_0^\$ I + L^\$ + A^\$$, then $i(\rho) = I$ and $t^\$(\rho) = (\rho - \rho_0)I - L$.

Region III: If $\bar{\rho}_{II} < \rho \le \bar{\rho}_{III} < \rho_1$, then $i(\rho) = L/(\rho - \rho_0) < I$ and $t^\$(\rho) = 0$.

Region IV: If $\rho > \bar{\rho}_{III}$, then $i(\rho) = 0$ and $t^\$(\rho) = 0$.

Consider first the top panel in figure 6.3. In region I, the liquidity shock ρ is so low that a firm can continue at full scale $i(\rho) = I$ with peso liquidity alone; no dollar liquidity is needed nor will it be used, since the shadow price of constraint (iii) in (6.10) is zero and (6.12) implies $\lambda_i \le \lambda_{ii}$. This is just saying that there is no point in wasting precious international liquidity if there is enough domestic liquidity. In region II, continuation is still at full scale, but the addition of dollar liquidity is required; constraint (iii) is binding and $\lambda_{iii}(\rho) = \lambda_{iii} > 0$ is constant, as seen from condition (6.12). As ρ increases, full-scale continuation is possible until the cumulative amount of dollar liquidity used in region II (the top triangle in the figure) reaches the total amount of available dollar liquidity. The economic intuition is straightforward: dollars, being scarce, will be allocated to states in decreasing order of productivity, which means in increasing order of ρ. In region III, the firm reverts back to using only peso liquidity because all dollar liquidity has been used up. The scale of continuation investment is now below I and decreasing in ρ. As in the model without international liquidity, there is credit rationing. Finally, beyond $\bar{\rho}_{III} < \rho_1$, it no longer pays to continue.

What about state prices? The prices that will support the centralized solution as an equilibrium are shown in the lower panel of figure 6.3.

Start with the price of peso liquidity. In the unconstrained region I, $s(\rho) = 1$, since there is an excess of peso liquidity even at full scale $i(\rho) = I$. In region III, only pesos are used, but now the continuation investment is below full scale. The price of liquidity must be such that the firm is persuaded to choose an interior value $i(\rho) < I$. Since the marginal value of a peso in region III is declining in ρ, so must its price $s(\rho)$.[3] At the left end of region III, we have $s(\bar{\rho}_{II}) = s^\$(\bar{\rho}_{II})$; the value of a peso equals the value of a dollar, since the next best use of a marginal dollar (in state $\bar{\rho}_{II}$) is to augment pesos in state $\bar{\rho}_{II} + \varepsilon$. At the right end of region III, we

---

3. If one goes back to the firm's program (6.9), one finds that the first-order condition for an interior solution for $i(\rho)$ requires that $s(\rho) = \varphi/(\rho - \rho_0)$, where φ is a constant.

have $s(\bar{\rho}_{III}) = 1$; since the firm is indifferent between continuing or not, the marginal peso does not command a premium. Note that throughout region III, the transfer constraint $t^{\$}(\rho) \geq 0$ is binding and the shadow price increasing. In region II both dollar liquidity and peso liquidity are employed, so $t^{\$}(\rho) > 0$. Since the shadow price on the transfer constraint is 0, both forms of liquidity must have equal value. In fact

$$s(\rho) = s^{\$}(\rho) = e_0 > 1 \qquad \text{throughout region II.}$$

The price of liquidity is constant in region II because a unit of liquidity, regardless of the state and the currency, will be used in the same manner, namely to increase the date-0 investment I, because the continuation investment equals I in this region. Furthermore liquidity prices must equal the exchange rate e_0 because exchanging e_0 pesos for a dollar at date 0 and using the proceeds to buy insurance on the international market against shocks in region II must return the same as buying insurance against these states in the domestic market.

The date-1 spot exchange rate, defined as the cost of a dollar good in terms of peso goods, equals 1 in all states, because domestic consumers are equally happy to consume either good. If $e_0 > 1$, the exchange rate therefore appreciates from date 0 to date 1. This is an artifact of the three-period model where the need for insurance only occurs in period 0. The inverse of the (contingent) forward exchange rate $1/e_1(\rho) = s(\rho)/s^{\$}(\rho) = s(\rho)/e_0$ will follow the pattern of $s(\rho)$.

6.3.3 Public Provision of Liquidity

We assumed a fixed, noncontingent amount of government supplied peso and dollar liquidity, L and $L^{\$}$. Referring to the analyses in chapters 4 and 5, we can derive some principles for how the government should optimally participate in the supply of liquidity considering the limited access to international liquidity. This depends on the government's objective and the implied cost of supplying liquidity. The simplest case occurs if consumers have no demand (or a noncontingent demand) for liquidity and the cost of supplying liquidity (taxing consumers) is constant across states. In that case the government should dispatch a constant amount of liquidity, just as in the figure, but the cutoff $\bar{\rho}_{II}$ will be determined by the marginal cost of liquidity supply instead of the exogenously given supply (e.g., it may be optimal for the government not to supply any liquidity if the marginal cost is high enough). A less obvious difference is that no outside liquidity will be supplied in

region III, which is eliminated. The reason for this is that partial continuation cannot be optimal other than at the boundary of region II.[4]
This explanation is consistent with the use of a state-contingent bond as
discussed in chapter 5 (see also Holmström and Tirole 1998).

More realistically, the government's supply function $\partial g(L; \omega)/\partial L$ is
increasing and also varies by state of nature because the cost of taxation
will depend on the consumer demand for liquidity. The logic behind our
analysis in this chapter gives a good indication of how this general case
works out. It will still be the case that international liquidity is most valuable because it is most flexible. Also the price of international liquidity
will be constant as a function of the state, else it would be reallocated to
its highest value. Therefore the price of domestic liquidity will also be
constant, except in states where no international liquidity is used. The
amount of domestic liquidity will, however, vary with the state ω to
reflect the marginal cost $\partial g(L; \omega)/\partial L$. The supply of corporate liquidity
would respond to the international price when international liquidity
is used and to the government price of liquidity where such is used.
Of course, in the end all of these prices and decisions are determined
jointly in a more complicated equilibrium than we have studied (i.e.,
one where the government's decisions affect the equilibrium.)

The main point is that with some of the pledgeable output nontradable, liquidity management by the government is again relevant. International investors make insurance cheaper, but they cannot provide all
of it when international collateral is scarce. International liquidity is
utilized most efficiently by having international investors supply the
marginal liquidity in high demand states. As before, there is capital
rationing at date 1 (a "planned crisis"), but with access to international
markets, the rationing will be less severe. Thus *the analysis of the value of
domestic outside liquidity in the previous chapter will be robust to the introduction of international capital markets.* This finding holds as long as some
outputs are nontradable. Had we assumed instead that all outputs at
date 1 were tradable, domestic liquidity supply would be entirely irrelevant. The reason for this disparity is again that dollars can be substituted
for pesos, but not the other way around.

---

4. Suppose that we had a region III. There would be partial continuation for all states ρ
such that $\rho_{II} < \rho < \rho_{III}$. Since the cost of government supplied liquidity, q, is constant, it
would be more efficient to move government liquidity from the high-ρ states in region III
to the low-ρ states in that region, bringing the low states to full scale. Consequently region
III cannot exist.

6.4 Concluding Remarks

This chapter studied liquidity management when firms have access to international financial markets and coordinate ex ante on the use of liquidity (second-best insurance). The main findings are the following:

• International markets will provide adequate insurance if there is sufficient international collateral. In that case domestic creation of liquidity will be unnecessary. In general, however, access to international markets does not obviate the need for domestic creation of liquidity because the amount of insurance that can be bought is limited by the amount of international collateral (tradable assets and income).

• Insurance will be incomplete (some states will not be covered) even when there is full parity between international and domestic liquidity. Optimal risk sharing, with limited entrepreneurial capital, leaves firms and therefore the country exposed to the possibility of financial crises. Financial crises are part of an optimal plan even in the best of circumstances.

• When international collateral is scarce, the analysis of domestic government policy is similar to that without international markets: the decision to supply liquidity in a state is determined by comparing state-contingent liquidity premia with the opportunity cost of providing liquidity in that state. International liquidity will be used as a last resort, in states where the cost of domestic outside liquidity exceeds the (domestic) cost of international liquidity. The cost of international liquidity is strictly positive on the domestic market whenever domestic dollar output is scarce, this despite the assumption that international liquidity is supplied at zero cost on international markets.

Even though the chapter is short and the analysis is presented in the form of simple examples, it reflects both the richness and the idiosyncratic character of our complete market approach. At its core, it is a study of optimal risk sharing under limited pledgeability of income, reflecting the view that the demand for liquidity is a demand for insuring risks. Our focus is on how different parties should optimally participate in the supply of risk sharing. In our analysis there are three parties: (1) the corporate sector, which optimizes the use of inside liquidity; (2) the government, which intermediates between consumers and the corporate sector in supplying outside liquidity; and (3) the international investors, who also provide outside liquidity. International insurance is limited by the international investors' willingness to accept only tradable goods (or in an alternative interpretation, by their limited information about and ability to monitor firms in a foreign country). At the same time, international investors are the most flexible and therefore the most valuable suppliers of liquidity. By assumption, they do not care about local risks because they can diversify away such risk. Both the scarcity of international insurance and the indifference it displays to local risks lead it to be used when the domestic, less flexible sources of insurance are in short supply, meaning too expensive. The conclusions in section 6.2 are all a simple consequence of this general perspective and can be readily extended to include shocks to pledgeable and nonpledgeable income as well as income shocks (as in section 6.1) along the lines discussed in section 4.3.

In reality, international investors do not seem to carry the most expensive domestic risk as suggested by our analysis. A possible reason for this is that while international investors have the capacity to insure, they do not have enough information to take on significant foreign risks. Another reason is that it is hard to write narrowly targeted, contingent insurance plans ex ante (see section 5.1.2). As a result international investors often invest in instruments guaranteed by the government, explicitly or implicitly (e.g., they invest through domestic banks), or they fund the government directly by buying government bonds. Even in this case, however, concerns about moral hazard problems—national governments can take advantage of foreign funding in a variety of ways—limit the sharing of exceptional risks.[5]

Unlike private investors, the International Monetary Fund (IMF) has significant monitoring capacity and also leverage over national governments (largely because private investors would pull out without the IMF). Therefore it can play an important role as a provider of insurance against sovereign tail risk. During the recent subprime crisis the IMF went well beyond orthodox interventions (just like central banks) and offered a variety of liquidity facilities to countries in trouble. These included special drawing rights, contingent credit lines, and systemic

---

5. For models of how the level and structure of sovereign and private borrowing affect government policies and for their implications for capital controls and the policies toward "original sin" features of borrowing (the issuance of debt claims, that are short-term and denominated in foreign currency), see for example, Amador (2008) and Tirole (2003); for an interesting alternative perspective on state opportunism, see Broner et al. (2010).

liquidity facilities. Nonetheless, the role played by the IMF seems rather different from that played by a Treasury or a central bank. The latter, both in practice and in theory (see chapter 5), act as lenders of last resort when there is a shortage of aggregate domestic liquidity. The problem for a country, by contrast, is not that there are not enough stores of value in the world but that the country may have a shortage of tradable goods that can be pledged to international investors. Also the IMF expects to get reimbursed, at least for its largest loans, so it does not provide liquidity unconditionally.

IMF support comes with strict conditions. The IMF writes and monitors covenants that make it more credible that a country reimburses its (sovereign and private) debts to foreigners. In the parlance of our model, most IMF interventions occur at date 1 when the country has faced a shock to its income or endowment. The covenants increase the country's date-2 international collateral at a cost that it can recoup by getting access to international capital markets, provided that the intervention is credible. And indeed this is how it should be if a more explicit contract were written between the country and the international community at date 0.[6] The IMF has also tried to venture into "ex ante monitoring," which in our model would correspond to writing covenants at date 0. In 1999 it introduced "contingent credit lines," which are meant to give a country automatic access to a credit line provided that certain criteria are met; unfortunately, as interesting as this idea is, no country has ever taken up those credit lines for fear of being stigmatized by the signal it would send to the market that it may encounter difficulties in the future.[7]

We conclude that the cost to monitor what is going on in foreign countries limits the amount of international risk sharing. The monitoring perspective can also be applied within a country as we have done in Holmström and Tirole (1997). In that paper, intermediaries are better informed than the public about the doings of firms and can more effectively limit the firms' ability to engage in moral hazard. To some extent, and as the recent eurozone crisis demonstrated, the same applies much

---

6. A thorny issue, though, is that the government may not behave in the citizens' best interests, and that hardships imposed by covenants—however well justified for the country as a whole at date 0—may unduly affect the poor at date 1.

See Tirole (2002) for further discussion of the raison d'être of the IMF.

7. Accordingly, the IMF in 2009 replaced these contingent credit lines by a new facility, the flexible credit line: see http://www.imf.org/external/np/sec/pr/2009/pr0985.htm.

more broadly: the willingness to share risk depends on the information and monitoring abilities of all parties involved. Much of the liquidity supply is local for this reason. For instance, what goes for good collateral in one country or one region of a country may not be worth much in another country or a distant region within the same country. The approach in this chapter could be used to study the role of such "local liquidity" more broadly.

IV Waste of Liquidity and Public Policy

In our study of aggregate liquidity shortages, we have assumed that the corporate sector can make efficient use of liquidity in each state of nature at date 1. One way in which efficient use of liquidity can be assured is to have a complete market of state-contingent claims on pledgeable income available for trade at date 0. This was illustrated by the LAPM model of chapter 4. As we discussed earlier, there may be many institutional solutions that achieve the same outcome, but our model is not rich enough to distinguish among them. In the real world, banks, conglomerates, and a variety of other intermediaries are the big players in the allocation of state-contingent aggregate liquidities to their best uses. How close these arrangements come to efficiency is an empirical matter. We view our model of complete contingent contracting that we developed in parts II and III as a helpful benchmark and reference point for such investigations.

In this fourth and final part of the book we depart from our benchmark model and analyze settings in which firms cannot pool their liquidity to achieve the complete market outcome. Instead they have to rely on *self-provision of liquidity*. To meet liquidity shocks that cannot be financed by issuing new claims at date-1 (funding liquidity)—that is, liquidity shocks that result in a negative net pledgeable income—firms have to invest in short-term assets that can be resold in the date-1 spot market (market liquidity). Firms operate in isolation, without coordinating either the acquisition or the use of liquidity. We assume further that firms cannot hold stakes in other firms. These assumptions are rather arbitrary, a problem shared by most models of incomplete markets. Our choices are guided by an interest in understanding when investments in short-term assets will be insufficient and when they will be excessive.

Chapter 7 explores two reasons why firms may overinvest in liquid assets. First, firms may hoard liquidity to overbid each other in auctions for distressed assets, resulting in wasteful competition for ex post rents. While such "predatory hoarding" is socially inefficient, public policy is not always able to increase welfare. Second, firms may hoard very liquid/safe assets such as Treasury bonds in the expectation of a freeze of the market for some other legacy assets that stand on their balance sheet and that they intended to resell (securitize). That is, an expectation of illiquidity in the market for the legacy assets encourages the hoarding of information-insensitive assets, whose market does not run the risk of collapsing. We show that precautionary hoarding of liquid assets is self-fulfilling, since it exacerbates adverse selection concerns in the legacy asset market.

Chapter 8 continues the analysis of having firms rely on secondary markets for their liquidity needs. It first analyzes when uncoordinated investments in "specialized assets" or "widgets" that are used to rescue long-term investments are inefficient. We find that despite a price discount in the secondary market, firms may still hoard the socially efficient amount of specialized assets to boost their capacity to acquire cheap specialized assets.

There are several possible interpretations of a specialized asset. The second part of the chapter explores an important one: reserves of foreign currency. It investigates whether the private sector has the proper incentives to hoard international liquidity and use international financial markets as a source of insurance.

We have so far assumed that the corporate sector makes efficient use of existing liquidity; that is, firms coordinate their liquidity provision through the pooling of liquid assets and the use of credit lines and other institutions that in effect dispatch available liquidity to those firms that need it most. This chapter and the next analyse situations in which firms fail to achieve such coordination. Rather, firms hoard liquid assets on their own balance sheet or count on the resale of relatively illiquid assets in the secondary market to meet their liquidity shocks.

This chapter explores the reasons why firms may hoard too much liquidity. We consider two models. In the first model (section 7.1), firms hoard liquidity in order to compete aggressively for the long-term assets of distressed firms. Our analysis of such *predatory hoarding* makes two main points: (1) the financial strength of the potential buyers increases the value of the distressed assets, contributing to liquidity at date 1; (2) uncoordinated purchases of short-term assets at date 0 may result in excessive hoarding of liquidity. During the subprime crisis (as in earlier crises) banks kept large amounts of excess reserves at the central bank (the Fed as well as the ECB). This is consistent with a strategy of strengthening their position to profit from fire sales of distressed assets.[1]

We will analyze the circumstances that lead to waste of liquidity due to lack of coordination and study government remedies that use the following two instruments:

• *Liquidity regulation*   The state can mandate minimum or maximum levels of liquidity. For example, many policy proposals following the subprime crisis called for a floor on the amount of liquidity hoarded by financial institutions. Our analysis suggests that a cap (or tax) on

---

1. Of course, there are other reasons for holding excess reserves. Banks may be concerned about survival in a worsening liquidity squeeze. They may also be waiting for the resolution of uncertainty that would reduce adverse selection.

liquidity hoarding may also be warranted, at least when the anticipation of fire sales makes it likely that financial institutions will stockpile on liquidity for predatory purposes.

• *Public provision of liquidity* As in chapter 5 the state can change the supply of liquidity. The rationale here is not to share aggregate risk, since there are no aggregate shocks in the model, but to influence the way the private sector manages its liquidity. The public supply of liquidity has an ambiguous impact if no separate liquidity regulation is in place. As in chapter 5, it lowers the cost of liquidity; however, it also facilitates rent-seeking.

The second model (section 7.2) focuses on *precautionary hoarding* of liquidity. In this framework, firms can use the secondary market to cover their future cash needs; namely they can sell/securitize legacy assets that they have hoarded on their balance sheets. If, however, the market for such assets is marred by asymmetric information, it may freeze, depriving the firms of access to market liquidity. To secure future funding, firms may instead hoard safe but low-yielding assets that are not subject to adverse selection, such as Treasury bonds. Interestingly the trade-off between relying on the securitization of legacy assets and hoarding safe assets can lead to multiple equilibria.[2] If firms invest mostly in safe assets, they are less dependent on being able to sell legacy assets in the secondary market. This creates adverse selection: legacy assets are primarily sold because their owners do not value them highly and want to get rid of them. In anticipation of such a date-1 "lemons market," firms indeed want to invest in safe assets at date 0.

Conversely, when firms do not expect a market freeze, they will prefer to invest in higher yielding assets. There is less adverse selection because asset sales are driven by liquidity shocks rather than purely by shocks to the value of the assets. This "liquid market" equilibrium dominates the "precautionary hoarding" equilibrium. Firms would be better off collectively if they could agree not to hoard safe assets.

7.1 Predatory Hoarding of Liquidity and Fire Sales

7.1.1 Parable of the Farmer and His Land

To put our analysis in perspective, we first review in this section some of the earlier work on asset redeployability. Shleifer and Vishny (1992),

---

2. See Malherbe (2009).

building on Williamson (1988), made several insightful observations about the limited ability of distressed firms to resell assets. To illustrate their reasoning, we offer the following parable.

A farmer has expertise in cultivating a certain crop but must borrow cash from a bank in order to purchase the land. Ex post, the farmer could prove competent or incompetent, or equivalently, the crop in which he has expertise could turn out to be suitable to the soil (or in high demand) or not (in low demand). If things go poorly, the land, which optimally is pledged as collateral to the bank, must be resold on the market. We have three possible circumstances for the reallocation of land:

• *Alternative use*   The land may be transformed by the buyer to serve another purpose, say, a baseball field. The issue with this type of sale is that the new use of land does not correspond to the best use of the land if farming yields a higher social value.

• *Deep-pocket investor*   The land is sold to investors with no farming expertise, who hire a farmer to plant and harvest crop. This approach has the advantage of maintaining the land in its best use but imposes an agency cost; it creates a wedge between the total value created and the price that the investors are willing to pay for the land.

• *Specialist*   To avoid the agency cost, the land could be resold to a farmer. Prospective buyers in this category, however, may not have the resources to buy the land, so they must borrow from nonspecialists, namely the same deep-pocket investors considered in the preceding type of sale.

Shleifer and Vishny argue that when assets must be managed by specialists, the wedge between the value of assets in specialist hands and the price that can obtained by selling the assets in the market is particularly high for industries in recession. Specialists tend to be found within a single industry and if that industry is in recession, the specialists are likely to be strapped for cash. Cash-strapped specialists may push the market price below its value in the best use.

This section develops a formal analysis of the three types of sales.

7.1.2 Coordinated Investment in Liquidity

Consider a continuum of entrepreneurial firms with unit mass. Firms are identical at date 0. Each has initial wealth A. At date 1, a fraction α of entrepreneurs is revealed to be *competent* and a fraction $1 - \alpha$ *incompetent*. *Intact firms* in this chapter are firms run by competent entrepreneurs, *distressed firms* are firms run by incompetent entrepreneurs. No one knows at date 0 which firms will be intact. At date 1, the entrepreneurs' types are privately revealed. The fraction α is known at date 0, so there is no aggregate uncertainty.

As before, all agents are risk neutral and indifferent over the timing of consumption, valuing their consumption stream

$$c_0 + c_1 + c_2.$$

Thus the consumer's required rate of return must be at least zero.

At date 0 the representative firm can invest in two types of assets:

1. *Long-term (LT) assets* If the firm invests I in LT assets at date 0, and the entrepreneur is revealed to be competent at date 1, the constant-returns-to-scale technology of section 3.1 applies: the LT asset delivers nothing at date 1; at date 2 it delivers total income $\rho_1 I$ and pledgeable income $\rho_0 I$, where

$$\rho_0 < 1 < \rho_1.$$

For simplicity, we assume that no reinvestment is needed at date 1.

If the entrepreneur turns out to be incompetent, the LT asset yields nothing ($\rho_0 = \rho_1 = 0$) under his management. Competent entrepreneurs can manage any number of assets, and LT assets may be transferred from incompetent to competent entrepreneurs. Assets transferred to competent entrepreneurs yield the same return as the entrepreneurs' original assets. LT assets may also be employed in an alternative use (e.g., converted to a baseball field), with a total return equal to the pledgeable income $\underline{\rho} I$, where $\underline{\rho} < 1$ can exceed or be smaller than ρ_0. An incompetent entrepreneur's assets will either be converted to the alternative use or be put under a competent entrepreneur's management.

2. *Short-term (ST) assets* A firm has also access to a storage technology. To obtain ℓ units of goods at date 1, the firm must invest $g(\ell)$ at date 0 in the ST asset, where

$$g'(0) = 1, \quad g'(\ell) > 1, \quad \text{and} \quad g''(\ell) > 0 \qquad \text{for all } \ell > 0.$$

Note that the the firm must pay a higher marginal cost the more it hoards liquidity.

For the purpose of this model, one can think of $g(\ell) - \ell$ as the physical depreciation of the storage good. But we have an alternative interpretation in mind in which the firms in this industry compete with firms in other industries for scarce (inside and outside) liquidity, and liquid assets command a premium $q - 1$, with $q = g'(\ell)$ in equilibrium.[3]

Coordinated Solution As a benchmark consider the second-best case whereby, at date 0, the entrepreneurs can agree among themselves and with investors (by forming a consortium or through contracting) on the levels of long-term and short–term investments and on the date-1 policy for redeploying the assets. Because there is no reinvestment need at date 1 and because liquidity is costly, the optimal coordinated policy is not to invest in ST assets at all:

$$\ell^* = 0. \tag{7.1}$$

Instead, firms agree in advance that the LT assets of the incompetent entrepreneurs will be turned over to the competent entrepreneurs. Because firms are identical ex ante and the entrepreneurs are risk neutral, there is no need for financial payments. In this case the optimal investment in LT assets, I^*, is given by the usual budget constraint equating investors' outlays with the pledgeable income:

$$I^* - A = \rho_0 I^*,$$

or

$$I^* = \frac{A}{1 - \rho_0}.$$

7.1.3 Self-provision of Liquidity and the Market for Distressed Assets

Suppose now that at date 0 each firm selects the pair (I, ℓ) independently, without coordinating its plan with the other firms.[4] At date 1 a spot market for assets opens, in which the entrepreneurs can sell (if they are incompetent) or buy (if they are competent) long-term assets. The price in the spot market is denoted p. Because a distressed firm can choose to put its assets in the alternative use, the date-1 price must satisfy $p \geq \rho$. If $p > \rho$, all the distressed assets are sold in the spot market; if $p = \rho$, some of the distressed assets may go into the alternative use. In either case the distressed firm will earn pI at date 1 from its LT investment. The model thus focuses on local liquidity in the sense that a limited set of players has the knowledge necessary to manage the assets or to buy the securities. Furthermore this set is financially constrained.

---

3. For this interpretation q should be taken as exogenous at the firm level.

4. Remember, we also assume that a firm cannot own shares of the other firms.

Intact firms have two potential sources of funds for purchasing distressed assets. They can sell their short-term assets ℓ, and they can issue new senior securities at date 1.[5] By fully diluting the initial shareholders, an intact firm can raise $\rho_0(I + j)$ at date 1, where I is the initial investment and j is the amount of assets purchased in the spot market. Together with the ST assets, the new issue has to cover the purchase of new assets, so the firm's investment plan has to satisfy the following date-1 *liquidity constraint*:

$$pj \leq \rho_0(I + j) + \ell. \tag{7.2}$$

The firm's investment plan also has to satisfy the date-0 *budget constraint*:

$$I - A + g(\ell) \leq \alpha \left[\rho_0(I + j) + \ell - pj \right] + (1 - \alpha) \left[\ell + pI \right]. \tag{7.3}$$

On the left-hand side are the costs of investments in LT and ST projects. On the right-hand side are the date-1 net returns. An intact firm will spend pj of its pledgable income on buying assets. A distressed firm will pay out to investors the returns from its ST assets plus what it gets by selling the LT assets in the date-1 spot market (or, alternatively, the returns it gets from putting the LT assets into the alternative use). When the liquidity constraint (7.2) binds, the first term on the right-hand side of (7.3) is zero. Then initial investors will only cash in on the liquidation of the distressed firms.

It may seem surprising that investors get something only when bad news is received. In other models of liquidity demand, such as the one considered in the next chapter, bad news means that more funds must be injected in order to avoid downsizing or closure; that is, investors provide funding liquidity by agreeing in advance to let their stakes be diluted and market liquidity by letting the firm's ST assets be sold. Good news (no liquidity shock) in these models make entrepreneurs and investors both better off. In the present case, by contrast, good news means an opportunity to purchase distressed assets, so good news creates a liquidity need. Funding liquidity and market liquidity are both employed in the good state, which ex post is beneficial to the entrepreneur but not to the investors.

For any given price p the representative firm will choose $\{I, j, \ell\}$ to maximize expected net utility:

---

5. Permitting dilution by intact firms is valuable from an ex ante point of view, since it is a cheaper form of liquidity than buying short-term assets.

$$U = \alpha \left[\rho_1(I+j) - pj \right] + (1-\alpha)pI - I - \left[g(\ell) - \ell \right], \tag{7.4}$$

subject to the liquidity constraint (7.2) and the budget constraint (7.3).[6]

An equilibrium in the date 1 spot market obtains when the demand for assets does not exceed the supply

$$\alpha j \leq (1-\alpha)I. \tag{7.5}$$

If the inequality is strict, $p = \rho$.

It follows immediately from the firm's maximization problem that

$$p > \rho_0. \tag{7.6}$$

Suppose, to the contrary, that $p \leq \rho_0$. The firm could then purchase boundless amounts of assets j, without the liquidity constraint or the budget constraint to constrain it. Therefore the purchase of date-1 assets would again be self-financing and entrepreneurial rents could be increased without bounds. This is inconsistent with equilibrium.

Note also that since $p \geq \underline{\rho}$, the option to put distressed assets into the alternative use is relevant only if

$$\underline{\rho} > \rho_0. \tag{7.7}$$

Otherwise, the purchase of distressed assets would again be self-financing. We will assume that (7.7) holds for now.

Next we argue that p must satisfy[7]

$$p \leq 1. \tag{7.8}$$

To see why, consider the following two investment options:

1. At date 1, the firm, when intact, buys an extra unit of distressed assets on the spot market at price p.

2. At date 0, the firm increases its investment I by one unit.

Let us ignore for the moment the firm's liquidity constraint and consider maximizing the firm's NPV subject only to the budget constraint (7.3). Letting $\lambda > 0$ be the Lagrange multiplier for the budget

---

6. Alternatively (from (7.3)):

$$U = \alpha(\rho_1 - \rho_0)(I+j) - A.$$

7. At first, one may think that ρ_1 is the upper bound for p, since that is the social value of an extra unit of the asset in the hands of a competent entrepreneur. However, this reasoning overlooks the alternative ways in which a firm can procure an asset for use at date 1.

constraint, we have the first-order conditions for choosing interior values of I and j:

$$\alpha\rho_1 + (1-\alpha)p - 1 - \lambda[1 - \alpha\rho_0 - (1-\alpha)p] = 0 \qquad \text{for } I, \qquad \text{(FOC-I)}$$

$$(\rho_1 - p) - \lambda(p - \rho_0) = 0 \qquad \text{for } j. \qquad \text{(FOC-j)}$$

The first-order condition (FOC-I) is increasing in p while (FOC-j) is decreasing in p. At $p = 1$ the two are equal. Because it is cheaper to buy date-1 assets through the spot market if $p < 1$ but not if $p > 1$, and because reintroducing the liquidity constraint can only work against buying assets through the date-1 spot market, the spot market can be in equilibrium only if $p \leq 1$. Note that this argument rests on the whole plan $\{I, j, \ell\}$ being agreed on between the investors and the firm.[8]

With these preliminaries, we turn to discuss equilibrium outcomes. Figure 7.1 describes the outcome when $\rho > \rho_0$. The spot market price p increases monotonically with the fraction α of intact firms, staying within the bounds ρ and 1. There are three possible regimes or regions of α. Let us look at the conditions under which each region applies, considering them in reverse order.

Region III ($\alpha > \alpha^* \equiv 1 - \rho_0$): No hoarding of assets (Efficient equilibrium)

Recall that the outcome is efficient if

- firms do not invest in ST assets ($\ell = 0$), and
- all the assets of distressed firms are transferred to the intact firms (none is put into the alternative use).

When most firms are intact (α is large), few LT assets are put on the market so supply is low. At the same time, demand is high because the aggregate purchasing power of intact firms (through dilution) is high.

Suppose that the assets put on the market command the maximum price $p = 1$ and that the firms invest nothing in outside liquidity ($\ell = 0$). To verify that this is an equilibrium, consider the two conditions that have to be met by the firm's choice $\{I, j, \ell\}$ and the price p. The firm's date-1 liquidity constraint implies that

$$j \leq \frac{\rho_0 I + \ell}{(p - \rho_0)}. \tag{7.9}$$

---

8. If the intact firms could bid for the date-1 assets by diluting shareholders at will, their purchasing power in region III of figure 7.1 would exceed the supply at $p = 1$ even without any investments in short-term assets. This would force the price up.

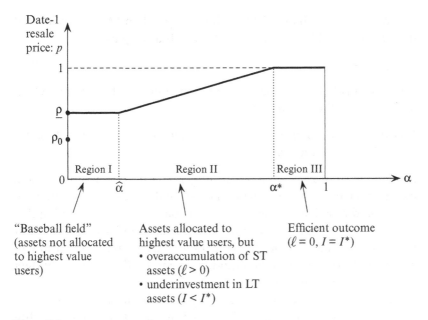

Figure 7.1
Redeployability in the absence of coordination

Also, because $p = 1 > \underline{\rho}$, the demand for assets is equal to the supply:

$$j = \frac{1 - \alpha}{\alpha} I. \tag{7.10}$$

Recall from (FOC-I) and (FOC-j) that a firm is indifferent between investing in I and j when $p = 1$. Therefore, when $p = 1$, we can adjust I and j so that supply equals demand regardless of α, and (7.9) is the key constraint. (Again, this is done in agreement between the firm and the investors at date 0—at date 1 the firm would like to expand purchases and full dilution would give enough purchasing power to do that.) Since no firm hoards liquidity ($\ell = 0$) in region III, they all invest the same amount as in the coordinated second-best solution:[9]

$$I = \frac{A}{1 - \rho_0} = I^*. \tag{7.11}$$

---

9. To obtain this expression, use the investors' breakeven constraint for $p = 1$, $I - A = \alpha[\rho_0(I + j) - j] + (1 - \alpha)I$ and the fact that supply equals demand: $\alpha j = (1 - \alpha)I$.

Substituting (7.10) into (7.9), noting that $p = 1$ and $\ell = 0$, we see that the efficient equilibrium (region III) prevails as long as

$$\alpha \geq \alpha^* \equiv 1 - \rho_0. \tag{7.12}$$

When α falls below α^* the liquidity constraint starts to bind, which moves us into the next regime.

Region II ($\hat{\alpha} \leq \alpha < \alpha^*$): Hoarding short-term assets to compete for LT assets at date 1 (Rent-seeking equilibrium)

In region II, since $\alpha < \alpha^*$, we can no longer have $p = 1$ as we just argued; we must have $p < 1$. Comparing (FOC-I) and (FOC-j), we see that the firm would now like to allocate all of its date-0 budget to buying distressed assets at date 1, choosing the maximal j, and setting $I = 0$. But this would violate the liquidity constraint (7.2). Therefore the firm will maximize (7.4) subject to the liquidity constraint (7.2) and the budget constraint (7.3), both binding.

The only purpose of hoarding costly liquidity at date 0 is to boost the firm's capacity to acquire distressed assets. Despite the liquidity premium, $g' - 1 > 0$, it is worth hoarding ST assets, since LT assets can be bought at a discount ($p < 1$) in the date-1 market. An intact firm's acquisition capacity j at date 1 is determined by the (binding) liquidity constraint

$$(p - \rho_0) j = \rho_0 I + \ell. \tag{7.13}$$

From the equilibrium condition (7.10) we find that the equilibrium price is

$$p = \frac{\rho_0}{1 - \alpha} + \frac{\alpha \ell}{(1 - \alpha)I}. \tag{7.14}$$

The first term is less than 1 because $\alpha < \alpha^* = 1 - \rho_0$. The second term reflects the fact that precautionary purchases of ST assets increase date-1 liquidity, boosting the price of assets relative to what it would be if $\ell = 0$ (but, of course, not so much that p gets pushed back up to 1).[10]

We can rewrite the firm's program in region II by substituting

---

10. Note that if we were to introduce uncertainty into the model, for example, in the form of a random fraction of intact firms α, then the point made by Shleifer and Vishny (1992) about price softness would hold: the asset price would fall during an industry recession (α low).

the binding liquidity constraint (7.2) into the budget constraint (7.3) to get

$$\max_{\{I,\ell,j\}} \{\alpha(\rho_1 - \rho_0)(I + j)\},$$

subject to

$$(1 - \alpha)(\ell + pI) - I + A - g(\ell) \geq 0$$

and

$$(pI + \ell) - (p - \rho_0)(I + j) = 0.$$

This can be further simplified to

$$\max \ [pI + \ell],$$

subject to

$$(1 - \alpha)(pI + \ell) - I + A - g(\ell) \geq 0,$$

which yields

$$g'(\ell) = \frac{1}{p}. \tag{7.15}$$

It follows that $\ell > 0$. In region II, entrepreneurs engage in wasteful competition for entrepreneurial rents by acquiring positive amounts of short-term assets. As we will see, this inefficiency can be reduced by discouraging liquidity hoarding.

A firm's maximum scale of investment, given that it purchases liquidity ℓ, is given by the budget constraint (7.3). Substituting expression (7.14) for p into the budget constraint, we see that a firm invests in equilibrium

$$I = \frac{A - [g(\ell) - \ell]}{1 - \rho_0} < I^*. \tag{7.16}$$

The inequality follows from $\ell > 0$. When the fraction of distressed firms is large (low α) the date-1 resale market is awash with assets. The price p falls when α falls, while firms respond by increasing ℓ and reducing I (buying assets in the spot market becomes increasingly attractive). To see this, suppose that p at some α were to (weakly) decrease with α. Then (7.15) implies that ℓ will (weakly) increase with α. From (7.16), I decreases with ℓ, so ℓ/I will (weakly) increase, which contradicts (7.14). Therefore p must be increasing in α in region II.

For some $\hat{\alpha} > 0$, determined by equations (7.13) through (7.16) and the firm's first-order condition for choosing I, the price eventually hits its lower bound:[11]

$$p = \underline{\rho} > \rho_0.$$

Region I ($\alpha < \hat{\alpha}$): Employing some assets in alternative use (Second-best equilibrium)

For values $\alpha < \hat{\alpha}$, a fraction of the distressed assets is converted to an alternative use. This situation is somewhat similar to the basic model considered in chapter 3 where (intact) consumers choose to consume rather than supply liquidity to firms. The reason why assets are inefficiently employed here is the same: there is a wedge between pledgeable and total income.

We summarize the analysis of this section as follows:

Proposition 7.1 Suppose that the assets of distressed firms are either sold to intact firms or converted to an inferior alternative use of value $\underline{\rho}$, and that firms procure their liquidity independently of each other by obtaining the right to issue new claims on their long-term assets at date 1 and by investing in costly short-term assets at date 0.

The price p at which LT assets are traded at date 1 is increasing in α. Furthermore there exist thresholds α^* and $\hat{\alpha}$, $1 > \alpha^* > \hat{\alpha} \geq 0$, such that

a. if $\alpha \geq \alpha^*$, the outcome is second-best efficient and $p = 1$;

b. if $\hat{\alpha} \leq \alpha < \alpha^*$, firms hoard excess liquidity ($\ell > 0$) and $p < 1$; when α decreases, ℓ increases, and p and I decrease.

c. if $\alpha < \hat{\alpha}$, firms hoard excess liquidity ($\ell > 0$) and $p = \underline{\rho}$, implying that some fraction of LT assets will be put into the (inferior) alternative use.

If $\underline{\rho} > \rho_0$, then $\hat{\alpha} > 0$. If $\underline{\rho} \leq \rho_0$, assets are never placed in the alternative use ($\hat{\alpha} = 0$), but parts a and b hold as stated.

If we interpret a lower α as reflecting a worse economic outlook, then the fact that the date-1 spot price p increases with α implies that there is more hoarding of liquidity when entrepreneurs become more concerned about the risk of distress and potentially also when they anticipate a less efficient use of LT assets[12].

---

11. At the lower bound, we must have $\ell > 0$ or else (7.13) will not hold for $p = \underline{\rho}$.

12. This property is obtained from the first-order conditions with respect to ℓ, I, and j in region II. In region I, set $p = \underline{\rho}$ and use (7.14) and (7.16).

7.1.4 Policy Implications

In the following discussion we ignore region III ($\alpha \geq \alpha^*$) because the uncoordinated solution in this case coincides with the coordinated (efficient) solution. For the other regions we study government interventions, with different values of α, keeping in mind that the value of α is fixed and known to the government at the time it decides on any intervention.

Liquidity Regulation: Imposing a Liquidity Cap (or Taxing Liquidity)?[13] Consider first region II ($\hat{\alpha} \leq \alpha < \alpha^*$). In this region all firms invest in liquidity and the intact firms buy all the long-term assets of the distressed firms at date 1. The ex post allocation is efficient, and the deadweight loss stems solely from liquidity hoarding. Furthermore, even without purchasing any liquidity, intacts can still buy all the long-term assets on sale, since the spot price will drop accordingly (until it hits its lower bound). This suggests that a liquidity cap of 0 could be an optimal intervention to eliminate rent-seeking without affecting the efficient transfer of assets.

To check this, note that—using (7.10) and (7.14)—the entrepreneur's net expected utility in this region is

$$U = \rho_1 I - I - [g(\ell) - \ell].$$

From (7.14) the firm's budget constraint (7.3) can be expressed as

$$I - A + [g(\ell) - \ell] \leq \rho_0 I.$$

Because $g(\ell) - \ell > 0$ is increasing in ℓ, hoarding more liquidity reduces welfare both directly and indirectly through the reduction in the investment level that investors are willing to grant. Thus as long as the LT asset is efficiently reallocated ex post, it is optimal to cap the use of liquidity as much as possible.

Let us imagine that the government bans liquidity hoarding altogether and sets $\ell = 0$. For which α values would intacts still be able to buy all the assets of the distressed? In region III of figure 7.1, firms privately choose $\ell = 0$, so the government cap has no effect. When α goes below α^*, firms would like to buy liquidity, but with the government cap they cannot. As a consequence their purchasing power in the

---

13. A steep tax on excess hoarding, starting at the level of the cap, achieves the same outcome as a cap. By contrast, an uncompensated tax on hoarding reduces entrepreneurial wealth.

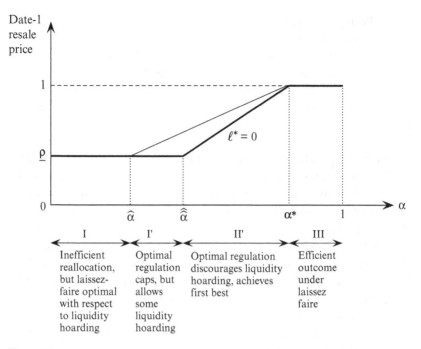

Figure 7.2
Regulation of liquidity

date-1 market is reduced, and the spot price is smaller than without government intervention as indicated in figure 7.2. Inserting $\ell = 0$ in (7.14), we see that the equilibrium date-1 price is

$$p = \frac{\rho_0}{1-\alpha} > \underline{\rho}, \tag{7.17}$$

as long as

$$\alpha > \hat{\hat{\alpha}} \equiv \frac{\underline{\rho} - \rho_0}{\underline{\rho}}. \tag{7.18}$$

Because the market clears when $p > \underline{\rho}$, the bound $\hat{\hat{\alpha}}$ in (7.18) defines the lower bound for α, such that there is a full transfer of assets from distressed to intacts when they cannot hoard any liquidity. Consequently, in region $\mathrm{II}' = [\hat{\hat{\alpha}}, \alpha^*]$ of figure 7.2, it is optimal (and essential) for the government to ban all liquidity hoarding ($\ell = 0$). Hoarding of liquidity serves no efficiency purpose and merely results in rent-seeking.

Next consider region $I = [0, \hat{\alpha}]$ in figure 7.2 (same as region I in figure 7.1). Firms hoard liquidity in this region, but hoarding is efficient because it does not affect the date-1 price. Hoarding serves efficiency by reducing the amount of long-term assets that get diverted to the alternative use. While some long-term assets still go to second-best use in region I, because liquidity hoarding is increasingly costly, the government cannot improve on the situation (other than reducing the cost of liquidity provision; see below). Formally, this can be seen by checking that in region I, the government's optimal program coincides with each firm's. (This is left to the reader.)

Finally, consider region $I' = [\hat{\alpha}, \hat{\hat{\alpha}}]$. Note first that we must have $\hat{\alpha} < \hat{\hat{\alpha}}$, because preventing firms from hoarding liquidity reduces their purchasing power in the date-1 market. Hence the date-1 price will be uniformly lower with than without liquidity hoarding. However, if the government sets $\ell = 0$, the long-term assets cannot all be transferred to the intacts, and some assets will go to the alternative use. Below we show that it is in the government's interest to allow some hoarding of liquidity. As long as hoarding does not raise the price in the date-1 market above $p = \underline{\rho}$, hoarding of liquidity will merely improve the transfer of assets from distressed to intacts. If the price rises above $\underline{\rho}$, however, we know that all assets are transferred and some of the liquidity is used for rent seeking. Hence the government's optimal policy in region I' is to allow enough hoarding of liquidity to permit full transfer of assets and keep the price from rising above $\underline{\rho}$.

Let

$$w(\ell, I) \equiv (1 - \alpha)I - \alpha j = (1 - \alpha)I - \frac{\alpha(\rho_0 I + \ell)}{\underline{\rho} - \rho_0}$$

denote the amount of LT assets placed in alternative use (with $w = 0$ and $\ell = 0$ at $\alpha = \hat{\alpha}$). Using the fact that $(1 - \alpha)\underline{\rho} > \rho_0$ in this region, we have

$$\frac{\partial w}{\partial \ell} < 0 \quad \text{and} \quad 1 > \frac{\partial w}{\partial I} > 0.$$

Welfare is reduced because of two forms of inefficiency, the waste of LT assets ex post and the inefficient buildup of liquidity ex ante, as seen from the social welfare function.

$$U = [\rho_1 I - I] - [\rho_1 - \underline{\rho}]w(\ell, I) - [g(\ell) - \ell]. \tag{7.19}$$

The social planner's budget constraint is

$$I - A + [g(\ell) - \ell] \leq \rho_0 I + (\rho - \rho_0)w(\ell, I). \tag{7.20}$$

Substituting this budget constraint into (7.19), we can write welfare as

$$U = (\rho_1 - \rho_0)[I - w(\ell, I)].$$

Let us ignore the constraint $w \geq 0$ for the moment, and substitute out $w(\ell, I)$ from U and the budget constraint (7.20). The social planner's problem can then be stated as

$$\max_{\{I,\ell\}} \left\{ \frac{\alpha}{\rho - \rho_0}(\rho I + \ell) \right\},$$

subject to

$$I = \frac{A - g(\ell) + (1 - \alpha)\ell}{1 - (1 - \alpha)\rho}.$$

The solution to this program is given by

$$g'(\ell) = \frac{1}{\rho}.$$

We define $\ell(p)$ by $g'(\ell(p)) = 1/p$, and rewrite the waste as a function of ℓ after substituting for I from the budget constraint, $\hat{w}(\ell, \alpha) \equiv w\left(\ell, [A - g(\ell) + (1 - \alpha)\ell]/[1 - (1 - \alpha)\rho]\right)$. This function $\hat{w}$ is a decreasing function of ℓ, so we have $\hat{w}(\ell(p(\alpha)), \alpha) = 0$ for $\alpha \in [\hat{a}, \hat{\hat{a}}]$, and $p(\alpha) > \rho$ in that range. Hence $\hat{w}(\ell(\rho), \alpha) < 0$, which violates the constraint $w \geq 0$. At the optimum therefore

$$w = 0.$$

As we asserted, the regulator caps ℓ at the level that just prevents wasting assets by converting them to the alternative use.

We can summarize these results succintly as follows:

• A cap on liquidity hoarding increases welfare as long as assets are reallocated efficiently with the cap.

• Firms choose the efficient level of liquidity whenever some of the assets are put into alternative use.

Public Provision of Liquidity We next investigate whether the state can improve welfare by increasing available stores of value. We only consider the impact of a marginal increase $\delta\ell$ in the supply per firm. We assume that the cost of taxation for the consumers at date 1 is $(1 + \lambda_0)\delta\ell$ and that the state at date 0 charges each entrepreneur $q_0 = (1 + \lambda_0)\delta\ell$. This keeps the welfare of the consumers constant, provided that the corporate tax is transferred to them. To make things interesting, we assume that $(1 + \lambda_0)$ is smaller than the marginal cost of private liquidity creation, $g'(\ell)$, in the uncoordinated, laissez-faire equilibrium studied above; otherwise, there would be no demand for public liquidity. Finally, we assume that there is no direct regulation of liquidity.

We begin with region I in which the LT asset is partly put into the alternative use $(\alpha < \hat{\alpha})$. An increase in the public supply of liquidity shifts the cost function downward

$$\hat{g}(\ell) = \begin{cases} g(\ell) & \text{if } g'(\ell) \leq 1 + \lambda_0, \\ g(\ell - \delta\ell) + (1 + \lambda_0)\delta\ell & \text{if } g'(\ell - \delta\ell) \geq 1 + \lambda_0. \end{cases}$$

The cost function $\hat{g}(\ell)$ is uniformly lower as δ is increased, so it raises the objective function in the social program above. Public supply of liquidity is (at the margin) welfare-enhancing.

In region II $(\hat{\alpha} \leq \alpha < \alpha^*)$ an increase in the supply of public liquidity has two opposing effects. As in region I, it reduces the cost of accumulating liquidity, but it also encourages rent seeking. Either effect may dominate as in the following two cases:

- *Public liquidity reduces welfare*   Suppose that $g(\ell) = q\ell$ for $\ell \leq \bar{\ell}$ and $+\infty$ for $\ell > \bar{\ell}$, where $q > 1 + \lambda_0$, and, in equilibrium without public liquidity, $\ell = \bar{\ell}$. Adding $\delta\ell$ of public liquidity increases the deadweight loss from $(q - 1)\bar{\ell}$ to $(q - 1)\bar{\ell} + \lambda_0\delta\ell$.
- *Public liquidity raises welfare*   Suppose that $g(\ell) = q\ell$, with $q > 1 + \lambda_0$.[14] The marginal cost of liquidity, and therefore the choice of ℓ, is unchanged by additional public liquidity. The deadweight loss is reduced from $(q - 1)\ell$ to $(q - 1)(\ell - \delta\ell) + \lambda_0\delta\ell < (q - 1)\ell$.

Proposition 7.2

a. *In region I*, some of the LT assets are wastefully redeployed in the alternative use, but firms hoard an optimal amount of liquidity, assuming that any reallocation of liquidity must be voluntary. Suppressing liquidity reduces welfare because it increases the volume of assets that are turned to the alternative use, whereas adding publicly provided liquidity is welfare enhancing.

---

14. This violates our assumption that $g'(0) = 1$ but is inconsequential for our argument.

b. *In region II'*, firms hoard excess liquidity under laissez faire, but LT assets are properly reallocated ex post. The tightest possible constraint on liquidity hoarding maximizes welfare. As a potential alternative to regulation, public provision of liquidity has an ambiguous impact: it reduces the firms' cost of hoarding liquidity, but it facilitates rent seeking.

Remark   In the introduction to this chapter we mentioned that many banks accumulated large amounts of reserves at the Fed and the ECB, possibly to take advantage of future fire sales, at the same time as other financial institutions and firms were in dire need of liquidity. In response to a near-zero federal funds rate, the Fed decided to raise the interest rate on bank reserves deposited at the central bank. This is the opposite of a policy that would encourage liquidity-rich institutions to invest their extra liquidity in the private sector. The welfare analysis in this section (regarding the benefits of a cap and the provision of liquidity) suggests that the Fed's policy may have been unwise.[15]

7.2   Precautionary Hoarding in Anticipation of a Market Freeze

This section draws on Malherbe (2009). We study his model of asymmetric information about the value of assets at date 1. Under asymmetric information resale markets may break down as buyers become concerned that lemons are offered for sale (Akerlof 1970). However, if buyers know that firms face liquidity shocks unrelated to the quality of their assets, and that firms do not have insurance against such shocks, buyers will be less concerned about lemons and date-1 markets will be liquid. Expecting that the secondary market will be liquid, firms do not need to self-insure as much. The rationale for putting the asset on the market may then be the firm's need for cash rather than privately known bad news about the asset's quality. The fraction of lemons will be low, confirming the expectation that markets are liquid.

An analogy may be useful here. Students who are moving abroad and selling their car or furniture make it clear that they are moving abroad. Similarly people selling their houses are inclined to reveal that they are moving out of town or that they move for change of life style reasons that make their current houses too small or too large. Sellers try to alleviate adverse selection by disclosing a legitimate reason for selling. A similar

---

15. The Fed's argument for paying interest on reserves was that this gave the Fed control of an interest rate that influenced credit. The Federal Funds rate had lost that role in the near-zero interest rate environment.

effect operates here as the sellers would want buyers to believe that they are selling an asset because of a fragile balance sheet rather than for opportunistic reasons.

7.2.1 The Model

To illustrate how adverse selection affects the hoarding of liquidity, we consider the following model (see figure 7.3):

Timing and actors   There are three periods, $t = 0, 1, 2$, and a continuum of firms.

Investment opportunity   At date 1 each firm will have a new (fixed sized) investment opportunity that, if undertaken, will deliver ρ_1 at date 2. To simplify notation, we assume that none of this value is pledgeable ($\rho_0 = 0$); this is inconsequential for the points we want to make. With probability α, the investment costs 0 and with probability $1 - \alpha$ it costs I. There are idiosyncratic liquidity shocks but no aggregate uncertainty. We note that investment I could alternatively be interpreted as a reinvestment on a project that started at date 0, in line with our earlier analyses.

Tradable legacy asset   Each firm owns a legacy asset that will deliver θ at date 2. The value θ is drawn from a cumulative distribution function $F(\theta)$ with support $[0, \rho_1]$ and mean $\bar{\theta}$.[16] The value of the legacy asset is independent of the cost of investment. No one knows the true value of θ at date 0. At date 1 the firm will have an opportunity to sell its legacy asset, knowing its true value, while the market will remain uninformed. (Later we will show that the conclusions are unchanged if a firm knows its θ and can sell the asset at date 0.)

Assumption 1   Without private information, the firm could finance the date-1 project in all states of nature by selling the legacy asset:

$$\bar{\theta} > I.$$

Stores of value   At date 0, firms can buy stores of value (ST assets) priced at $q \geq 1$ per unit that deliver 1 per unit at date 1. We continue to assume that the firms' capital insurance decisions are separate, that is there is no pooling of liquidity. Let ℓ denote the short-term investment by the representative firm at date 0.

---

16. The upper bound ρ_1 simplifies expressions but is not crucial to the analysis.

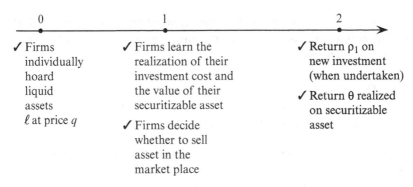

Figure 7.3
Precautionary hoarding and market freezes

Assumption 2   At date 1 the legacy asset is indivisible; it must be sold as a single unit.

This assumption simplifies the analysis and avoids some technical complications.[17]

Assumption 3   A firm's purchase of ST assets is not observed by outsiders.

The third assumption can be motivated in two ways. First, as banking regulators know well, it is difficult to apprehend the liquidity position of a bank, since the liquidity position depends on many hard to observe factors: the correlation of the risks on the bank's balance sheet, the quality of its assets, the reliability of its counterparties, the banks's reputation, its contracts in OTC markets, its pledges for liquidity support, and so forth.

Second, and anticipating our analysis, firms would like to prove that they have not hoarded liquidity, since this makes them more reliable trading partners at date 1. However, it can be difficult to demonstrate to the market that one is selling due to liquidity needs rather than strategic reasons. We capture both of these considerations simply by assuming that the firm's choice ℓ is unobserved by the market.

---

17. We are making the same indivisibility assumption as Akerlof did in his paper. When a good for sale is divisible and subject to exclusivity (i.e., the seller must trade with a single buyer or none), a pure-strategy equilibrium in the market for lemons often does not exist, as was shown by Rothschild and Stiglitz (1976). By contrast, the equilibrium in the market for a divisible good under nonexclusive competition (shares may be sold to different buyers) always exists and is the Akerlof equilibrium; see Attar, Mariotti, and Salanié (2009).

We will now demonstrate that market liquidity is endogenous and that multiple equilibria, one with sufficient market liquidity and the other with a market freeze, may co-exist.

7.2.2 Equilibrium with a Liquid Market (No Hoarding)

Consider an equilibrium with a liquid secondary market, where firms do not hoard any liquidity at date 0:

$$\ell = 0.$$

Instead, firms count on selling their legacy asset if they need funds at date 1. Let $p(\alpha)$ be the equilibrium price of the assets in the date 1 market (α is the fraction of intact firms). It is defined by[18]

$$p(\alpha) = \frac{\alpha \int_0^{p(\alpha)} \theta dF(\theta) + (1-\alpha)\bar{\theta}}{\alpha F(p(\alpha)) + (1-\alpha)}. \tag{7.21}$$

The equation above sets the date-1 price equal to the expected value of the assets put on sale, provided that all distressed firms sell their asset, along with the intact firms that have an asset worth less than $p(\alpha)$, as reflected in the numerator. The denominator is the total fraction of assets sold.

The value of $p(\alpha)$ in (7.21) is decreasing in α as pictured in figure 7.4. The higher the fraction of intact firms, the more there is adverse selection and the lower is the price. There are two premises behind (7.21). The first

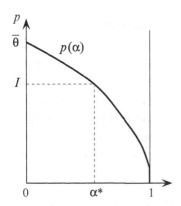

Figure 7.4
Equilibrium price when the market is liquid

---

18. It can be shown that $p(\alpha)$ is unique.

is that distressed firms sell their legacy asset regardless of the asset's realized value θ. This will be true if and only if

$$p(\alpha) \geq I \quad \text{or} \quad \alpha \leq \alpha^*, \tag{7.22}$$

where α^* is defined by $p(\alpha^*) = I$ (see figure 7.4). Since we assumed that the unconditional expected value of the legacy asset is higher than I, we have $p(0) > I$. Also, since the market is one with pure adverse selection when $\alpha = 1$, we have $p(1) = 0$. Because $p(\alpha)$ is strictly decreasing, it follows that $\alpha^* \in (0, 1)$.

The second premise behind (7.21) is that firms do not hoard any liquidity at date 0. The firm's net expected utility without liquidity hoarding ($\ell = 0$) is

$$U^{\text{no insurance}} = \rho_1 + \alpha \left[p(\alpha) + \int_{p(\alpha)}^{\rho_1} (\theta - p(\alpha)) dF(\theta) \right]$$
$$+ (1 - \alpha)(p(\alpha) - I).$$

This utility must exceed the utility that the firm obtains by choosing $\ell = I$ (choosing $\ell \in (0, I)$ is useless because of our indivisibility assumption, and $\ell > I$ is wasteful), which is

$$U^{\text{insurance}} = -qI + \rho_1 + \alpha \left[I + p(\alpha) + \int_{p(\alpha)}^{\rho_1} (\theta - p(\alpha)) dF(\theta) \right]$$
$$+ (1 - \alpha) \left[p(\alpha) + \int_{p(\alpha)}^{\rho_1} (\theta - p(\alpha)) dF(\theta) \right].$$

Thus the second condition for a liquid market equilibrium is

$$(q - 1)I \geq (1 - \alpha) \int_{p(\alpha)}^{\rho_1} [\theta - p(\alpha)] dF(\theta). \tag{7.23}$$

This condition is intuitive. It says that the cost of capital insurance, $(q - 1)I$, must exceed the savings, $\theta - p(\alpha)$, associated with not selling an undervalued asset ($\theta > p(\alpha)$) when distressed. Note, in particular, that a liquidity premium $q - 1 > 0$ is required to sustain an equilibrium without ex ante hoarding of liquidity.

7.2.3 Equilibrium with a Market Freeze (Hoarding of Liquidity)
In an equilibrium with a market freeze, no transactions take place at date 1. The only way for a firm to finance an investment is to self-insure

by buying short-term assets at date 0 in the amount $\ell = I$. The condition for an equilibrium with a market freeze is therefore

$$U^{\text{insurance}} = -qI + \rho_1 + \alpha I + \bar{\theta} \geq U^{\text{no insurance}} = \alpha \rho_1 + \bar{\theta},$$

or

$$(1 - \alpha)(\rho_1 - I) \geq (q - 1)I. \tag{7.24}$$

This condition simply says that the net cost of ex ante insurance, $(q - 1)I$, must be smaller than the value of the forgone investment opportunity, else firms would not want to hoard liquidity.

Because firms already have all the liquidity they need, there are no gains from trade at date 1. The date-1 market is a pure lemons' market, clearing at a zero price with no trade:

$$\hat{p}(\alpha) = E[\theta | \theta \leq \hat{p}(\alpha)] \Longrightarrow \hat{p}(\alpha) = 0.$$

Multiple equilibria arise whenever $\alpha \leq \alpha^*$, and conditions (7.23) and (7.24) both hold. Combining these two conditions, we get

$$\rho_1 - I \geq \int_{p(\alpha)}^{\rho_1} [\theta - p(\alpha)] dF(\theta), \tag{7.25}$$

where $p(\alpha)$ is defined by (7.21). Inequality (7.25) is a necessary condition for having both an equilibrium without any hoarding of liquidity ($\ell = 0$, $p(\alpha) \geq I$) and an equilibrium with a market freeze ($\ell = I$, $p(\alpha) = 0$).

There may also exist intermediate equilibria between these two extremes. In such equilibria $0 < p < I$ and $0 < \ell < I$, such that $p + \ell = I$. The price is no longer determined by (7.21), since some of the distressed firms will not sell their legacy asset. In particular, only distressed firms with $\theta \leq \rho_1 - \ell = \rho_1 + p - I < \rho_1$ will sell; the rest prefer to keep their legacy asset. As a result the fraction of assets sold for strategic reasons will be higher, leading to more adverse selection and a price $p < I$. Again, the more firms procure liquidity in advance, the more severe the adverse selection will be and the lower the price. The intermediate equilibrium, as long as it exists, is unique for a given α, since the price decline per unit of increase in ℓ is less than 1.

Because hoarding liquidity is costly, the Pareto-optimal equilibrium, given a fixed α, is the one with a liquid market and no hoarding. The worst equilibrium is the one where the market freezes and firms have to arrange all of the liquidity in advance. In between these two is the mixed equilibrium. These comparisons are, of course, relevant only when they exist for a given α.

7.2.4 Discussion

Public Policy   Government supplied liquidity can help or harm depending on circumstances. To see this, suppose $\alpha > \alpha^*$ so that the market for legacy assets alone cannot support the firm's investment (because $p(\alpha) < I$; see figure 7.4). Firms would then like to hoard liquidity in advance so that they can invest at date 1 as discussed above. If there are no private stores of value, the government can improve matters by supplying liquidity for this purpose. More generally, if there is a fixed but insufficient supply of private stores of value, the ex ante insurance market will push the liquidity premium up to the point where firms become indifferent between hoarding and not hoarding liquidity. If the liquidity premium in this equilibrium is higher than the government's cost of supplying stores of value, the government can improve welfare.

By contrast, when $\alpha \leq \alpha^*$, it is socially optimal not to issue government securities (or more generally to lower the yield on such securities so that (7.23) is violated), because the equilibrium without hoarding is more efficient than any other equilibrium. Issuing more liquidity may make no difference to the equilibrium, but would be wasteful (there is a deadweight loss from taxation). If anything, the government may want to reduce the supply of liquidity, raising its price, which could make the no-hoarding equilibrium more likely.

The general point here is that an increased supply of liquidity will lower the cost of liquidity and encourage hoarding. This makes adverse selection in the asset market worse, inhibiting the functioning of the date-1 market. In this light, the policy of central banks to accommodate the flight to quality during the subprime crisis (they welcomed deposits at the central bank) might have had the unintended consequence of delaying the recovery of asset markets. This conclusion is similar to our earlier point about the advisability of paying interest on reserves (see section 7.1.4) Our analysis underlines the exceptional informational requirements for a good public policy.

Market versus Funding Liquidity   Instead of relying on market liquidity by selling assets, as we have assumed so far, firms could rely on funding liquidity by issuing securities. We could have developed our analysis in this alternative context. At date 1, suppose that firms have no assets and hold private information about the value ρ_0 of their date-2 pledgeable income, which is now drawn from a distribution $G(\rho_0)$. Suppose further that the entrepreneurs keep all claims on pledgeable income until date 1 with the intent to raise funds by selling the claims at date 1 (this could be a cheaper way of saving). Then those firms that sell claims because of liquidity needs will on average offer higher quality claims than those who sell to unload impaired claims. A formula akin to (7.21) obtains: If the market for funding liquidity does not break down, shares will trade at price $p(\alpha)$ such that (with double use of notation)

$$p(\alpha) = \frac{\alpha \int_0^{p(\alpha)} \rho_0 dG(\rho_0) + (1-\alpha)\bar{\rho}_0}{\alpha G(\rho_0) + (1-\alpha)}.$$

By contrast, if firms were to invest in stores of value, the market for funding liquidity would dry up (under conditions similar to those discussed earlier).

Stigma   One of the potentially counterintuitive features of the analysis presented above is that a firm benefits from appearing fragile. Having stored little liquidity and being forced to go to the asset market for more, rather than being selective about selling, is reassuring to potential buyers. Yet, common wisdom as well as empirical evidence suggests that issuing securities or being forced to sell assets entail a stigma. For this reason financial institutions typically avoid turning to a government agency for help, even if the agency does not associate stigma with its lending. For instance, banks are often reluctant to borrow at the discount window and countries are often reluctant to apply for contingent credit lines (CCF) from the IMF. How can we reconcile the theory with this evidence?

A potential story has the following two ingredients. First, the bank or the country typically needs to borrow from other lenders than the central bank or the IMF, respectively, so borrowing from the discount window or a CCL may send a signal of fragility to these lenders. Second, we need to explain why borrowing from a public body conveys bad news about an institution. One possible reason is that the need for cash is due to the unwillingness of better informed lenders and counterparties to continue funding the institution. Whatever is the reason, our analysis is clearly picking up only a limited aspect of the story.

Securitization at Date 0   We have assumed that securitization (the sale of legacy assets) occurs at date 1.[19] Would the outcome be different if the firm could securitize at date 0, knowing the value of its legacy assets (the realization of θ), but not yet knowing the cost of the new investment opportunity? To address this issue, let p_0 and p_1 denote the date-0 and date-1 equilibrium prices of the legacy asset. Because legacy assets represent a claim that can be resold at date 1, the date-0 price p_0 is equal (if there is a demand for liquidity at price q) to q times the expected dividend conditional on the legacy asset being sold at date 0. We consider possible equilibria in this new situation.

An equilibrium *without hoarding at date 0* is observationally equivalent to the no-hoarding equilibrium when only date-1 securitization is feasible. As before, $p_1 = p(\alpha) \geq I$ (assuming that $\alpha \leq \alpha^*$, of course). Firms wait until date 1 to sell their legacy asset and do so if they are distressed or if they are intact and face a liquidity shock and $\theta \leq p_1$. There is no trade of the legacy asset as long as $p_0 - (q - 1)I \leq p_1$, that is, as long as there are no gains to trading early even if firms knew that they will sell at date 1, regardless of the liquidity shock. In particular, there is an equilibrium with $p_0 = 0$ and no trade, supported by the off-equilibrium belief that any attempt to sell at date 0 has a purely strategic motive.

Thus the no-hoarding equilibrium in the earlier model is robust to the possibility of date-0 trading of the legacy asset under adverse selection.

In a *hoarding equilibrium*, $p_0 = p_1 = 0$ without any trading of assets. Firms will hoard their own liquidity (which requires (7.24) to be satisfied). Like the no-hoarding equilibrium, the hoarding equilibrium is robust to early trading.

Could there be *other equilibria*? Intuitively there are two forces that determine the equilibrium price. First, we would expect "more adverse selection" at date 0, since at date 1 there are at least some potential sellers who experience a liquidity shock. Ceteris paribus, the sellers with low-quality assets are more eager to sell at date 0 (i.e., unconditionally) than those who have better quality assets and are more willing to wait to see

---

19. One possible justification is that the firm is in the process of creating an asset that is not yet ready to be traded at date 0 (e.g., because of severe asymmetric information). This raises interesting avenues for extending the model. As has been demonstrated empirically, the prospect of issuing securities creates moral hazard (see Keys et al. 2009). So we would expect the distribution $F(\theta)$ to be less favorable in the securitization equilibrium than in the market freeze equilibrium. (For more on this, see Aghion, et al. 2004, who take a mechanism design approach to securitization under moral hazard. See also Faure-Grimaud and Gromb 2004; Parlour and Plantin 2008.)

whether they will end up distressed or intact at date 1. Second, selling claims at date 0 creates stores of value for the buyers, and this has social value since $q > 1$. The premium charged on stores of value could favor date-0 trading, though the benefit of saving by not selling also needs to be taken into consideration.

Let us look for an equilibrium in which some trade occurs at date 0. We are led to consider two cases:

Case 1: $p_1 < I$ There are no gains from trade at date 1, so the only market for assets is at date 0. A firm that wants to invest at date 1 will have to buy liquidity at date 0, regardless of whether it sells the asset at date 0 or holds it to maturity. Type θ decides to sell at date 0 rather than hold the asset to maturity if and only if

$$p_0 - (q-1)I + [\rho_1 - (1-\alpha)I] \geq \theta - (q-1)I + [\rho_1 - (1-\alpha)I] \qquad (7.26)$$

or

$$p_0 \geq \theta.$$

The term on the left-hand side of (7.26) includes the proceeds from selling at date 0, the cost of buying I units of liquidity to weather a low shock at date 1, and the net benefit of investing at date 1. The right-hand side has a corresponding interpretation, reflecting the value of investing and holding the asset to maturity. Let θ^* be the cutoff for selling the asset. Note that $p_0 = qm^-(\theta^*)$, where $m^-(\theta^*) = E(\theta|\theta \leq \theta^*)$ is the expected value of the assets put up for sale. The equilibrium cutoff, if it is interior, satisfies

$$qm^-(\theta^*) = \theta^*.$$

For a uniform distribution, $m^-(\theta^*)/\theta^* = 1/2$, so trade occurs at date 0 (and involves all types) if and only if $q \geq 2$.

Case 2: $p_1 \geq I$ There is a need to buy liquidity at date 0 only if the asset is sold at date 0. If it is sold at date 1, the price at date 1 is sufficient to cover the investment need.

On the one hand, selling at date 0 yields, as before,

$$p_0 - (q-1)I + [\rho_1 - (1-\alpha)I].$$

On the other hand, the value of holding off on selling until date 1 is

$$[\rho_1 - (1-\alpha)I] + p_1 \quad \text{if} \quad \theta \leq p_1,$$

and

$$[\rho_1 - (1-\alpha)I] + \alpha\theta + (1-\alpha)p_1 \quad \text{if } \theta \geq p_1.$$

Again, only types below some cutoff θ^* sell at date 0. Futhermore, a necessary condition for trade at date 0 is

$$p_0 - (q-1)I \geq p_1.$$

Since only types above θ^* can sell at date 1, we must have $p_1 \geq \theta^*$, and therefore an equilibrium of the assumed kind exists only if there is a θ^* such that

$$qm^-(\theta^*) - (q-1)I = p_1(\theta^*),$$

where $p_1(\theta^*)$ is the solution to

$$p_1 = \frac{\alpha \int_{\theta^*}^{p_1} \theta dF(\theta) + (1-\alpha) \int_{\theta^*}^{p_1} \theta dF(\theta)}{\alpha \left[F(p_1) - F(\theta^*)\right] + (1-\alpha)[1 - F(\theta^*)]}.$$

Mixing Financial Muscle and Adverse Selection   Bolton, Santos, and Scheinkman (2009) argue that adverse selection may increase liquidity hoarding, but for a somewhat different reason. Their model involves two sets of players: long-term arbitrageurs (sovereign wealth funds, pension funds, etc.) that hoard costly liquidity to buy assets at cash-in-the-market prices (i.e., at a discount) and firms that face a liquidity need before the date of reckoning (i.e., before the final return on a project is realized). Uncertainty about the final profit of each firm unfolds gradually, and efficient trade involves trading as late as possible before the date of reckoning. Delaying trade reduces the quantity hoarded by long-term investors, as they do not have to acquire intermediate dividends.[20] However, late trading may not be feasible since Bolton et al. posit that adverse selection increases over time. The prospect of a market freeze then forces early trading and therefore more liquidity hoarding. Increasing adverse selection provides incentives for early

---

20. The paper assumes all-or-nothing trades, that is, a firm's cash flow cannot be split into securities with different maturities. Otherwise, the long-term investors could economize on costly liquidity hoarding by purchasing only the securities' late dividends, and not the early ones.

   In the paper, there are four dates: 0, 1, 2, 3. The ST traders have preferences $c_0 + c_1 + c_2 + \delta c_3$ with $\delta < 1$. Thus ST traders do not need to trade before date 2, at which date they need to sell only the claim to the last dividend.

trading, which, if tranching is infeasible, induces an inefficient amount of liquidity hoarding.

7.3 Summary

As this chapter showed, the inability of firms to write state-contingent contracts on the available supply of liquidity at date 1 may lead to excess investments in liquidity at date 0 as well as to a wrong allocation of assets at date 1. When liquidity is used to buy distressed assets, investments in liquidity tend to be excessive due to wasteful competition for ex post rents. However, our analysis of predatory hoarding of liquidity also shows that decentralized choices regarding liquidity do not necessarily cause inefficiencies. With our particular structure, spot markets are often capable of replicating the fully coordinated solution. And even when spot markets cannot duplicate the coordinated solution, the government is not always able to increase welfare by regulating liquidity. If the problem is a reluctance on the part of firms with excess resources to reallocate these resources to distressed firms, then increasing government supplied liquidity may simply lead to more assets being employed suboptimally at date 1.

We also showed that precautionary hoarding of liquidity may have the unintended consequence of a market freeze. Buyers may question the sellers' motives for selling their assets if they know that the sellers have a sufficiently large cushion of cash. Liquidity hoarding encourages market freezes (and conversely). While the laissez-faire outcome may involve excessive liquidity hoarding, in some circumstances precautionary hoarding is desirable. Distinguishing between the two cases with such radically different policy implications requires detailed information and makes the policy task very challenging.

An extension that would be interesting and relatively straightforward to explore is to have the fraction of intact firms be random. This would be one way of introducing an aggregate shock.[21] Given that the shock is aggregate, it should be possible to write contracts on the state. The characteristics of an optimal supply of liquidity (e.g., by government) when the idiosyncratic shocks must be handled through spot markets would be interesting to explore.

While the two motives leading to overhoarding of liquidity (predatory and precautionary hoarding) seem realistic, we certainly do not believe

---

21. Allen and Gale (1994, 2005) allow for such aggregate shocks in their models.

overhoarding is the rule. Indeed the subprime crisis appears to have been triggered in part by underhoarding of liquidity and excess leverage among financial institutions. Many commercial and investment banks (and insurance companies, e.g., AIG) relied on short-term financing for continued funding, instead of investing in short-term assets that could have been used when liquidity got scarce. These institutions, which benefited from cheap sources of capital thanks to an implicit guarantee from the governments, took increasingly risky gambles with more severe maturity mismatches despite warnings. As Farhi and Tirole (2009b) argue, maturity mismatches are subject to strategic complementarities. Central banks are unlikely to maintain interest rates low in order to keep a single institution alive. By contrast, when faced with a widespread maturity mismatch, the centrals banks have no choice but to keep the interest rate very low, at the cost of substantial distortions to the economy, and so they did.

8   Specialized Inputs and Secondary Markets

In this chapter we continue to analyze the implications of firms relying exclusively on secondary markets for their liquidity needs. As in the previous chapter we assume that firms do not coordinate their balance sheet choices and that there are no aggregate shocks. Firms hoard an input, which we will call a "widget." This input is needed to keep long-term assets operative. A widget is a generic term that can stand for many things. It could literally be a mechanical part that is needed for continuing production, it could be a service or knowledge that is needed to make the asset productive, or it could stand for collateral secured on international financial markets (an application we discuss in section 8.2).

We begin in section 8.1 with ex ante identical firms that invest both in illiquid long-term assets and in widgets. Widgets are used at date 1 to help those firms that end up being distressed to weather the shock. Widgets, however, need not be in the right hands, and so in the absence of an ex ante coordinated pooling arrangement, a secondary market will open to allow transfers of widgets held by intact firms to distressed firms. As in section 7.1, buyers may not have enough financial resources to acquire the needed widgets at a price that dominates the alternative use of widgets. Therefore financial constraints may lead to an inefficient reallocation of widgets through the secondary market. A central question we address in section 8.1 is whether firms will tend to underhoard widgets. Intuitively one might reason that a low resale price should discourage investments in widgets: A firm that ends up on the sell side would have to sell widgets at a discount relative to the social value. A firm that ends up on the buy side would get widgets at a discount. Both forces would seem to favor less hoarding and more reliance on the date-1 market. We will show, however, that this intuition is wrong in our model. In equilibrium there is no underhoarding, even though the date-1 widgets sell at a discount.[1]

In section 8.2 we apply the model in section 8.1 to an international context. Widgets refer to dollars, meaning international liquidity. The focus is on international liquidity (dollars) as an input in the production process. Like the widgets in section 8.2, dollars are needed for reinvestment. We are interested in possible inefficiencies arising from the firms' uncoordinated purchase of dollars at date 0—in particular, the possibility that firms will not secure enough dollars at date 0 (or equivalently, that they will borrow excessively on the international markets).

8.1 Secondary Markets for Specialized Inputs

8.1.1 Model and Two Benchmarks

We assume that firms are ex ante homogeneous but ex post heterogeneous. Our model is again one where distressed assets are salvaged by intact firms. But we turn the model of section 7.1 on its head by assuming that distressed firms do not sell their assets to intacts, but rather that intact firms sell their assets to distressed firms. Those in distress buy rather than sell. The secondary markets will deal in liquid short-term (ST) assets rather than illiquid long-term (LT) assets. And liquid assets rather than illiquid ones will sell at a discount relative to their date-0 price.

At date 0, a representative entrepreneur has wealth A and invests in both LT and ST assets:

• I in LT assets delivers, at date 2, $\rho_1 I$ in total income and $\rho_0 I$ in pledgeable income, provided that the assets are still in use at date 2.

• ℓ in ST assets (widgets) is the number of units received at date 1 in return for a date-0 investment $g(\ell)$.

For simplicity, we assume that the marginal cost of producing widgets is constant, that is, $g(\ell) = q\ell$, where $q \geq 1$. Firms that invest in the LT asset also have access to the ST widget technology.

At date 1, a firm will be intact or distressed:

• *Intact* (which has probability α) means that the firm does not need any widgets. Its long-term investments will deliver total value $\rho_1 I$ and pledgeable income $\rho_0 I$ at date 2.

---

1. Caballero and Krishnamurthy (e.g., 2001, 2002) explain underhoarding using this kind of intuition. We will discuss why the "cheap widget" intuition fails in our setting.

• *Distressed* (which has probability $1 - \alpha$) means that it takes one widget per unit of long-term investment to deliver the date-2 returns of intact firms. A distressed unit that does not get a matching widget at date 1 generates no income at date 2.

As in chapter 7, there is no aggregate uncertainty. Widgets at date 1 can be converted to an alternative use (the "baseball field" of the parable in chapter 7) with per unit value[2]

$$\underline{\rho} < q.$$

Only an intact firm will face the choice of converting its widgets to the alternative use.

Second-Best Benchmark (Full Coordination) As a benchmark we begin with policies in which firms coordinate their date-0 investments and the date-1 use of widgets. Because there is no aggregate uncertainty and the investment and use of widgets are fully coordinated, there is never any excess accumulation of widgets. No widgets are converted to the alternative use (since $\underline{\rho} < q$), so we can, without loss of generality, assume that widgets are only used by the distressed firms.

How much will the firms invest in widgets (ST assets)? Intuitively it is worth investing in widgets whenever they are cheap enough (q is small) or the probability of distress ($1 - \alpha$) is high. To demonstrate this formally, consider the following social planning program:

$$\max_{\{I,\ell,m\}}\{(\rho_1 - \rho_0)\,[\alpha I + (1 - \alpha)(\ell + m)]\}, \tag{8.1}$$

subject to

(i) $\alpha\ell \geq (1 - \alpha)m,$

(ii) $I + q\ell - A \leq \alpha\rho_0 I + (1 - \alpha)\rho_0(\ell + m),$

(iii) $\ell + m \leq I.$

The choice variables are the date-0 investments I in LT assets and ℓ in ST assets (widgets) and the date-1 amount m of widgets received by distressed firms from intact ones. The objective is to maximize the representative entrepreneur's gross utility, which is equal to the social surplus, since the budget constraint must bind at an optimum. The first constraint is the date-1 aggregate resource constraint; it requires

---

2. In this model, unlike the one in chapter 7, there will be no inefficiencies without this outside option.

that the transfer of widgets to the distressed firms cannot exceed the supply of widgets by the intact firms. As noted above, this constraint can be written as an equality because it would be wasteful to hoard more widgets than will be used by the intacts (recall that there is no aggregate uncertainty). The second constraint is the date-0 resource, or budget constraint. The third constraint is technological: the continuation scale cannot exceed I.

Let the date-1 continuation scale be $i = \ell + m$. Constraint (i), as an equality, implies that $m = \alpha i$ and $\ell = (1 - \alpha)i$. We can then rewrite the social program (8.1) as

$$\max_{\{I,i\}}\{\alpha I + (1 - \alpha)i\}, \tag{8.2}$$

subject to

(i) $I + q(1 - \alpha)i - A \leq \alpha\rho_0 I + (1 - \alpha)\rho_0 i,$

(ii) $i \leq I.$

In this program the firm chooses the initial scale I and the continuation scale i with the continuation i assured by choosing m and ℓ according to $m = \alpha i$ and $\ell = (1 - \alpha)i$. The budget constraint, as an equality, allows us to subtitute out I and write the social objective (dropping constants) as

$$\max_{i}\{[\alpha(\rho_0 - q) + (1 - \alpha\rho_0)]i\}.$$

It follows that when

$$\alpha q \lesssim 1, \tag{8.3}$$

it is socially optimal to continue at full scale (choose $i = I$). As a weak inequality, the condition is necessary for buying widgets at date 0 ($\ell > 0$). As one would expect, liquidity hoarding is more desirable when the probability of distress is higher and the acquisition of liquidity is cheaper.

Another Useful Benchmark: The Autarky Case   Even though we will allow a spot market for reallocating widgets shortly, it is also useful to study the autarky case as a benchmark. Clearly, for very low levels of ρ_0, distressed firms have little with which to pay for widgets. Therefore, even in the presence of a secondary market, trade will be minimal and the outcome will resemble the autarky outcome.

In autarky each firm provides for its own widgets: there is no coordination or reallocation of widgets. Given the linear technology, a firm has two relevant choices. It can bet all its money on being intact and use its capital to maximize the initial scale without any investment in widgets. Alternatively, it can allocate its capital equally between the initial investment I and widgets $\ell = I$ so that it can continue at full scale even when it ends up in distress. The latter strategy will waste part of the initial investment in widgets because a firm that ends up being intact recovers only $\underline{\rho} < q$ per unit. However, the former strategy will waste the initial investment if the firm ends up in distress.

With the first strategy the maximal scale and the entrepreneur's *gross* payoff are

$$I_I = \frac{A}{1 - \alpha \rho_0}, \tag{8.4}$$

$$\tag{8.5}$$

$$U_I^g = \frac{(\rho_1 - \rho_0)A}{(1/\alpha) - \rho_0}. \tag{8.6}$$

The maximal scale associated with investing in widgets (the second strategy) is given by

$$I + qI \le A + \rho_0 I + \alpha \underline{\rho} I,$$

yielding

$$I_{II} = \frac{A}{1 + q - (\rho_0 + \alpha \underline{\rho})}. \tag{8.7}$$

So the *gross* payoff to the entrepreneur is

$$U_{II}^g = \frac{(\rho_1 - \rho_0)A}{1 + q - \rho_0 - \alpha \underline{\rho}}. \tag{8.8}$$

Comparing U_I^g and U_{II}^g, we find that hoarding is optimal in autarky if and only if

$$\alpha(1 + q) - \alpha^2 \underline{\rho} < 1. \tag{8.9}$$

There is an important difference between the coordinated hoarding criterion (8.3) and the autarky hoarding criterion (8.9). In autarky the firm is forced to hoard the initial investment ($\ell = I$) in order to continue at full scale, while in the coordinated solution it suffices to hoard $\ell = (1 - \alpha)I$, because liquidity is optimally shared. So hoarding is more costly in autarky and the cutoff criterion for hoarding therefore more stringent. If there is hoarding in autarky, there will be hoarding in the coordinated case as well. Moreover there is a region of α for which there is no hoarding in autarky even though there is hoarding in the coordinated case.[3]

8.1.2 Self-provision of Liquidity with Resale

Suppose now that at date 1 a spot market opens in which the intact firms may sell their widgets (for which they have no use) to distressed firms. The distressed firms pay for these widgets by issuing claims on their pledgeable income. In addition the distressed firms can rescue long-term assets by using widgets procured at date 0. We first investigate the case where widgets have no alternative use and hence are all sold to distressed firms.

No Alternative Use for Widgets ($\underline{\rho} = 0$)   We first show that without an outside option for liquidity—a "baseball field" in the parable of the introduction to chapter 7—trading in a date-1 spot market always achieves the second-best outcome. To this purpose we show that the firm's optimization program is equivalent to the second-best, full-coordination program described in section 8.1.1 above.

Let p be the date-1 spot price for widgets. The firm's problem is solved by the program

$$\max_{\{I,\ell,m\}}\{(\rho_1 - \rho_0)\,[\alpha I + (1-\alpha)(\ell + m)]\}, \tag{8.10}$$

subject to

(i) $pm \le \rho_0(\ell + m)$,

(ii) $I + q\ell - A \le \alpha(\rho_0 I + p\ell) + (1-\alpha)[\rho_0(\ell + m) - pm]$,

(iii) $\ell + m \le I$.

Constraint (i) is the firm's date-1 liquidity constraint, which limits purchases m to no more than the pledgeable income. Constraint (ii) is

---

3. Let $\tilde{\alpha}(\rho)$ denote the solution of

$$\alpha(1 + q) - \alpha^2\rho = 1.$$

Note that $\tilde{\alpha}(q) = \frac{1}{q}$ (the cutoff found in the perfectly corrdinated solution), that $\tilde{\alpha}(0) = \frac{1}{1+q}$, and that for all $\underline{\rho} < q, \tilde{\alpha}(\underline{\rho}) < \frac{1}{q}$. The region with hoarding only in the coordinated case is the interval $(\tilde{\alpha}(\underline{\rho}), \frac{1}{q})$.

the date-0 budget constraint and constraint (iii) limits the continuation to the initial scale of investment. The objective function maximizes the entrepreneur's gross utility; because the budget constraint will bind, the entrepreneur obtains all the social surplus.

Since an intact firm has no other outlet for its stored widgets than the spot market, all the widgets must in the date-1 equilibrium be transferred from the intact firms to the distressed firms (without aggregate uncertainty, there is no point in buying more widgets than are needed in equilibrium). This gives the equilibrium condition

$$\alpha \ell = (1 - \alpha)m. \tag{8.11}$$

Adding up the individual firms' liquidity constraints (i) and the date-1 market-clearing condition (8.11) yields the following condition that p must satisfy:

$$p \leq \frac{\rho_0}{\alpha}. \tag{8.12}$$

To build some intuition for the solution, it is helpful to consider the relative attractiveness of investments in short-term and long-term assets, ignoring the liquidity constraint (i) and the feasibility constraint (iii). That is, we look at the benefit of investing in ℓ, m, and I relative to the budget expenditure.

Consider first the choice of acquiring widgets in the *primary* versus the *secondary* market: a firm can procure widgets ℓ at date 0 for price q or widgets m at date 1 for price p. Suppose $p > q$ and $m > 0$, and consider the effect of substituting a unit of ℓ for a unit of m in the firm's program (8.10). This will loosen the firm's budget constraint (ii) by $(p - q) > 0$, loosen the firm's liquidity constraint (i) by p, and leave the firm's objective and the technological constraint (iii) unaltered. The entrepreneur could therefore do strictly better by reducing m all the way down to 0. But at zero demand, the date-1 equilibrium price cannot be positive, a contradiction. So in equilibrium we must have $p \leq q$. Running the substitution argument in reverse, we see that $p < q$ implies that the liquidity constraint (i) of (8.10) must bind, else the entrepreneur could do better by substituting m for ℓ. Note also that the liquidity constraint (i) of (8.10) can bind only if $p \geq \rho_0$. We have established that the equilibrium price must satisfy

$$\rho_0 \leq p \leq q. \tag{8.13}$$

With these preliminaries we proceed to analyze the four regions of α that characterize the solution to program (8.10), and show that in the absence of an alternative use for liquidity at date 1, the outcome will be efficient.

Region I $(0 < \alpha \le \rho_0/q)$:   *Widgets resold at their purchase price*

In this region there are few intact firms (α is small), so widgets are in high demand and command a high price in the secondary market. For this reason we conjecture that the equilibrium price will be at its upper bound, $p = q$, (see (8.13)). We also conjecture that the firm's liquidity constraint is slack at this price and relax the firm's program by ignoring this constraint. We will come back to verify that both conjectures are true in equilibrium in the indicated range of α.

When $p = q$ the firm's budget constraint (ii) of (8.10) can be written

$$I + q(1 - \alpha)(\ell + m) - A \le \alpha\rho_0 I + (1 - \alpha)\rho_0(\ell + m). \tag{8.14}$$

In the relaxed program, where the firm's liquidity constraint is dropped, only the choices I and $i = \ell + m$ matter. We can therefore impose the additional constraint

$$m = \alpha i \quad \text{and} \quad \ell = (1 - \alpha)i \tag{8.15}$$

and restrict the firm to chosing ℓ and m along this ray. Substituting (8.15) and $p = q$ into the firm's liquidity constraint, we get

$$\alpha q \le \rho_0 < 1. \tag{8.16}$$

We see that on the ray (8.15) the validity of the liquidity constraint does not depend on i. The constraint (8.16) will be satisfied if and only if $\alpha \le \rho_0/q$, which is the upper bound of region I. So the solution to the relaxed program (without liquidity constraint) satisfies the liquidity constraint in region I when $p = q$. Finally, it is immediate that the market equilibrium condition (8.11) holds whenever the firm chooses ℓ and m along the ray (8.15); indeed the ray condition is equivalent to the market equilibrium condition as we noted earlier.

We have verified that the equilibrium in region I entails $p = q$ with the representative firm choosing $m = \alpha I$, $\ell = (1 - \alpha)I$, where (using the budget constraint)

$$I = \frac{A}{1 + q(1 - \alpha) - \rho_0}. \tag{8.17}$$

In region I the firm's liquidity constraint will be slack until α hits its upper bound. Conversely, note that if the liquidity constraint is slack, we must have $p = q$ or else the firm would do better either by buying all its liquidity at date 0 or at date 1, violating the equilibrium condition. The ex post competition for scarce liquidity goes hand in hand with a nonbinding liquidity constraint.

It is more surprising that the uncoordinated equilibrium in region I is actually the same as the second-best solution obtained by coordinating liquidity purchases (as in the benchmark model discussed earlier). This can be verified directly by solving the second-best program (8.1). But it is more instructive to check that the firm's program (8.10) is identical with the second-best program when $p = q$. Notice that the liquidity constraint in the firm's program is irrelevant in region I. Condition (8.15) assures that the date-1 resource constraint in the second-best program is satisfied regardless of i. When one substitutes $p = q$ and (8.15) into the firm's budget contraint (8.14) and the second-best program (8.1), the two programs can be seen to be identical. Finally, note that $\alpha q < 1$, so the second-best program has $i = I$.

Region II $(\rho_0/q < \alpha < \rho_0/\underline{\rho})$: *Resale at a discount*

When $\alpha > \rho_0/q$, the solution in region I no longer works because it violates the firm's liquidity constraint. In region II we therefore expect the liquidity constraint to bind. We proceed with this conjecture and verify that it is true in equilibrium.

The binding liquidity constraint $pm = \rho_0(\ell + m)$, together with the market-clearing condition $\alpha\ell = (1 - \alpha)m$, implies that the market price must be

$$p = \frac{\rho_0}{\alpha} < q. \tag{8.18}$$

The inequality follows from the lower bound of region II. If we insert this equilibrium price into the firm's liquidity constraint then we get $m = \alpha i$, implying that $\ell = (1 - \alpha)i$. So the liquidity constraint at the equilibrium price coincides with the date-1 resource constraint of the second-best program. The firm's budget constraint becomes

$$I + q(1 - \alpha)i - A \leq \alpha\rho_0 I + (1 - \alpha)\rho_0 i + [\alpha p\ell - (1 - \alpha)pm] \\ = \alpha\rho_0 I + (1 - \alpha)\rho_0 i. \tag{8.19}$$

Therefore the budget constraint in the firm's program is identical to the budget constraint in the social program (8.2). We conclude that the firm and the social programs coincide again, and hence the solution in region II will be efficient. The investment I will be given by (8.17) and $i = I$. In particular, firms will buy a strictly positive amount of widgets at date 0.

It may seem surprising that efficiency obtains in region II despite an undervalued resale price ($p < q$). After all, intact firms sell their widgets at too low a price and distressed firms buy them up at an equally low price. Either way, ex ante firms should have an incentive to underhoard widgets. However, this reasoning misses the point that widgets relax the liquidity constraint of distressed firms: The more widgets distressed firms own, the higher their funding liquidity, and consequently the more widgets they can purchase: see the firms' liquidity constraint (i) of (8.10). And the lower the secondary market price p, the more distressed firms can lever up the pledgeable income that stems from their own widgets. As a result, under constant returns to scale there is neither underhoarding nor overhoarding.[4]

Widgets with Alternative Use ($\underline{\rho} > \rho_0 q$)   Without the outside option, region II would extend all the way to $\alpha = 1/q$. The uncoordinated solution would coincide with the coordinated solution for all α. To introduce a source of inefficiency, we assume that there is an alternative use for widgets (a "baseball field" in the langue of chapter 7) that intact firms can make use of. The value of this use is assumed to be $\underline{\rho} > \rho_0 q$, so that $\rho_0/\underline{\rho} < 1/q$, which is the point at which it becomes inefficient in the second-best program to continue.

In region II, as α increases, the equilibrium price $p = \rho_0/\alpha$ falls. The alternative use of widgets implies that

$$p \geq \underline{\rho}. \tag{8.20}$$

---

4. A related issue is what would happen if relatively cheap stores of value (Treasury bonds) were available as well. Would they crowd out widget hoarding by offering a better yield while allowing firms to obtain refinancing? We have not attempted a full analysis, but our guess is that the answer is "no". If widgets are expected to be cheap in the secondary market, then firms will hoard substantial amounts of Treasury bonds to take advantage of fire-sale prices. This will raise the price of widgets until the firms are indifferent between hoarding widgets and hoarding Treasury bonds.

When Treasury bonds are costless (their price is equal to 1), the liquidity constraint is not binding because firms have access to costless liquidity. Then, regardless of the value of other parameters, the widgets trade at no discount in the secondary market: $p = q$.

This constraint binds whenever

$$\alpha > \frac{\rho_0}{\underline{\rho}}, \tag{8.21}$$

which defines the upper bound of region II.

Region III $(\rho_0/\underline{\rho} < \alpha < \alpha_0 < 1/q)$: *Widgets in part converted to the alternative use[5]*

Other things equal, ρ_0 has to be sufficiently small to satisfy (8.21) A small ρ_0 means that the purchasing power of the distressed firms is small; the smaller it is, the more of the intact firms' widgets will go to the alternative use. To be more precise, the liquidity constraint will allow a firm to purchase widgets (at price $p = \underline{\rho}$) up to the amount

$$m = \frac{\rho_0 \ell}{\underline{\rho} - \rho_0}. \tag{8.22}$$

Consider an equilibrium in which some liquidity is converted to the alternative use so that the market price for liquidity is equal to the value of this alternative use:

$$p = \underline{\rho}.$$

There are two cases to consider:

1. *The firm does not withstand the shock.* This strategy, as usual, yields gross utility:

$$U_I^g = \frac{(\rho_1 - \rho_0)A}{(1/\alpha) - \rho_0}.$$

2. *The firm withstands the shock.* The firm then purchases the maximal amount (8.22) and so, as $\ell + m = I$,

$$\ell = \frac{\underline{\rho} - \rho_0}{\underline{\rho}} I.$$

This yields gross utility

$$U_{II}^g = \frac{(\rho_1 - \rho_0)A}{1 + q[(\underline{\rho} - \rho_0)/\underline{\rho}] - \alpha \underline{\rho}}.$$

---

5. The upper limit α_0 will be defined shortly.

For firms to be willing to accumulate liquidity, one must have

$$U_{II}^g \geq U_I^g$$

or

$$1 + q\frac{\rho - \rho_0}{\rho} - \underline{\alpha}\rho \leq \frac{1}{\alpha} - \rho_0. \tag{8.23}$$

Let α_0 be the highest α satisfying (8.23), implicitly defined by

$$1 + q\frac{\rho - \rho_0}{\rho} - \alpha_0\underline{\rho} = \frac{1}{\alpha_0} - \rho_0.$$

Last we need to check that there is enough liquidity on the market to support the suggested solution. This requires that

$$\alpha\ell \geq (1 - \alpha)m,$$

which holds, by (8.22), whenever

$$\alpha \geq \frac{\rho_0}{\underline{\rho}}, \tag{8.24}$$

which together with $\alpha \leq \alpha_0$ from (8.23), defines region III.

If (8.24) is slack, then there is excess liquidity in the market and some of the widgets will be converted to the alternative use. The wasted amount is found (after some manipulations) to be

$$w = \alpha\ell - (1 - \alpha)m = \frac{\alpha\rho - \rho_0}{\rho}I$$

$$= \left(\frac{\alpha\underline{\rho} - \rho_0}{\underline{\rho}}\right)\left(\frac{A}{1 + q\left[(\underline{\rho} - \rho_0)/\underline{\rho}\right] - \alpha\underline{\rho}}\right).$$

With some simple computations, we conclude that

$$\frac{\partial w}{\partial \rho_0} < 0.$$

So a smaller pledgeable income leads to more waste of liquidity.

Region IV $(\alpha > \alpha_0)$: *No investment in liquidity*

Firms may not find it attractive to hoard liquidity at all when the spot price is $\underline{\rho}$. This arises when (8.23) is violated. Firms will not invest in liquidity when $\alpha > \alpha_0$. Note that

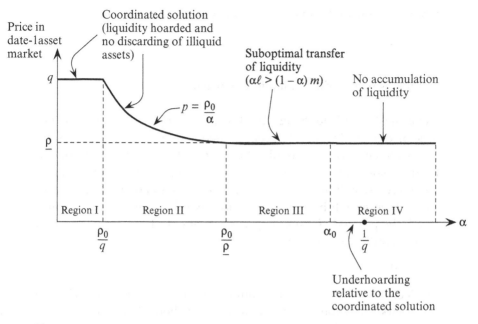

Figure 8.1
Attractive alternative use ($\underline{\rho} > q\rho_0$)

$$\alpha_0 < \frac{1}{q}.$$

Thus the region over which there is investment in liquidity is smaller than that in the coordinated case, giving rise to an inefficiency.

We summarize these findings in figure 8.1 and in

Proposition 8.1 Suppose that there is a date-1 spot market and that the liquidity (widgets) of intact firms can either be turned to an alternative use (with per-unit value $\underline{\rho}$) or be sold to distressed firms. Then

a. Uncoordinated investment in liquidity (self-provision) will replicate the second-best solution if $\alpha \le \rho_0/\underline{\rho}$. The resale price equals the purchase price ($p = q$) if $\alpha \le \rho_0/q$. Otherwise, it involves a discount ($p < q$).

b. Liquidity is wasted (turned into alternative use) when

$$\frac{\rho_0}{\underline{\rho}} < \alpha < \alpha_0,$$

where α_0 is the highest value of α satisfying (8.23), and hence

$$\alpha_0 < \frac{1}{q}.$$

c. There is no hoarding of liquidity when $\alpha > \alpha_0$.

Example: Very Little Pledgeable Income   Suppose that there is very little pledgeable income. The coordinated and uncoordinated cases are then different. Without coordination, a firm that wants to continue in the distressed state can count on getting m widgets from the spot market and therefore will buy at most $\ell = I - m$ widgets at date 0. If ρ_0 is very small, then m will be very small and ℓ will be close to I. If $\underline{\rho}$ is also small, the proceeds from selling widgets at date 1 will be small. So in the uncoordinated case for

$$\rho_0 \simeq 0,$$

the decision whether to hoard liquidity or not at date 0 is very close to the autarky decision, where the firm had to choose between $\ell = I$ and $\ell = 0$. In the autarky case and in the absence of alternative use, we found that the firm would not buy any widgets if $\alpha \geq 1/(1+q)$.[6] This is a lower cutoff than the second-best $\alpha \geq 1/q$. So, if $\rho_0 \simeq 0$, and $\underline{\rho} \simeq 0$, we will have a range of α such that firms in the spot market choose not to buy any widgets, while firms in a coordinated market would buy $\ell = (1 - \alpha)I$. In this limited range $\left(1/(1+q), 1/q\right)$, there is underhoarding of widgets relative to the second best. Conversely, when $\alpha < 1/(1+q)$, we know that the firm will procure $\ell = I$ widgets in the autarky solution, and hence $\ell = I - m \approx I$ when $\rho_0 \simeq 0$. Now there is overhoarding of widgets relative to the second best.

8.1.3   Policy
Regions I and II deliver the coordinated solution, so no policy intervention is called for. Similarly the optimal solution ($\ell = 0$) prevails when $\alpha \geq 1/q$, which is a subset of region IV.

Liquidity is wasted in region III. However, encouraging firms to hoard more liquidity can only reduce welfare, since the problem is that the secondary market price is too low ($p = \underline{\rho}$). Any extra liquidity will only be wasted as it goes to the alternative use. Indeed underhoarding and overhoarding refer to equilibrium investments in liquidity relative to

---

6. Notice that for $\rho_0 = 0$, (8.23) is equivalent to $\alpha \leq 1/(1+q)$ as $\underline{\rho}$ tends to 0.

the second-best, coordinated benchmark studied in section 8.1.1. Therefore liquidity regulation, provided that it is feasible, does not improve welfare.

When overhoarding occurs, the government could force firms to hoard less than I, say, on the second-best level $(1 - \alpha)I$. For ρ_0 small, the distressed firms would not be able to buy liquidity to make up the shortage (e.g., acquire αI when the liquidity is constrained to the coordinated level). Likewise forcing firms to hoard more if they are underhoarding does not help because the extra liquidity does not get transferred at date 1. De facto there is autarky because firms cannot count on buying widgets when distressed.

8.1.4 Asymmetries and Underhoarding

In a two-sector variant of the previous model, the liquidity produced by one group of firms at date 0 is needed by another group of firms at date 1. Because the latter may have little to offer in exchange for liquidity, the former may produce (or procure) insufficient amounts of liquidity. Due to the asymmetry the production of liquidity will have no direct benefit for the producers, and this eliminates the countervailing effect that rules out underhoarding in the symmetric model of the previous section.

An example of such a two-sector economy is given in figure 8.2. Sector 1 consists of a continuum of identical entrepreneurial firms of the type studied in section 3.1. A representative entrepreneur in this sector has initial wealth A and borrows $I - A$ to invest I in LT assets. At date 1, the firm faces a deterministic demand for liquidity. It needs one widget

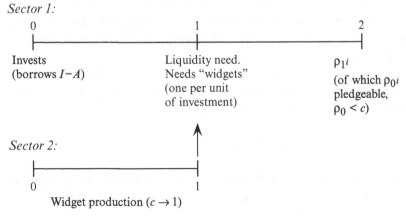

Figure 8.2
Consumers and producers of widgets

per unit of investment in order to continue. Investments, with widgets as inputs, yield, per unit of investment, ρ_1 at date 2, of which ρ_0 is pledgeable. The investment unit costs c with $\rho_1 > 1 + c$ and $c > \rho_0$.

Sector 2 is composed of a continuum of competitive intermediaries that specialize in the production of widgets. They have a technology that transforms c units of the consumption good at date 0 into 1 widget at date 1. The economy is such that:

• Widgets have no alternative use at date 1. Widgets produced by sector 2 are of no value to consumers; neither do they have any value to sector-2 firms (so inefficient date-1 allocations of the type studied in the previous sections do not arise).

• Firms in sector 1 have no access to the widget-producing technology. In particular, widgets in this sector should not be thought of as Treasury bonds or other liquid assets; actually, we will shortly assume that no such store of value is available in the economy. Nor can firms in sector 1 secure in advance a supply of widgets through contracts or cross-ownership of firms in sector 2. Trading of widgets can only occur on a date-1 spot market.

• There is no outside liquidity, and hence no stores of value that firms in sector 1 could use to pay for widgets at date 1.

It is easy to see that no production can take place in this economy. The only way firms in sector 1 can pay for widgets on the date-1 spot market is by offering their securities to sector-2 firms, that is offering claims on their pledgeable income. But because $\rho_0 < c$, a sector-1 entrepreneur cannot pledge enough to make it worthwhile for sector-2 entrepreneurs to invest. In the anticipated absence of widgets, sector-1 entrepreneurs do not invest either. Yet, investment is desirable (and would occur if the two sectors could coordinate their plans at date 0) as long as $\rho_1 > 1 + c$.

Compare this with the case where firms can coordinate plans. The consolidated net present value for the economy is $(\rho_1 - 1 - c) I$. The representative firm in sector 1 invests I, where

$$(1+c)I - A = \rho_0 I \quad \text{or} \quad I = \frac{A}{1 + c - \rho_0}.$$

Sector 1 finances the date-0 investment in widgets by issuing claims on its future income and by transferring date-0 endowment so as to make up for the shortfall $(c - \rho_0)I$.

Note that the coordination failure highlighted here—the failure to contract at date 0—differs from the standard, multiple-equilibrium coordination failure developed in the literature on strategic complementarities (e.g., Hart 1979). In our example there is only one equilibrium. Relatedly, if ρ_0 were greater than c, the problem we have identified would be moot, but the standard coordination failure could still arise—a bad equilibrium in which sector 1 does not invest because it anticipates that sector 2 will not invest, and conversely.

Policy If date-0 contracting proves infeasible, the creation at date 0 of outside liquidity (stores of value) that can be hoarded by firms in sector 1 and traded at date 1 against the widgets produced by sector 2 improves welfare provided that the standard coordination failure is avoided: firms in sector 2 invest in widgets at date 0 if they expect firms in sector 1 to invest in liquid assets and make up for the income shortfall $c - \rho_0$ per unit, and conversely.

A Possible Interpretation The logic of our example can be used to illustrate a key distinction between intermediated and direct finance. A large theoretical and empirical literature emphasizes the need for firms with serious agency problems to resort to costly monitoring by intermediaries as a way to alleviate the agency problem and to create more pledgeable income (e.g., see Diamond 1984; Gorton and Whinton 2003; Holmström and Tirole 1997). Firms with low agency costs, in contrast, have direct access to (cheaper) market finance. In this context, the situation depicted in figure 8.2 can be given the following interpretation: At date 1, firms may face a shock that aggravates the agency problem. For example, new opportunities for misbehavior may appear, or bad news that the entrepreneur's stake in the firm has decreased may make him more prone to waste resources or to gamble for resurrection. Continuation then calls for monitoring by intermediaries. Monitoring at date 1, however, requires that intermediaries hoard resources ("widgets") at date 0, since they must build human capital (c represents the cost of dedicating personnel who are specialized in sector 1). Nevertheless, intermediaries will not have the incentive to invest in monitoring expertise because the firms lack pledgeable income with which to pay for intermediary services at date 1 (we are assuming here that firms cannot arrange for intermediary services in advance, the same way that sector-1 entrepreneurs could not contract in advance with sector-2 producers of widgets in the formal treatment above).[7]

---

7. This interpretation points to a difficulty one is likely to encounter when trying to measure aggregate liquidity in an industry or a country. Liquidity is provided by the stock of

To assume that no production can take place in the absence of monitoring (our interpretation of widgets) is a bit extreme. More generally, one could follow Holmström and Tirole (1997) and assume that monitoring reduces moral hazard and thereby increases pledgeable income. But for the sake of simplicity, consider the case where nothing is pledgeable in the absence of monitoring. The entrepreneurs in sector 1 can then invest $I = A$ in the absence of monitoring and $I = A/(1 + c - \rho_0)$ with monitoring and coordination. If a firm waits until date 1 to secure monitoring, it can invest only $I = A$, since at that point it is unable to pay monitors. As a result monitors will not invest at date 0.

8.2 Application to Uncoordinated International Liquidity Provision

8.2.1 Framework and the Coordinated Benchmark

We begin with a brief review of the international liquidity model of chapter 6.

Goods and Preferences   There are two kinds of goods:

• *Tradable goods*, which are consumed by foreigners as well as domestic residents. These goods will at times be called *dollar goods* or simply dollars.

• *Nontradable goods*, which only domestic residents consume. These goods are called *peso goods* or pesos.

Variables with the superscript "$" refer to dollars, and all variables without superscripts refer to pesos.

There are three periods, $t = 0, 1, 2$. We assume that economic agents only care about their total consumptions at the three dates, and therefore demand a zero expected rate of return on investments. Mainly for convenience, we have domestic residents view tradables and nontradables as perfect substitutes. Thus a foreigner's utility from the consumption stream $\{c_t^\$\}_{t=0,1,2}$ is

$$\sum_{t=0}^{2} c_t^\$,$$

---

knowledge held by intermediaries about the industry (or in the context of international crises, by the foreign financial institutions about the country's firms and markets), as well as by their own financial strength. Such variables are by no means easy to measure.

while a domestic resident's utility from the consumption stream $\{(c_t^\$, c_t)\}_{t=0,1,2}$ is

$$\sum_{t=0}^{2} \left[c_t^\$ + c_t \right].$$

We use date-0 pesos as our numéraire. All uncertainty is revealed at date 1.

Technologies and Timing   There is a continuum of ex ante identical domestic firms of mass 1. Ex post (date 1) a known fraction α of them remain *intact* and the remaining fraction $(1 - \alpha)$ will be *distressed*. To simplify notation, intact firms do not have to make any additional investments at date 1 ($\rho_L = 0$), whereas distressed firms are hit by a high liquidity shock normalized to have value $\rho_H = 1$.

The flows of tradable (dollar) and nontradable (peso) goods for a representative firm are depicted in figure 8.3.

The representative firm has an endowment $A^\$ > 0$ of pledgeable dollar goods at date 0. All investments are in dollars and all outputs in pesos. The technology is constant returns to scale. At date 0, the firm invests $I^\$$ dollars in a long-term project, leaving $\ell^\$ = A^\$ - I^\$$ dollars in reserve. We let the parameter values be such that it is optimal in the coordinated solution to continue at full scale, $I^\$$, even in the high shock state. At date 2, the firm produces $\rho_1 I^\$$ of which $\rho_0 I^\$$ is pledgeable, all in pesos. We have deliberately chosen a specification in which all inputs are tradable to ensure (as will become evident) that there is no role for government-provided liquidity if firms coordinate their use of liquidity.[8]

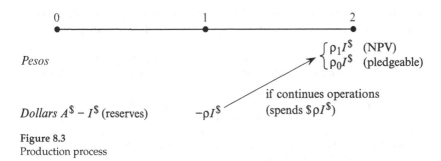

Figure 8.3
Production process

---

8. This is very different from the model in chapter 6. There we focused on the value of international collateral in supporting second-best insurance. Also note that the firm does

Full Coordination   Our benchmark is the fully coordinated solution, which we calculate first. Since shocks are idiosyncratic, date-1 aggregate demand for liquidity is deterministic. Given our special assumptions $\rho_L = 0$ and $\rho_H = 1$, the aggregate demand is $\ell^\$ = (1 - \alpha)I^\$$ if firms want to continue at full scale. Foreigners must be paid in dollars. The only source of dollars is the representative firm's pledgeable endowment $A^\$$, which is split between the initial investment $I^\$$ and reinvestment $A^\$ - I^\$$. The budget constraint is

$$I^\$ + (1 - \alpha)I^\$ = A^\$, \tag{8.25}$$

implying that

$$I^\$ = \frac{A^\$}{1 + (1 - \alpha)}. \tag{8.26}$$

The representative firm's gross utility, if it holds enough reserves to cover the high liquidity shock, is

$$U^g = \frac{\rho_1}{2 - \alpha}A^\$.$$

The policy of holding no reserves would yield investment $I^\$ = A^\$$ and a gross value $U^g = \alpha\rho_1 A^\$$. Provided that $1 > \alpha(2 - \alpha)$, it is optimal to hoard reserves.

To meet the high liquidity shock, the corporate sector must have $(1 - \alpha)I^\$$ dollars at date 1 and find a way to dispatch liquidity to those firms hit by the high shock. As in the previous chapter, we assume that institutions for coordinating liquidity use are not available. [9] Instead, liquidity will be allocated in a spot market at date 1.[10]

8.2.2   No Coordination: A Date-1 Spot Market
When firms act on their own without any advance agreements on how liquidity is to be used, the date-1 spot market determines how excess

---

not borrow at date 0, as (1) domestic investors cannot buy dollar goods and (2) foreign investors can lend dollar goods but will demand them back, a wash in terms of access to tradables.

9. Even though there is only aggregate risk, so that all firms are hit by the same shock, the second-best solution is the same as for the idiosyncratic case discussed above. However, international investors may find it easier to insure country shocks, since these are more readily identified. If foreign investors can insure country shocks, there is no need for firms to coordinate their liquidity purchases.

10. Because there is no aggregate uncertainty, there is no need for state-contingent government bonds.

dollar reserves get reallocated. The market is similar to the spot market for liquidity in section 8.1. Intact firms can do one of two things. They can hand over their dollar reserves to distressed firms in exchange for date-2 peso goods (paid out of the $\rho_0 I^\$$ income); alternatively, they can choose to consume their dollar reserves, which they value the same as peso goods. However, consumption is an inferior use of dollar reserves, just like the "baseball field" was an inferior use of land in chapter 7. The value of consumption implies that the inferior use of dollars is worth

$$\rho = 1 < \rho_1.$$

Let e_1 be the date-1 real exchange rate, defined as the price of the dollar good in terms of the peso good. The real exchange rate must fall in the range

$$1 \leq e_1 \leq \rho_1. \tag{8.27}$$

The lower bound holds because the entrepreneurs of intact firms would prefer to consume the tradable good if e_1 fell below 1. The upper bound holds because a distressed firm does not want to pay more for salvaging a unit of the project than what that unit can produce at date 2. Next we analyze the date-1 spot market.

• *Demand for dollar goods at date 1*   A distressed firm, holding $\ell^\$$ units of dollar reserves, can buy up to $m^\$$ units of dollar goods at date 1, subject to the liquidity constraint

$$e_1 m^\$ \leq \rho_0(\ell^\$ + m^\$). \tag{8.28}$$

The left-hand side of this inequality is the total cost, expressed in peso goods, of buying dollar goods on the spot market. The right-hand side is the amount of peso goods that can be promised in exchange, namely the pledgeable income on salvaged assets ($\ell^\$ + m^\$$). As long as the exchange rate falls within the bounds (8.27), the demand for dollar reserves is given by

$$m^\$ \leq \min\left(\frac{\rho_0 \ell^\$}{e_1 - \rho_0}, I^\$ - \ell^\$ \right). \tag{8.29}$$

Note that the right-hand side of (8.29) is well defined, since $e_1 \geq 1 > \rho_0$. For technological reasons the firm has to choose $m^\$$ so that the reinvestment scale does not exceed the initial investment level:

$$i^\$ \equiv \ell^\$ + m^\$ \leq I^\$ \Leftrightarrow m^\$ \leq I^\$ - \ell^\$. \tag{8.30}$$

• *Supply of dollar goods at date 1*   As in section 8.1.4 intact entrepreneurs are the only agents who can rescue distressed firms. They have dollar reserves and are willing to trade dollars for peso consumption if the spot price is at least as high as the value of consumption. By assumption, domestic consumers do not have dollar reserves. Foreigners do have dollars, but they are unwilling to supply dollars for pesos because they cannot convert peso claims into dollar goods at date 2.

• *Investment in production and in dollar reserves at date 0*   The date-0 gross utility of a representative firm that chooses investments $I^\$$ and $\ell^\$ \leq I^\$$ at date 0 is[11]

$$U^g = \alpha \left[\rho_1 I^\$ + e_1 \ell^\$ \right] + (1 - \alpha) \left[\rho_1 (m^\$ + \ell^\$) - e_1 m^\$ \right]. \tag{8.31}$$

We have grouped the entrepreneur's utility into two terms. The first term is the return when the firm is intact, which happens with probability α; an intact firm produces $\rho_1 I^\$$ and gets $e_1 \ell^\$$ from selling (or consuming) its dollar reserves, which it does not need to continue operations. The second term is the return when the firm is in distress, which happens with probability $1 - \alpha$; a distressed firm can salvage $\ell^\$$ units using its own dollar reserves and $m^\$$ units by buying dollars in the spot market. From (8.29) we see that the firm can purchase dollars in the amount $m^\$ = \rho_0 \ell^\$ / (e_1 - \rho_0)$ as long as the total does not exceed $I^\$ - \ell^\$$.

The entrepreneur will have to pay investments up front because all the investments are in dollars while all the returns are in pesos. Foreigners will not accept pesos as payment, and domestic investors do not, by assumption, have dollars for the investments. The entrepreneur's date-0 budget constraint is therefore simply

$$I^\$ + \ell^\$ \leq A^\$. \tag{8.32}$$

• *Equilibrium in the date-1 spot market*   Supply must weakly exceed demand in the date-1 spot market for dollar goods, so

$$\alpha \ell^\$ \geq (1 - \alpha) m^\$. \tag{8.33}$$

An equilibrium in the date-1 spot market is achieved with the price of dollar goods e_1 set at a level such that when the representative firm maximizes (8.31) subject to (8.29) and (8.32), the inequality (8.33) is satisfied, and holds as an equality whenever $e_1 > 1$. It is easy to see that an equilibrium always exists.

---

11. Recall that the firm does not borrow at date 0.

At a firm optimum, the budget constraint (8.32) is always binding. Substituting $I^\$ = A^\$ - \ell^\$$ into the objective function (8.31), we find that the derivatives of the objective function with respect to $\ell^\$$ and $m^\$$ are

$$\alpha e_1 + (1 - 2\alpha)\rho_1$$

and

$$(1 - \alpha)(\rho_1 - e_1) \geq 0,$$

respectively. Note that whenever

$$e_1 < \rho_1,$$

the derivative with respect to $m^\$$ is positive (purchasing liquidity is cheap), so the liquidity constraint must be binding:

$$(e_1 - \rho_0)m^\$ = \rho_0 \ell^\$. \tag{8.34}$$

Also there would be no activity in the date-1 market if e_1 were above ρ_1, verifying formally the upper bound of (8.27).

No Ex post Waste of Liquidity Suppose $e_1 > 1$. Then (8.33) is an equality as supply must equal demand. Combining the market equilibrium condition with a binding liquidity constraint gives the following price for the equilibrium in the date-1 dollar market:

$$e_1 = \frac{\rho_0}{\alpha}. \tag{8.35}$$

This equilibrium price prevails, provided that e_1 falls in the interval (8.27), that is,

$$1 < \frac{\rho_0}{\alpha} < \rho_1. \tag{8.36}$$

Substituting (8.35) into (8.34), we see that $(1 - \alpha)m^\$ = \alpha \ell^\$$ or equivalently that $m^\$ = \alpha i$ and $\ell^\$ = (1 - \alpha)i^\$$, where $i^\$ \equiv m^\$ + \ell^\$$ is the continuation scale of distressed firms. The technology requires $i^\$ \leq I^\$$. When we insert the expressions for $\ell^\$$ and $m^\$$ into the firm's objective function, we see that it is optimal to choose $i^\$ = I^\$$. The representative firm's gross utility then becomes

$$U^g = \rho_1 I^\$ = \rho_1(A^\$ - \ell^\$).$$

We note in passing that when the price given by (8.35) prevails, the amount that the intact firms make on selling dollars at date 1 equals the amount that the distressed firms pay for the dollars, regardless of the level of continuation investment $i^\$$. This is, of course, always the case in equilibrium if all the dollars get transferred from intact to distressed firms. Because $\ell^\$ = (1 - \alpha)I^\$$, the equilibrium allocation coincides with the second-best allocation, in analogy with the analysis in section 8.1.2. There is no waste of dollars.

The price given by (8.35) has to fall within the bounds defined by (8.36). For $\alpha \leq \rho_0/\rho_1$, the date-1 price is at its upper bound

$$e_1 = \rho_1.$$

In this region

$$U^g = \alpha\rho_1 A^\$ + (1 - \alpha)\rho_1 \ell^\$,$$

where $\ell^\$$ is determined by the liquidity and budget constraints after substituting $I^\$ = A^\$ - \ell^\$$. The representative firm's utility is

$$U^g = \frac{\rho_1 A^\$}{2 - \alpha}.$$

We conclude that also in this case the uncoordinated solution coincides with the coordinated solution.

Ex post Waste of Liquidity   We finally consider the case where the equilibrium occurs on the boundary $e_1 = 1$, in which case some dollar reserves are consumed rather than transferred to salvage distressed assets. For $\alpha > \rho_0$, the exchange rate given by (8.35) lies below 1, so we must have

$$e_1 = 1.$$

In this price regime it can be optimal for firms not to buy any liquidity at all at date 0. This happens if α is high enough and the pledgeable income low. If firms do buy liquidity, supply will exceed demand:

$$\alpha\ell^\$ > (1 - \alpha)m^\$.$$

The excess supply of liquidity is consumed by the intact entrepreneurs, who are indifferent between selling into the market and consuming when $e_1 = 1$. Putting liquidity to an inferior, alternative use is, of course, wasteful from a social perspective. Note, however, that distressed firms will be able to continue at full scale. Knowing that they

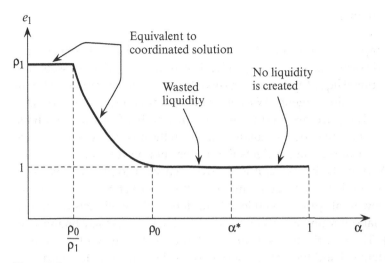

Figure 8.4
Exchange rate when liquidity is not coordinated

cannot afford to buy much in the market (despite the price being as low as it can go), they hoard more liquidity at date 0. In the limit, as ρ_0 goes to zero, and distressed firms have no purchasing power at date 1, the situation will be the same as in autarky—either firms hoard $\ell^{\$} = A^{\$}/2$ of liquidity or they do not buy any. When the distressed firms have a bit of purchasing power ($\rho_0 > 0$), they can reduce $\ell^{\$}$ a bit.

It is tedious, but straightforward, to determine when firms opt to buy liquidity and when they do not. The optimum either occurs at the intersection of the budget and the liquidity constraint or at the origin. We have

(i) $\ell^{\$} = m^{\$} = 0$ and $U^{g} = \alpha \rho_1 A^{\$}$

if $\alpha > \dfrac{\rho_1 + (\rho_1 - 1)\rho_0}{2\rho_1 - 1}$,

(ii) $\ell^{\$} = \dfrac{1 - \rho_0}{2 - \rho_0} A^{\$}$, $m^{\$} \equiv \dfrac{\rho_0}{2 - \rho_0} A^{\$}$, and $U^{g} = \left[\dfrac{\alpha + \rho_1 - \rho_0}{2 - \rho_0}\right] A^{\$}$,

if $\dfrac{\rho_1}{2\rho_1 - 1} < \alpha \leq \dfrac{\rho_1 + (\rho_1 - 1)\rho_0}{2\rho_1 - 1}$.

Our results are summarized in figure 8.4, which is, for obvious reasons, similar to figure 8.1.

8.3 Summary

This chapter explored incentives for uncoordinated investments in specialized assets—or widgets (e.g., physical inputs, knowledge assets, and international liquidity)—that can serve to rescue the operations of financially constrained agents. Widgets trade at a discount in the secondary market. The price discount raises the concern that firms will not have the right incentive to accumulate widgets. If the secondary-market price is low, a firm reselling widgets that it does not need will face a capital loss. And on the buy side, it is relatively cheaper to purchase widgets in the secondary market than in the primary market. So it would seem that a low resale price would lead to undersupply of widgets relative to the social optimum, a key conclusion in Caballero and Krishnamurthy (2001). The surprising result in this chapter is that when firms are ex ante identical and the only imperfection is their inability to coordinate in advance the purchase and use of liquidity, the price of widgets will remain high enough to encourage efficient hoarding.

While it is correct that a suboptimal price discourages hoarding widgets, the reasoning above misses another effect: in the absence of alternative stores of value (e.g., Treasury bonds), hoarding widgets provides date-1 funding liquidity (beyond the ability to dilute the initial investors—with their ex ante consent—by issuing new securities). This relaxes the liquidity constraint and creates an additional incentive to hoard widgets as a store of value. The incentive is higher, the lower the secondary-market price, and in our model the incentive to hoard widgets is in the end socially optimal. The only situation where self-provision of widgets does not replicate the coordinated outcome is when the distressed firms have so little aggregate purchasing power that some of the widgets will be turned into the alternative use. In this case there is nothing the government can do to improve welfare.

One reason why we get efficiency, whereas Caballero and Krishnamurthy (2001) could conclude that investment in liquidity (investment in dollars, to be more specific) is suboptimal, is that our investors have more commitment power. In particular, our investors allow firms to issue new shares when liquidity is needed. Because intact firms have no use for additional funds, this right will not be abused. One could argue that it would be more realistic to assume that intact firms would abuse the right to dilute initial shareholders (as in appendix 2A and in Caballero and Krishnamurthy 2001). Nevertheless, our analysis, when juxtaposed with Caballero and Krishnamurthy's analysis, identifies the inability to control the firms' use of funds as a key assumption in their underinvestment result.

Underinvestment occurs, perhaps more naturally, when there is a separation between the producers of widgets and the users of widgets as suggested by the asymmetric case discussed in section 8.1.4. The shortage of pledgeable income of the buyers of widgets discourages the sellers from investing in widgets, as in the intuitive reasoning above. The extra effect on funding liquidity is missing. We showed that there may be scope for policy intervention, in particular, the creation of stores of value that would make it possible for the buyers of widgets to pay a high enough price to sellers thanks to higher savings.

The findings in this chapter are still tentative. While we have delivered some new insights into policy intervention, we have not attempted to deliver clear guidelines. Moreover we have not yet investigated whether the reasons for the absence of forward markets could interact with the overall logic of this chapter. So the analysis of this chapter should be read with caution when it comes to drawing policy recommendations.

Epilogue: Summary and Concluding Thoughts on the Subprime Crisis

We started our research on liquidity over fifteen years ago with the aim of understanding the role of liquidity (collateral) shortages in financial crises.[1] We close this book with some reflections on what our approach can tell us about the ongoing subprime crisis. We begin by summarizing the key themes and insights of the book, before getting into the crisis itself.

The Main Ingredients and Insights

Our approach is based on two key premises. The first is that income streams are not fully pledgeable.[2] Only part of the pie that a firm creates can be credibly pledged to investors,[3] and consumers cannot pledge any of their future income without collateral or through government taxation.[4] The second premise is that arbitrary, state-contingent contracts can be written on pledgeable income as in the standard Arrow–Debreu general equilibrium model. The critical departure from the Arrow–Debreu model is the first assumption that there is a wedge between total income and pledgeable income. Introducing a wedge extends the

---

1. We were inspired by the severe financial crises in Scandinavia in 1991–92 and later in Asia in 1997.

2. Recall that *pledgeable income, liquidity,* and *collateral* are terms used interchangably in this book, including this epilogue.

3. Firms have to give up some of the income to management, workers, and monitors (e.g., venture capitalists) who share in the rents created by firms; how much depends on many factors that we lump together into an nonpledgeable share of the pie.

4. This modeling assumption is a caricature of reality, of course. Unsecured consumer debt in the form of credit cards, for instance, is not trivial but still relatively small in comparison with collateralized debt such as housing.

standard complete market model to a slightly more realistic setting with surprisingly powerful implications.[5]

The first implication is that firms and financial institutions will have a demand for liquidity despite everyone being risk neutral. In contrast to the Arrow–Debreu model, where firms can fund all positive net present value projects on a pay-as-you-go basis, in our model firms have to arrange funding in advance to avoid credit rationing in states where their pledgeable income is insufficient to fund desirable continuation investments. The firms' demand for liquidity is a demand for insurance against future credit rationing. With a limited net worth, the firm has to choose how much of its capital to spend on future liquidity and how much on current investment. In general the trade-off results in the firm being credit rationed both today and in the future.

A second implication of partial pledgeability of income is that it reduces the supply of liquidity. Investors (and financial institutions) need collateral to back up their promises for future funding of firms. If the corporate sector's pledgeable income in some state of nature is too small, there will be a shortage of aggregate inside liquidity in that state. It is the potential for aggregate liquidity shortages and their consequences for liquidity premia, investment decisions, and government policies that constitute the central and most original part of our analysis.

If the private sector is a net lender, or if it is subject to significant aggregate shocks, there is always insufficient inside liquidity. However, when the private sector is a net borrower and shocks are idiosyncratic, the private sector is self-sufficient. The second-best solution nonetheless requires state-contingent insurance that transfers liquidity from the intact to the distressed firms in an efficient way. Firm-specific credit lines offered by a financial intermediary that holds a well-diversified market portfolio of securities can achieve the required reallocation of liquidity, as can a variety of other state-contingent mechanisms, including the option that firms themselves hold claims in the market portfolio.

In states where there is a shortage of aggregate liquidity, there is a liquidity premium on its supply. The price of liquidity and the value of assets can be determined using a liquidity asset pricing model (LAPM). The value of an asset has two components: the consumption value of its cash flow plus the value (or cost) of the collateral that it produces or requires as part of its investment plan. We study asset pricing using

---

5. We still refer to our model as one with complete markets because the market is complete with respect to the pledgeable income.

techniques familiar from standard general equilibrium models. We find that the equilibrium is efficient subject to the constraint that all contracts must be secured by pledgeable income.

The government can play a key role in making up for aggregate liquidity shortages. Its unique access to current and future consumer income through taxation allows it to act as an intermediary between consumers and firms. It can raise welfare by transferring liquidity from consumers (current and future) to firms in states where the value of such transfers is higher than the shadow cost of public funds. The marginal value of government transfers can be inferred from the state-contingent prices for liquidity in LAPM.

In practice, the government supplies contingent liquidity through a variety of policies and interventions, including the conduct of monetary policy, the provision of deposit insurance, the occasional bailout of commercial banks, investment banks, pension funds and other financial institutions like Freddie Mac and Fannie Mae. Also a whole range of social insurance programs (unemployment insurance and social security, etc.) and of implicit catastrophe insurance (earthquakes, nuclear accidents etc.) play an important role in influencing the amount of aggregate liquidity in the economy.

It is important to stress that government transfers can be seen as part of an explicit or implicit insurance plan. Having taxpayers get involved because private insurance is constrained by limits on aggregate liquidity, makes perfect sense, at least in theory. Moreover the government enjoys an advantage over private parties because it can supply liquidity on a contingent basis. The private sector has to decide ex ante how much liquidity it creates, often by making investments in short-term, physical assets (or just biasing investments in the direction of income that is more readily pledgeable). In contrast, the government can supply liquidity once the need has materialized, saving significantly on the cost of investing in lower-yielding projects. This implies that the state has a particularly strong comparative advantage in offering insurance against unlikely and extreme shocks hitting the economy.

International markets can also alleviate domestic liquidity shortages. However, international markets will not in general eliminate a country's liquidity shortages, even if there is more than enough international liquidity to meet its needs. A country has its own pledgeability limitations: nontradable output, while exchangeable in markets with tradable goods, must in the end go to domestic consumers and has little appeal to international investors as such. When there is a shortage of international liquidity (tradable output), domestic liquidity supply and liquidity management by the government remain effective policies just as in a closed economy.

Assuming that contingent claims markets are complete is, of course, unrealistic. But in return it offers simplicity and discipline. It also provides an upper bound on the supply of aggregate liquidity. When markets are incomplete, aggregate liquidity shortages tend to become accentuated, as coordination problems prevent the efficient use of available liquidity. The burgeoning literature on financial crises employs almost exclusively incomplete market models. By way of illustration, we studied a few models of this sort in part IV. We found that despite market incompleteness, the equilibrium can sometimes be efficient, replicating the outcome of complete contingent contracting. When the equilibrium is inefficient, it may exhibit:

• overhoarding of liquidity before a crisis, because firms invest in liquidity to be able to compete for distressed assets in the future;

• insufficient transfers of liquidity during the crisis to firms whose management cannot be replaced (due to specific knowledge) as firms with excess liquidity prefer to invest in low-productivity projects rather than in firms that need liquidity, but do not have enough pledgeble income to attract the excess liquidity;

• consumer savings behavior that may be too short-termist because consumers are employees of firms and are afraid of being laid off;

• fire-sale prices that deprive the sellers of liquidity when they need it;

• possible underhoarding of liquidity relative to the complete contingent market case, though forcing firms to invest more in liquidity may not solve the problem if the extra reserves can be put to alternative, inferior use (because the spot price is low).

Relating Our Model to the Subprime Crisis

Our understanding of the causes of the subprime crisis is still limited. While it is easy to list a variety of factors that must have played some part in the collapse, there is still disagreement on the major drivers. We will focus on four factors that seem to us particularly central and that form a relatively coherent view of the crisis. These are (1) the global imbalances and the savings glut, (2) the growth of the US shadow banking system in response to the savings glut, (3) the collapse of the wholesale funding market that supported shadow banking, and (4) regulatory deficiencies.[6]

The Savings Glut

There is wide spread agreement that the increasingly large current account deficits that the United States ran up in the new millennium (growing steadily from 4.4 percent of GDP in 2000 to 6.2 percent in 2006) were a major cause of the crisis. Why did the account deficits grow so large? The traditional argument would suggest that US consumers lived beyond their means, needing ever more funds to support their consumption habits. But there is an alternative view, originally put forward by Ben Bernanke, the current chairman of the Federal Reserve. In a widely noticed speech in 2005, he suggested that the problem stemmed from a global savings glut, caused largely, but not exclusively, by excess savings in the emerging markets of Asia. Foreign investors were looking for a safe place to park their excess funds and found it in the United States. The view that money was pushing its way into the United States, rather than being pulled in by a demand for capital, has received wider acceptance lately. One argument in its favor is that interest rates kept falling as the US current account deficit grew. This seems inconsistent with the notion that the US consumer was driving the growth of the deficit.[7]

The notion that Asian money was looking for safe investment opportunities in the United States fits well with our basic premise that a country can have a shortage of aggregate liquidity if pledgeable income is low. In developing economies poorly developed financial markets and political and legal uncertainties generally make the pledgeable income of firms small. Paired with exceptionally high savings ratios, this may well have caused much of the savings to be channeled toward countries with higher fractions of pledgeable income and greater safety.[8]

---

6. Our interpretation of events draws on Adrian and Shin (2008), Caballero et al. (2008), Rochet (2008b), Hellwig (2009), Holmström (2008), Gorton (2008, 2010), chapter 3 in Gylfasson et al. (2010), and Dewatripont et al. (2010), among others.

7. See Caballero et al. (2008) for the "parking space" hypothesis. However, Taylor (2009) has argued that global imbalances played a minor role relative to US monetary policy, which was too lax, keeping interest rates low for too long.

8. These observations fit well with Forbes's (2010) empirical demonstration that foreigners hold greater shares of their investment portfolios in the United States if they have less developed financial markets. She further shows that foreigners, who invested a cumulative $6.2 trillion between 2002 and 2006 in the United States earned substantially lower returns on their US investments than US investors earned abroad, and that diversification motives do little to explain the patterns of foreign investments in the United States.

The savings glut also could have made it easier for the US housing bubble to emerge.[9] Bubbles augment the stock of stores of value, albeit in a very imperfect way. They risk bursting, and what is worse, they burst at the wrong time for those institutions that seek liquidity from the bubble: when a bubble bursts, not only does it have a negative effect on these institutions' solvency (a wealth effect), it also deprives them of collateral at a moment when it is most valuable (because when liquidity becomes scarcer, interest rates fall, and leveraging one's collateral becomes more attractive).[10]

The Rise of Shadow Banking

Global imbalances, as such, do not explain why the bulk of excess savings flowed into the United States rather than into Europe, for instance.[11] One reason could be the US consumer's willingness to go deep into debt, especially in the low interest rate environment maintained by the Fed at the time. Another possibility is that the United States was especially well positioned to absorb the global savings glut because its financial markets were (and still are) the most advanced in the world. In particular, the United States had come up with a financial innovation that enabled it to absorb huge inflows of capital in a short period of time—the shadow banking system.

The shadow banking system is usually defined as that part of banking (intermediation of credit) that is not explicitly insured by the government.[12] It is comprised of a network of players—investment banks, hedge funds, money market mutual funds (MMMF) and government sponsored entities (GSEs) like Freddie Mac and Fannie Mae among

---

9. There is always some difficulty in identifying empirically the existence of a bubble. In the recent real estate bubble it could be argued that the very large subsidies to house ownership (both direct—e.g., the tax deductibility of interest—and indirect—e.g., low interest rates, the lenient regulatory treatment of asset backed securities, or the implicit insurance given to Freddie Mac and Fannie May) made the fundamentals of real estate very strong if these subsidies were expected to last. See, however, Shiller (2008) for a rather convincing case for the existence of a bubble. For important historical perspectives on bubbles and financial crises, see Kindelberger (1989) and Reinhart and Rogoff (2009).

10. See Farhi and Tirole (2009a); other recent work on bubbles includes Kocherlakota (2009) and Ventura (2010). The latter argues that bubbles can substitute for imperfect capital flows and appear in countries in which productivity is low relative to the rest of the world.

11. The European private sector invested substantial amounts in the United States during the same period.

12. See Potzar et al. (2010).

others—all helping to intermediate credit through the market. The shadow banking system is based on wholesale funding rather than deposits, making it potentially more vulnerable to runs.

The liabilities of the shadow banks grew rapidly from less than 10 percent of total bank liabilities in 1980 to about 60 percent in 2008.[13] The growth rate was especially strong after 1995. That the yearly growth of gross liabilities was of the same order of magnitude as the yearly US trade deficits suggests that shadow banks must have played a central role in intermediating the vast amounts of money that flowed into the United States.

The shadow banking system has been widely implicated in the crisis. Many see the whole system as a scam, driven by excessive short-term incentives for bankers on Wall Street. Some of these accusations are certainly valid. But the original driver of the growth of shadow banking must, in the first instance, have been its ability to respond to the international demand for safe investment opportunities. In particular, the repo market, which is at the core of shadow banking, offered a form of secured lending that emulated many of the features of demand deposits in commercial banking.

To understand how, let us briefly discuss the repo market. A repo (repurchase agreement) consists of two simultaneous transactions. In the first, party A buys a security (almost always debt) from party B at a price that typically is below the value of the security (the difference is called the "haircut"). In the second transaction, party B agrees to buy back the security for a slightly higher price at a later date (the next day, in case of an overnight repo). By rolling over an overnight repo until one or the other party withdraws, the repo becomes similar to a deposit. If party A decides not to roll over an overnight repo, the effect is the same as the withdrawal of the deposit. However, unlike traditional banking, the repo market was designed to secure hugely bigger deposits—typically millions or even hundreds of millions of dollars in a single trade.

Federal deposit insurance would provide minimal protection for investments of this size. In contrast, the repo market, by selling a security in exchange for the deposit, could provide insurance on the appropriate scale. There is a key legal detail in the repo contract that makes it so effective: if party B (the borrower) cannot repurchase a security when party A (the investor) demands it (i.e., pay back A's deposit), party A

---

13. Figure 1 in Potzar et al. (2010).

owns the security and is immediately free to sell it or use it as collateral in another repo transaction. Structuring things as a purchase and repurchase agreement is ingenious because it avoids having a multimillion dollar deposit tied up in a bankruptcy process if party B defaults. Unlike traditional banking, repo markets were highly scaleable without much (apparent) risk. The only limitation was really the supply of securities and the assets underlying them.

The raw material for creating new securities came mostly from housing. There are several reasons for this. Housing is by far the largest consumer asset. But before the era of modern financial engineering, housing was an underdeveloped asset. Keeping mortgages on the books of regional banks was like operating a severely underutilized financial parking lot: mortgages that could serve as collateral for millions of investors with billions more money were serving just a fraction of the potential investor demand. Likewise US homeowners who had paid off their mortgages were denying foreign investors the opportunity to park their money in US houses with minimal risk. The enormous growth of home equity loans in the 1990s unleashed some of the housing potential. Securitization, especially of mortgages but later on of just about any other kind of asset (car loans, student loans, credit card loans, etc.), made the most of this opportunity. Securitization could deliver highly rated (AAA) bonds out of relatively marginal assets using tranching.[14] The combination of the repo market with asset-backed, highly rated securities created a formidable intermediation machine, one that in appearance no other country could match in terms of legal safety and capacity.

How does securitization and shadow banking fit our theory? A plausible interpretation is that the shadow banking system strived to, and perhaps came close to, replicating the state-contingent use of collateral that is the central ingredient in our model (see chapter 4). By mixing securities to create portfolios that diversified away much of the idiosyncratic risk, parties were left trading aggregate risk. Relatively liquid markets in such risk made it possible to use state-contingent aggregate liquidity more efficiently, as the theory suggests one should. In this view,

---

14. The creation of structured products involves two steps: first, pooling of assets (e.g., mortgages) and, second, issuing of claims against these assets—mainly debt—with varying credit ratings. The second step is tranching. Gorton (2008, 2010) describes in detail how structured products are created. Coval et al. (2009) contains an excellent analysis of how much AAA-rated securities can be created from low subprime mortgages, depending on the correlation of the underlying assets.

securitization created investment instruments that used collateral much more effectively than if the funds had been parked for long periods in nontraded instruments.[15]

The tri-party repo system, which in the United States is a major part of the repo market, illustrates the contingent use of aggregate liquidity.[16] Each day the dealers (borrowers) in the tri-party repo market place collateral (securities) with the clearing banks. The clearing banks provide a number of services, including assistance in optimizing the allocation (and reallocation) of a dealer's collateral to its investors. There are only two banks, JP Morgan Chase and Bank of New York Mellon, which act as clearing banks for tri-party repos, possibly because economies of scale are critical for the allocation of collateral. Bilateral, over-the-counter repos do not offer the same matching efficiencies.[17] Intraday large payment systems, such as the Clearing House Inter-bank Payment System (CHIPS) the main privately held clearing house for large-value transactions in the United States, similarly are designed to make efficient use of limited collateral while concurrently trying to contain systemic risk.[18]

To sum up, the financial innovations that have been so decried lately should, in principle, have raised welfare by allowing a much better use of collateral in the economy. So what is being questioned is not the ideas themselves, but how they were and can be implemented in practice. The collateral underlying the state-contingent claims was not what it was supposed to be. We turn to possible explanations for this failure.

The Panic

We now know that the reliance on wholesale funding, especially on the increasing fraction of overnight lending in the shadow banking system, proved much riskier than investors had imagined. In August

---

15. Regulatory arbitrage was another powerful driver. By moving capital off their balance sheets, commercial banks could evade onerous capital constraints. Capital charges were reduced roughly by a factor of ten when assets were moved into special purpose vehicles (SPVs).

16. For an in-depth analysis of tri-party repos, see the report of the Payments Risk Committee (2010).

17. The tri-party system is not without its problems because the clearing banks are highly exposed during the day, effectively providing huge bridge loans to the broker-dealers. This poses big risks for the clearing banks, which may react abruptly to news about the credit worthiness of their clients. By raising haircuts, or in the extreme, by refusing to roll over a bridge loan for a counterparty, whose risk has increased (e.g., Lehman), they can quickly do significant damage to the position of broker-dealers. See Tuckman (2010).

18. See Rochet and Tirole (1996b) for a description of the working and properties of intraday payment systems.

2007, the market for asset-backed commercial paper (ABCP) collapsed.[19] While the ABCP market was not big enough to set off a panic, the collapse elevated the level of risk as measured by Libor-OIS spreads, for instance. The much larger repo market, mostly secured by AAA-rated products, initially held up, though haircuts increased and the terms of funding became shorter. But when Lehman fell, in September 2008, the myth of repos as secure deposit-like contracts unraveled. Markets for asset-backed securities, which had been very liquid, froze quickly as banks began to question not just the underlying value of mortgage-backed securities but, more important, the counterparty risks caused by impaired mortgage-backed assets. A full-blown panic ensued.

It is difficult to judge whether the asset-backed security ratings were flawed from an ex ante perspective (even though the existence of conflicts of interest makes us suspect that they were) or whether investors were hit by a highly unlikely tail event. Given that many people were concerned about the real estate bubble bursting at some point, too little attention was apparently paid to the consequences of an aggregate shock that could bring down the value of housing across the nation. That said, a drop in the average nominal price of US housing had not occurred since the Great Depression, making it difficult to assess aggregate risks and forecast a 30 percent drop in prices. Also it is clear that the standard mechanics of a balance sheet driven crisis—funding and margin spirals caused by and causing fire sales of assets, flight to quality and strategic hoarding of liquidity—all contributed to the large collapse in prices. This systemic risk, or at least its size, was largely overlooked.

Our complete market model views the panic as an exogenous tail event; it says nothing about how a panic might unfold, since all contracts are made at the beginning.[20] However, it can explain why firms may choose not to buy insurance against rare events. In our model, firms may cut down production dramatically (in the absence of government assistance) when an aggregate shock hits because liquidity is so scarce and the ex ante returns from investing in private insurance to cover such

---

19. See Covitz et al. (2009). The ABCP market was much smaller than the repo market and ABCPs were not tranched (only one type of claim was issued). Banks provided liquidity backstops for the ABCP market, which helped prevent a panic. Subsequently such backstops contributed greatly to the spread of the crisis into commercial banking.

20. A large literature (e.g., Allen and Gale 2000; Caballero and Simsek 2009) shows how one bank's default may propagate in a financial system in which institutions are interdependent through cross-exposures (e.g., in interbank or derivatives markets). The magnitude and impact of the resulting contagion effects depend on the completeness

an eventuality is low. Liquidity could also be scarce because of adverse selection in the market for collateral as illustrated by the analysis in section 7.2. Finally, liquidity could be scarce in states where it is valuable (ex post), but the states are so hard to define that the insurance must be broad and therefore expensive.

The subprime crisis fits these conditions. Arguably, adverse selection, driven by uncertainty about counterparty risks, froze many markets.[21] And even if many saw the possibility of a collapse in house prices, the fact that so few did something about it suggests that either they believed that the consequences would be relatively benign or, as we discuss next, they deliberately gambled on the tail event. Also buying insurance against a catastrophic event may be hard because there is insufficient liquidity (collateral) to back up such insurance. From this point of view, our approach of modeling the collapse as an exogenous event is not an unreasonable starting point for analyzing some aspects of the crisis.[22]

One of the key implications of our model is that there is a role for government in redistributing wealth ex post. Transfers from taxpayers (i.e., consumers) to the corporate sector—including bailouts of banks, to the extent banks are the efficient channel for such transfers—can be rationalized if the government can make pledges on behalf of consumers (including consumers who are not yet born). In practice, such plans take a variety of forms. A looser monetary policy lowers interest rates and transfers resources from consumers to entrepreneurs, by lowering the cost of reinvestments and by providing capital gains for those who own government debt (entrepreneurs buy government bonds in our model).

---

of the structure of claims, on a common understanding of these claims (securities traded in OTC markets can have unforeseen or complex consequences) and on the opaqueness of bilateral exposures (as participants need to know the solvency not only of their counterparties, but also that of their counterparties' counterparties, etc.). While this literature obtains a number of useful insights, cross-exposures are taken as exogenous; in particular, they are unaffected by the regulatory environment (i.e., the centralization and transparency of intra-day payment systems—see Rochet and Tirole 1996b for a description—or the current regulatory push toward central clearing houses for derivative products). Relatedly it is interesting to study the benefits of decentralized systems (in Rochet and Tirole 1996a the benefit is associated with mutual monitoring). We are not aware of research showing how cross-exposures and shortages in aggregate liquidity feed back on each other, but the work of Caballero and Simsek (2009), for example, suggests that fear of propagation may lead liquidity to dry up rather quickly.

21. See, for instance, Acharya and Richardson (2009) and Caballero and Simsek (2009).

22. Of course, at a more detailed level, the crisis was the consequence of many factors, including the (deliberately) complex way the securitized contracts were structured. There is every reason to try to gain a good understanding of how the panic actually evolved.

Also, at a conceptual level, the numerous liquidity facilities provided by the Fed to jump start frozen asset markets in the shadow banking system (TARP, TALF, TLGP, etc.) receive support from our model, though it does not speak to the relative merits of any given liquidity facility.

Regulatory Weaknesses

Of course, government transfers and insurance come with well-known costs. We considered the deadweight losses from taxation but did not consider the moral hazard problems associated with subsidized insurance, especially bailouts that the government was forced to undertake ex post. It is clear that the subprime crisis revealed very significant weaknesses in the regulatory systems that were meant to keep in check moral hazard and other dysfunctional actions. We have taken a normative viewpoint—analyzing how the state should manage aggregate liquidity—rather than a positive one—analyzing the political economy of domestic liquidity management. Our analysis therefore misses a crucial element of the recent subprime crisis. Let us briefly consider how we could embody the positive considerations into our analysis.

Take first the role of the state in the traditional banking sector. One view of regulation has it that the state monitors financial institutions on behalf of retail depositors, clients of insurance companies, pension funds, or MMMFs, making sure that financial institutions are adequately capitalized and operate proper risk management processes so as not to leave the economic agents—or the deposit insurance fund—with an empty shell.[23] Yet in many countries, the state, by ignoring off-balance sheet vehicles, by accepting (at the international level) low capital requirements for the trading book, and by permitting (or failing to check) other actions that circumvented capital requirements, allowed regulated institutions to overlever themselves. The US government also provided many subsidies for real estate investments, including the indirect subsidies to Freddie Mac and Fannie Mae. Subsidies promote excess investment, which according to our models sows the seeds for a subsequent liquidity shortage, because financial institutions trade off how much to invest in productive assets and how much in liquidity (insurance).

Take next the role of the state in the shadow banking sector. Large investment banks were largely unregulated. Yet they and their creditors felt that they could count on a bailout with taxpayer money if the

---

23. This view is developed in more detail in Dewatripont and Tirole (1994).

investment banks got into trouble—indeed the financial markets were stunned when the US authorities let Lehman go under. This implicit access to taxpayers' money has dramatic consequences as it implies that troubled institutions can access funds with little or no market discipline. Observers sometimes point out that many wealthy managers and investors in the shadow banking system lost their shirt and take this as evidence against the moral hazard argument. The point, though, is that the implicit insurance of short-term funding allowed them to gamble with taxpayer money and to continue receiving financing, when they should have de-levered or even shut down.

But why were states eager to rescue institutions in which no small depositor had invested? The answer is "systemic risk," the fear that a default might propagate through the financial system. The combination of interconnectedness and opaqueness of cross-exposures made a default particularly troubling for the financial system, which after the collapse of Lehman had little clue as to how subsequent episodes would unfold and therefore chose safety over almost any risk. The regulators were on the whole too tolerant when they acquiesced to large exposures in opaque OTC derivative markets and thereby accepted that regulated entities would be heavily exposed if large unregulated institutions defaulted. This led to substantial additional commitments of taxpayers' money, which unregulated institutions took advantage of. It would have been wiser to require that derivative contracts between regulated and unregulated institutions be traded in exchanges with a well-capitalized central clearing house as the counterparty. In short, the state supplied liquidity in a way that created moral hazard. Needless to say, our theoretical conclusions on the role of the state as provider of liquidity presume that liquidity is injected in a way that limits moral hazard.

We mentioned above that repo markets may well have strived to emulate the optimal state-contingent use of aggregate liquidity or at least significantly improved the use of the collateral. This comment applies to orderly times in the market. The crisis suggests that coming close to efficiency in normal times may provide no guarantees against a crisis in exceptional times. Put differently, trading systems that emulate contracts are not as good as real contracts, when times get tough. This has been seen many times. Long-Term Capital Management (LTCM) collapsed because its trading strategy did not work in all states of nature. Had there been explicit contingent contracts, perhaps LTCM would have protected itself against the collapse, though it is also possible that it relied on a government bailout. The same was true when portfolio insurance strategies led to mass sales of securities in 1987. The programs that functioned so beautifully against idiosyncratic risks in peaceful times proved worthless, or worse, in the face of a big aggregate shock.

This raises the question of transparency of financial claims and markets and the role of clearinghouses and other financial institutions. With organized markets there is more transparency and better information about outstanding positions and risks (though the portfolio insurance collapse suggests that parties can create complex strategies that are completely hidden from the eyes of the market—intentions are not easily inferred from the way people trade even in organized markets). However, exactly how and where transparency should be provided is not obvious. There is a fundamental paradox embedded in liquidity provision. In order to function well, liquidity providing markets are designed to minimize the need for information acquisition. Debt is the dominant instrument because it is information insensitive.[24] Parties that trade in debt that is sufficiently overcollateralized need not worry about adverse selection stemming from private information about the underlying collateral. It is sufficient to know that there is enough collateral. But, if the purpose of debt is to provide little incentives for information acquisition about credit risk, it is hard to see how debt markets can properly reflect the price of systemic risk. The suddenness with which financial crises typically appear is consistent with lack of information about systemic risk. To remedy the situation, the government will have to find a way to produce such information (e.g., through periodic stress tests) or come up with some way to make the markets produce better information (e.g., by requiring trade in instruments that are more information sensitive).

---

24. Gorton and Penacchi (1990) argued that banks, by issuing riskless debt, allow depositors to avoid the costs of adverse selection. Dang et al. (2010) analyze a model where risky debt is optimal because it is least information sensitive in the sense that parties will have the lowest incentive to collect information. For this reason debt maximizes the amount of wealth that can be transported from one period to the next. The paper also shows that bad news about the aggregate state of the economy (e.g., lower housing prices) will result in write-downs of debt sometimes exceeding the reduction in the fundamental value of debt to prevent costly information acquisition. So the reduction in trade is amplified by bad news, which is one of the manifestations of a crisis.

The transition from an information-insensitive to an information-sensitive security helps us understand why trading partners were so ill informed about the complex securities they were trading before the crisis and why they wanted to know so much more about the securities once the crisis broke out. In the logic of the model, this is privately rational. See also Pagano and Volpin (2009).

In order to understand the role of systemic risk, how it should be measured and what types of transparency will provide information about it, one has to move away from the complete market model to a model that offers a deeper understanding of how crises erupt and what kinds of warning signs about the systemic risk one should follow. Building the conceptual foundation for measuring systemic risk remains a challenging task.

Bibliography

Acharya, V., and M. Richardson. 2009. *Restoring Financial Stability: How to Repair a Failed System*. Hoboken, NJ: Wiley-VCH.

Acharya, V., D. Gale, and T. Yorulmazer. 2009. Rollover risk and market freezes. Working paper. Federal Reserve Bank of New York.

Adrian, T., and H. Shin. 2008. Financial intermediaries, financial stability and monetary policy. *Maintaining Stability in a Changing Financial System, Proceedings of the 2008 Jackson Hole Conference*. Kansas City, MO: Federal Reserve Bank of Kansas City: 287–34.

Aghion, P., P. Bolton, and J. Tirole. 2004. Exit options in corporate finance: Liquidity vs. incentives. *Review of Finance* 3: 327–53.

Akerlof, G. 1970. The market for lemons, qualitative uncertainty and the market mechanism. *Quarterly Journal of Economics* 84: 488–500.

Allais, M. 1947. *Economie et intérêt*. Paris: Imprimerie Nationale.

Allen, F., and D. Gale. 1994. Liquidity preference, market participation and asset price volatility. *American Economic Review* 84: 933–55.

Allen, F., and D. Gale. 1998. Optimal financial crises. *Journal of Finance* 53: 1245–84.

Allen, F., and D. Gale. 2000. Financial contagion. Journal of Political Economy 108: 1–33.

Allen, F., and D. Gale. 2004. Optimal currency crises. *Carnegie-Rochester Conference Series on Public Policy* (Elsevier) 53: 177–230.

Allen, F., and D. Gale. 2005. From cash-in-the-market pricing to financial fragility. *Journal of the European Economic Association* 3 (2–3): 535–46.

Allen, F., and D. Gale. 2007. *Understanding Financial Crises*. Oxford: Oxford University Press.

Amador, M. 2008. Sovereign debt and the tragedy of the commons. Working paper. Stanford University.

Arrow, K. 1970. *Essays in the Theory of Risk Bearing*. Amsterdam: North-Holland.

Attar, A., T. Mariotti, and F. Salanié. 2009. Non-exclusive competition in the market for lemons. *Econometrica*, forthcoming.

Barro, R. 1974. Are government bonds net wealth? *Journal of Political Economy* 82: 1095–117.

Bernanke, B. 2005. The global savings glut and the U.S. current account deficit. Sandridge Lecture.Virginia Association of Economics, Richmond, VA; available on Federal Reserve Board website: http://www.federalreserve.gov/boarddocs/speeches/2005/200503102.

Bernanke, B., and M. Gertler. 1989. Agency costs, net worth and business fluctuations. *American Economic Review* 79: 14–31.

Biais, B., Mariotti, T., Plantin, G., and J. C. Rochet. 2007. Dynamic security design: Convergence to continuous time and asset pricing implications. *Review of Economic Studies* 74 (2): 345–90.

Biais, B., T. Mariotti, J. C. Rochet, and S. Villeneuve. 2010. Large risks, limited liability and dynamic moral hazard. *Econometrica* 78 (1): 73–118.

Blanchard, O., and S. Fischer. 1989. *Lectures on Macroeconomics.* Cambridge: MIT Press.

Bolton, P., and D. Scharfstein. 1990. A theory of predation based on agency problems in financial contracting. *American Economic Review* 80: 93–106.

Bolton, P., T. Santos, and J. Scheinkman. 2009. Outside and inside liquidity. Mimeo. Columbia University and Princeton University.

Boot, A., A. Thakor, and G. Udell. 1987. Competition, risk neutrality and loan commitments. *Journal of Banking and Finance* 11: 449–71.

Broner, F., A. Martin, and J. Ventura. 2010. Sovereign risk and secondary markets. *American Economic Review,* forthcoming.

Brunnermeier, M., and L. Pedersen. 2009. Market liquidity and funding liquidity. *Review of Financial Studies* 22 (6): 2201–38.

Bryant, J. 1980. A model of reserves, bank runs, and deposit insurance. *Journal of Banking and Finance* 43: 749–61.

Caballero, R., and A. Krishnamurthy. 2001. International and domestic collateral constraints in a model of emerging market crises. *Journal of Monetary Economics* 48 (3): 513–48.

Caballero, R., and A. Krishnamurthy. 2002. A dual liquidity model for emerging markets. *American Economic Review Papers and Proceedings* 92 (2): 33–37.

Caballero, R., and A. Krishnamurthy. 2003a. Excessive dollar debt: Financial development and underinsurance. *Journal of Finance* 58: 867–93.

Caballero, R., and A. Krishnamurthy. 2003b. Smoothing sudden stops. *Journal of Economic Theory* 119 (1): 104–27.

Caballero, R., and P. Kuralt. 2009. The "surprising" nature and origins of the financial crisis: A macroeconomic proposal. *Financial Stability and Macroeconomic Stability, Proceedings of the 2009 Jackson Hole Conference.* Kansas City, MO: Federal Reserve of Kansas City, forthcoming.

Caballero, R., and A. Simsek. 2010. Fire sales in a model of complexity. Working paper. Department of Economics, MIT.

Caballero, R., E. Fahri, and P.-O. Gourinchas. 2008. An equilibrium model of global imbalances and low interest rates. *American Economic Review* 98 (1): 358–93.

Castiglionesi, F., F. Feriozzi, and G. Lorenzoni. 2010. Financial integration and liquidity crises. Mimeo. Tilburg University and MIT.

Conning, J. 2004. Monitoring by delegates or by peers? Joint liability loans under moral hazard. Working paper. Department of Economics, Hunter College.

Coval, J. D., J. Jurek, and E. Stafford. 2009. The economics of structured finance. *Journal of Economic Perspectives* 23 (1): 3–25.

Covitz, D. M., N. Liang, and G. A. Suarez. 2009. The evolution of a financial crisis: Panic in the asset-backed commercial paper market. Finance and Economics Discussion Series 2009-36. Federal Reserve Board, Washington, DC.

Daley, B., and B. Green. 2010. Waiting for news in the market for lemons. Mimeo. Duke University and Northwestern University.

Dang, T. V., G. Gorton, and B. Holmström. 2010. Financial crises and the optimality of debt for liquidity provision. Working paper. Yale University.

DeMarzo, P., and M. Fishman. 2007a. Agency and optimal investment dynamics. *Review of Financial Studies* 20 (1): 151–88.

DeMarzo, P., and M. Fishman. 2007b. Optimal long-term financial contracting. *Review of Financial Studies* 20 (6): 2079–2128.

DeMarzo, P., M. Fishman, Z. He, and N. Wang. 2009. Dynamic agency and the q theory of investment. Mimeo. Stanford University, Northwestern University, University of Chicago, Columbia Business School.

de Soto, H. 2003. *The Mystery of Capital: Why Capitalism Triumphs in the West and Fails Everywhere Else.* New York: Basic Books.

Dewatripont, M., and J. Tirole. 1994. *The Prudential Regulation of Banks.* Cambridge: MIT Press.

Dewatripont, M., J. C. Rochet, and J. Tirole. 2010. *Balancing the Banks.* Princeton: Princeton University Press.

Diamond, D. 1984. Financial Intermediation and Delegated Monitoring. *Review of Economic Studies* 51 (3): 393–414.

Diamond, D. 1997. Liquidity, banks, and markets. *Journal of Political Economy* 105 (5): 928–56.

Diamond, D., and P. Dybvig. 1983. Bank runs, deposit insurance, and liquidity. *Journal of Political Economy* 91: 401–19.

Diamond, D., and R. Rajan. 2009. Fear of fire sales and the credit freeze. Mimeo. University of Chicago.

Diamond, P. 1965. National debt in a neo-classical growth model. *American Economic Review* 55: 1126–50.

Dow, G., G. Gorton, and A. Krishnamurthy. 2005. Equilibrium asset prices and investment under imperfect corporate control. *American Economic Review* 95 (3): 659–81.

Farhi, E., and J. Tirole. 2009a. Bubbly liquidity. Mimeo. Harvard University and Toulouse School of Economics.

Farhi, E., and J. Tirole. 2009b. Collective moral hazard, maturity mismatch and systemic bailouts. Mimeo. Harvard University and Toulouse School of Economics.

Farhi, E., Golosov, M., and A. Tsyvinski. 2009. A theory of liquidity and regulation of financial intermediation. *Review of Economic Studies* 76 (3): 973–92.

Faure-Grimaud, A., and D. Gromb. 2004. Public trading and private incentives. *Review of Financial Studies* 17: 985–1014.

Forbes, K. 2010. Why do foreigners invest in the United States? *Journal of International Economics* 80 (1): 3–21.

Froot, K. A., D. A. Scharfstein, and J. C. Stein. 1993. Risk management: Coordinating corporate investment and financing policies. *Journal of Finance* 48 (5): 1629–58.

Fudenberg, D., and J. Tirole. 1985. Preemption and rent equalization in the adoption of new technology. *Review of Economic Studies* 52: 383–402.

Geanakoplos, J. D., D. A. Zame, and P. Dubey. 1995. Default, collateral, and derivatives. Mimeo. Cowles Foundation, Yale University.

Goldstein, I., and A. Pauzner. 2005. Demand-deposit contracts and the probability of bank runs. *Journal of Finance* 60 (3): 1293–1328.

Gompers, P., and J. Lerner. 1999. *The Venture Capital Cycle*. Cambridge: MIT Press.

Goodhart, C. 2008. Liquidity risk management. *Banque de France Financial Stability Review* 11: 39–44.

Gorton, G. 2008. The panic of 2007. *Maintaining Stability in a Changing Financial System, Proceedings of the 2008 Jackson Hole Conference*. Kansas City, MO: Federal Reserve Bank of Kansas City: 131–262.

Gorton, G. 2010. *Slapped in the Face by the Invisible Hand: The Panic of 2007*. Oxford: Oxford University Press.

Gorton, G., and G. Pennacchi. 1990. Financial intermediaries and liquidity creation. *Journal of Finance* 65 (1): 49–71.

Gorton, G., and A. Whinton. 2003. Financial intermediation. In G. Constantinides, M. Harris, and R. Stultz, eds. (with the help of A Whinton), *Handbook of the Economics of Finance*. Amsterdam: Elsevier.

Gottschalk A. O. 2008. *Net Worth and the Assets of Households: 2002. Current Population Reports*. Washington, DC: US Census Bureau.

Gurley, J., and E. Shaw. 1960. *Money in a Theory of Finance*. Washington, DC: Brookings Institution.

Gylfasson, T., B. Holmström, S. Korkman, V. Vihriälä, and H. Tson Söderström. 2010. *Nordics in Crisis: Vulnerability and Resilience*. Research Institute of the Finnish Economy. Helsinki: Taloustieto.

Hart, O. 1979. Monopolistic competition in a large economy with differentiated commodities. *Review of Economic Studies* 46: 1–30.

He, Z., and A. Krishnamurthy. 2009. A model of capital and crises. Working paper. Northwestern University.

Hellwig, M. 1994. Liquidity provision, banking, and the allocation of interest rate risk. *European Economic Review* 38 (7):1363–90.

Hellwig, M. 2000. Financial intermediation with risk aversion. *Review of Economic Studies* 67: 719–42.

Hellwig, M. 2009. Systemic risk in the financial sector: An analysis of the subprime-mortgage financial crisis. *De Economist* 157: 129–207.

Hicks, J. 1967. *Critical Essays in Monetary Theory.* Oxford: Oxford University Press.

Holmström, B. 2008. Commentary: "The panic of 2007." *Maintaining Stability in a Changing Financial System, Proceedings of the 2008 Jackson Hole Conference.* Kansas City, MO: Federal Reserve Bank of Kansas City: 263–73.

Holmström, B., and J. Tirole. 1997. Financial intermediation, loanable funds, and the real sector. *Quarterly Journal of Economics* 112: 663–92.

Holmström, B., and J. Tirole. 1998. Private and public supply of liquidity. *Journal of Political Economy* 106: 1–40.

Holmström, B., and J. Tirole. 2000. Liquidity and risk management. *Journal of Money, Credit and Banking* 32 (3): 295–319.

Holmström, B., and J. Tirole. 2001. LAPM: A liquidity-based asset pricing model. *Journal of Finance* 56 (5): 1837–67.

House, C., and Y. Masatlioglu. 2010. Managing markets for toxic assets. Mimeo. University of Michigan.

Ivanisha, V., and D. Scharfstein. 2010. Bank lending during the financial crisis of 2008. *Journal of Financial Economics* 97: 319–38.

Jacklin, C. 1987. Demand deposits, trading restrictions, and risk sharing. In E. Prescott and N. Wallace, eds., *Contractual Arrangements for Intertemporal Trade.* Minneapolis: University of Minnesota Press.

Kaplan, S., and P. Strömberg. 2003. Financial contracting theory meets the real world: An empirical analysis of venture capital contracts. *Review of Economic Studies* 70: 281–315.

Kayshap, A., R. Rajan, and J. Stein. 2008. Rethinking capital regulation. *Maintaining Stability in a Changing Financial System, Proceedings of the 2008 Jackson Hole Conference.* Kansas City, MO: Federal Reserve Bank of Kansas City: 431–71.

Keynes, J. M. 1936. *The General Theory of Employment, Interest and Money.* London: Macmillan.

Keys, B., T., Mukherjee, A. Seru, and V. Vig. 2010. Did securitization lead to lax screening? Evidence from subprime loans. *Quarterly Journal of Economics* 125: 307–62.

Kilenthong, W. T., and R. M. Townsend. 2010. Market based, segregated exchanges with default risk. Working paper. MIT.

Kindelberger, C. 1989. *Manias, Panics, and Crashes: A History of Financial Crises.* New York: Basic Books.

Kiyotaki, N., and J. Moore. 1997. Credit cycles. *Journal of Political Economy* 105 (2): 211–48.

Kocherlakota, N. 1996. The equity premium: It's still a puzzle. *Journal of Economic Literature* 34: 42–71.

Kocherlakota, N. 2001. Risky collateral and desposit insurance. *Advances in Macroeconomics* 1, art. 1 (1).

Kocherlakota, N. 2009. Bursting bubbles: Consequences and cures. Presented at the Macroeconomic and Policy Challenges Following Financial Meltdowns Conference hosted by the International Monetary Fund Washington, DC.

Krishnamurthy, A., and A. Vissing-Jorgensen. 2010. The aggregate demand for Treasury debt. Working paper. Northwestern University.

Kurlat, P. 2010. Lemons, market shutdowns and learning. Mimeo. MIT.

Lacker, J., and J. Weinberg. 1989. Costly state falsification. *Journal of Political Economy* 97 (6): 1345–63.

Lagos, R. 2006. Inside and outside money. Federal Reserve Bank of Minneapolis Research Department Staff Report 374. Federal Reserve Bank of Minneapolis and New York University.

Landier, A., and D. Thesmar. 2009. Contracting with optimistic entrepreneurs. *Review of Financial Studies* 22 (1): 117–50.

Laux, C. 2001. Limited liability and incentive contracting with multiple projects. *Rand Journal of Economics* 32 (3): 514–26.

Levine, R. 1997. Financial development and economic growth: Views and agenda. *Journal of Economic Literature* 35: 688–726.

Lorenzoni, G. 2008. Inefficient credit booms. *Review of Economic Studies* 75 (3): 809–33.

Malherbe, F. 2009. Self-fulfilling liquidity dry-ups. Mimeo. ECARES, Université Libre de Bruxelles.

Mayer, C. 1988. New issues in corporate finance. *European Economic Review* 32 (5): 1167–83.

Meltzer, A. 2009. What happened to the "Depression"? *Wall Street Journal*, August 31.

Modigliani, F., and M. H. Miller. 1958. The cost of capital, corporation finance, and the theory of investment. *American Economic Review* 48: 261–97.

Morris, S., and H. Shin. 1998. Unique equilibrium in a model of self-fulfilling currency attacks. *American Economic Review* 88: 587–97.

Pagano, M. 1993. Financial markets and growth: An overview. *European Economic Review* 37: 613–22.

Pagano, M., and P. Volpin. 2009. Securitization, transparency and liquidity. Mimeo. University of Naples and London Business School.

Payments Risk Committee. 2010. *Report of the Task Force on Tri-Party Repo Infrastructure.* Federal Reserve Bank of New York and SEC.

Parlour, C., and G. Plantin. 2008. Loan sales and relationship banking. *Journal of Finance* 63 (3): 1291–1314.

Philippon, T., and V. Skreta. 2010. Optimal interventions in markets with adverse selection. Working paper 15785. National Bureau of Economic Research, Cambridge, MA.

Pozsar, Z., T. Adrian, A. Ashcraft, and H. Boesky. 2010. Shadow banking. Federal Reserve Bank of New York Staff Report 458.

Rampini, A., and S. Viswanathan. 2010. Collateral, risk management, and the distribution of debt capacity. *Journal of Finance*, forthcoming.

Rajan, R., and L. Zingales. 1998. Financial dependence and growth. *American Economic Review* 88: 559–86.

Reinhart, C., and K. Rogoff. 2009. *This Time Is Different: Eight Centuries of Financial Folly*. Princeton: Princeton University Press.

Rochet, J. C. 2008a. Commentary: Rethinking capital regulation. *Maintaining Stability in a Changing Financial System, Proceedings of the 2008 Jackson Hole Conference*. Kansas City, MO: Federal Reserve Bank of Kansas City: 473–83.

Rochet, J. C. 2008b. *Why Are There So Many Banking Crises? The Politics and Policy of Bank Regulation*. Princeton: Princeton University Press.

Rochet, J. C., and J. Tirole. 1996. Interbank lending and systemic risk. *Journal of Money, Credit and Banking* 28: 733–62.

Rochet, J. C., and J. Tirole. 1996b. Controlling risk in payment systems. *Journal of Money, Credit and Banking* 28: 832–62.

Rochet, J. C., and X. Vives. 2004. Coordination failures and the lender of last resort: Was Bagehot right after all? *Journal of the European Economic Association* 2 (6): 1116–47.

Rothschild, M., and J. Stiglitz. 1976. Equilibrium in competitive insurance markets: An essay in the economics of imperfect information. *Quarterly Journal of Economics* 90: 629–50.

Sahlman, W. 1990. The structure and governance of venture capital organizations. *Journal of Financial Economics* 27: 473–521.

Samuelson, P. 1958. An exact consumption-loan model of interest with or without the contrivance of money. *Journal of Political Economy* 66: 467–82.

Shiller, R. 2008. *The Subprime Solution: How Today's Global Financial Crisis Happened, and What to Do about It*. Princeton: Princeton University Press.

Shleifer, A., and R. Vishny. 1992. Liquidation values and debt capacity: A market equilibrium. *Journal of Finance* 47: 1343–65.

Shleifer, A., and L. Summers. 1988. Breach of trust in hostile takeovers. In A. J. Auerbach, ed., *Corporate Takeovers: Causes and Consequences*. Chicago: University of Chicago Press, 33–56.

Simsek, A. 2010. When optimists need credit: Asymmetric disciplining of optimism and implications for asset prices. Mimeo. MIT.

Stein, J. 2003. Agency, information, and corporate investment. In G. Constantinides, M. Harris, and R. Stulz, eds., *Handbook of the Economics of Finance*. Amsterdam: Elsevier, 111–65.

Strahan, P. J., E., Gater, and T. Schuermann. 2006. How do banks manage liquidity risk? Evidence from deposit and equity markets in the fall of 1998. In M. Carey and R. Stulz, eds., *Risks of Financial Institutions*. Chicago: NBER/University of Chicago Press, 105–27.

Sundaresan, S. M., and Z. Wang. 2004. Public provision of private liquidity: Evidence from the millennium date change. Working paper. Columbia University.

Taylor, J. 2009. *Getting off Track: How Government Actions Caused, Prolonged and Worsened the Financial Crisis*. Stanford, CA: Hoover Institution Press.

Terviö, M. 2009. Superstars and mediocrities: Market failure in the discovery of talent. *Review of Economic Studies* 72 (2): 829–50.

Tirole, J. 2002. *Financial Crises, Liquidity and the International Monetary System*. Princeton: Princeton University Press.

Tirole, J. 2003. Inefficient foreign borrowing: A dual-and common-agency perspective. *American Economic Review* 93 (5): 1678–1702.

Tirole, J. 2006. *The Theory of Corporate Finance*. Princeton: Princeton University Press.

Tirole, J. 2010. Overcoming adverse selection: How public intervention can restore market functioning. Mimeo. Toulouse School of Economics.

Tuckman, B. 2010. Systemic risk and the tri-party repo clearing banks. Policy paper. Center for Financial Stability, New York.

Van den Steen, E. 2004. Rational overoptimism (and other biases). *American Economic Review* 94 (4): 1141–51.

Ventura, J. 2010. Bubbles and capital flows. Mimeo. CREI, University Pompeu Fabra.

Vissing-Jorgensen, A. 2002. Limited asset market participation and the elasticity of intertemporal substitution. *Journal of Political Economy* 110 (4): 825–53.

Von Thadden, E. L. 1995. Long-term contracts, short-term investment and monitoring, *Review of Economic Studies* 62 (4): 557–751.

Wicksell, K. [1898] 1936. *Interest and Prices: A Study of the Causes Regulating the Value of Money* (trans. R. F. Kahn). Jena: G. Fischer.

Williamson, O. 1988. Corporate finance and corporate governance. *Journal of Finance* 43: 567–92.

Woodford, M. 1990. Public debt as liquidity. *American Economic Review, Papers and Proceedings* 80: 382–88.

Index